CHEZ JOEY

By Joe Flaherty

MANAGING MAILER

FOGARTY & CO.

CHEZ JOEY

Chez Joey

The World of Joe Flaherty

Introduction by Wilfrid Sheed

Coward, McCann, & Geoghegan, Inc., New York

For
Jeanine Johnson, Dan Wolf, Paul Schiffman, and
His Sugarship Mr. Butler.
The classiest quartet to be found this side of Car-
negie—or Murderers' Row.

Contents

Three: Mug Shots

Four: Fancy Flights

Introduction

To dispose of the logrolling charge right away—this is a logroll. Joe Flaherty would be a man to my taste if he'd never written a word. Whether he is hiding a broken heart at the track or demonstrating samurai strokes at the bar, Joe improvises on life and letters with the same high style and low mind, which I take to be the correct human combination. There is absolutely nothing middle-class about Flaherty; he goes straight from the poolroom to the royal Enclosure without passing through respectability. Lordly, profane, an eighteenth-century sportsman with the latest in street smarts.

My chief excuse for rolling this particular log is that I admired Flaherty's work even before I knew him (much logrolling has this innocent explanation), and for the same reasons. The man you meet on the page is precisely the one you meet in real life, and not some literary persona cooked up for the occasion.

This is partly a matter of integrity (a word Joe would never use about himself). Some writers will give you *macho* monosyllables at the bar and purple champagne at the typewriter, but not Flaherty. A triple-decked metaphor can turn up in his conversation as easily as a swear word in his copy. Likewise, he won't suddenly pull a warm working-class heart on you or a Celtic rage or any of those stale literary devices: If he doesn't feel it during off hours, he doesn't start feeling it at his desk. When Joe does strike a pose, it is strictly for laughs or some other esthetic effect. His major distinction, in a field where showing off is mandatory and where marginal idiosyncrasies are cultivated like sick plants, is that he is always himself.

Such honesty rings pleasantly in the cattle market and to some extent determines Flaherty's role there. His principal enemy, or let's say his favorite straight man, is false emotion, and he goes after professional Irishmen, professional saints, professional anythings, like Groucho lunging upon Mrs. Rittenhouse. The effect on his contemporaries has to be tonic. With Flaherty leering out there, you think twice before letting on how hard you cried at Martin Luther King's last birthday: OK, if you really did, and can prove you weren't drunk at the time, but let's not cheapen the currency around here. Joe's contribution to the New Journalism is a strict emotional precision, based on a lacerating self-awareness. Readers of his novel *Fogarty & Co.* will remember the boot camp of an Irish conscience he goes through regularly himself; after that it's a rare Holy Willy or spiritual con man who can slip anything past him.

All this could be pretty painful if it wasn't so funny. Joe may be cursed with the liverish eye of a satirist, but he is twice blessed with the heart of a clown. Pretension, false feeling, the unhousetrained ego—all these fripperies move him to mirth, not anger. Laughter is harder to fake than tears, and Joe is taking no chances. He isn't mad at anybody, only operatically outraged, and this is a great source of strength in his writing. Yet his laughter can be as merciless as another man's rage.

Of course, to have all this and have not talent would availeth one damnall. But fortunately talent is the least debatable of Joe's virtues. In the course of a travesty of a radio show we once did together, the host tried to get him to say that a love of New York was his ruling passion. Joe hemmed and hawed as only he can hem and haw (Charles Laughton in a thunderstorm gets you close) and allowed as how New York was fine if you like that kind of thing. Then he looked the poor wretch in the eye and said, "But I really love words."

Check. And they return his affection. To observe a word lecher at large, staging an orgy a paragraph, turn the page. If Joe has a defect, it's an occasional excess of wordolatry, a reaching for the extra-spatial metaphor or the world's worst pun, a playfulness in the cause of his passion. But in return you get a feast of the unexpected, the colorful, and the precisely right—not to mention the finest in terse description when that's called for.

The other thing you get is a Rabelaisian quickening of life as Flaherty stalks his subject, whether it be a Super Bowl or some luckless politician or a quiet afternoon at home. Like all fine writers, Flaherty has his own world, but it's not a made-up Runyonesque world; it's the real one, with a robust art laid on top of it. Taking an analogy from left field and with no embarrassing comparisons intended (Joe respects the dead): Dickens' London is frequently a simple masterpiece of reporting, yet no one else had seen it that way before. So too with Flaherty's New York or Flaherty's liver or Flaherty's universe.

I won't do your work for you by citing my favorite pieces—so much depended on how I felt when I picked up the *Village Voice* that week, whether in Beckett-like gloom or just regular despair; in either event, Joe carried the mood to farce and lightened it—but if you like the one about his fellow grain handlers, I won't argue with you; if you thrill to the twilight world of Harold Nederland, the somewhat different sex object, by my guest; or if you dig the third dimension of Howard Cosell—a marvel of sympathetic rendering—be my guest. I could nominate another three just by sticking a pin in the table of contents.

I'd like to end on a more controversial note, as befits the subject. Flaherty was read out of the Irish race (which takes some reading) when he lowered the boom on St. Paddy's and the New York Irish renaissance. Yet Joe never wrote a more Irish piece than that. Seeing through their own bullshit is the height of Irish attainment (or anyone else's—but with the Irish it's a form of genius), and those who don't think so must have been over here too long. Anyone who's seen the inside of a County Clare farmhouse or the backside of a Dublin slum knows that Irish sentimentality never came out of there. Blarney was always for the tourist trade anyway. For home consumption, you'd better see it straight and tell it straight and have a sense of your stinking situation. After that, you can laugh, if you still have the stomach for it.

So don't give Flaherty Emerald Isles or ould sods, and renascence him no renascences. He's the other kind of Irishman: the kind who has looked despair in the eye, and seen the dark side of the moon through the bottom of a glass, and came out cracking wise. I give you the ould sod himself, Mr. Joe Flaherty.

—WILFRID SHEED

JOEY: Drunks tossing pennies—that's the story of my life. . . . Just between you and me I've been thinking about opening my own little place. Something very intimate, and quite—classy. Maybe have a quartet of violins.

VERA: What are we going to call it? How about—Chez Joey?

JOEY: Chez Joey! That's very good. That's perfect. I like that. It's even French. Chez Joey—a place with real class. I might even appear in white tie and tails. I might even wear an opera hat.

—Selected dialogue from the Columbia
Pictures' film of John O'Hara's
Pal Joey.

Author's Preface

As Edward G. Robinson proclaimed in the final reel of *Little Caesar,* "My God, can this be the end for Rico?" I, too, never thought I'd wind up this way. Journalism, "new" or old, never entered my mind back then.

Perhaps the best way to explain is to flash back to "back then." I was born in 1936 in Brooklyn, the third son (of four) to John Flaherty of the County Galway ("herring-chokers") and Maggie Casey of the County Tipperary ("stone-throwers").

My nook of Brooklyn was called Windsor Terrace, an Irish and Italian concrete principality that sleepily came to rest between the pastoral boundaries of Greenwood Cemetery and Prospect Park. The houses were mostly two-family affairs, and their occupants seemed to know every nuance of each other's lives. It wasn't the hip rendition of Brooklyn one came to expect from Hollywood but, in fact, a small town that could be found in mid-America. If Dorothy's twister had lifted Windsor Terrace from its roots and deposited it a thousand miles inland, I've always felt the windfall could go unnoticed.

Surely this is an oversimplification. The burghers of another burg would be horrified by our slaughter of the Queen's tongue, our duck's ass haircuts, our pistol pocket pants, and our ever-present talisman, the hip pocket comb. And our swearing would baffle them as Elizabethan oaths confound contemporary readers. (I'm sure nobody in Ohio said, "Up your kazoo!") But where it mattered, in our career aspirations, in our moribund relationships, in our love lives, we were closer to cornball than cosmopolite.

My father, like the fathers of many of my friends, worked the docks for a living. The other places where immigrants hustled for a buck were shipyards, breweries, construction sites, Con Ed, and the telephone company. The closest you ever came to a professional man was the Jewish doctor who treated your family. This is in no way set forth as a lament;

these were fine, tough, honest men who realistically dealt with the immigrant's lot. Their Yankee-born sons ("narrowbacks" we were scornfully labeled) would follow in their fathers' steps or, it was hoped, move on to civil service jobs—as cops, firemen, or sanitation men. Thus, the snailing down of the American Dream.

Civil service jobs meant security and, better yet, that Utopia for immigrants—pensions. Poverty in old age was a European nightmare to be guarded against. So when one of my friends passed a civil service test, there was a celebration—a beer racket. We "Yankees" were on the move.

Culture was a languid malady of the leisure class. I would like to report that as boys we read Yeats and Joyce in my home, but it was more like the *Daily News* and the Catholic paper, the Brooklyn *Tablet*. (The latter was our invaluable guide to what we supposed were horny movies. The Legion of Decency once condemned a Betty Grable-Dan Dailey opus because they were contemplating divorce. In retrospect we must have been the original *Deep Throat* for swallowing such fantasies.)

Nor did my Italian friends' fathers spend their idle hours listening to the strains of Puccini and Verdi. Strain had a much more sweaty interpretation. Relaxation for the old-timers came on summer nights when they would sit in their undershirts on stoops drinking tap beer from tin buckets obtained from the "beer garden," while their sons played stickball in the streets. Once again, if you were to substitute porch for stoop, lemonade for suds, and baseball for stickball, the specter of the small town rises.

We also had our version of barn raisings. In a sense of community we would gather to paint or wallpaper the apartment of a friend who was getting married. He was odds-on to marry a neighborhood girl and, more important, one of his "own kind." That is, the Irish married Irish, and the Italians married Italians. The blacks and Puerto Ricans had not yet been heard from, so even our prejudices were parochial. An Italian-Irish merger was our version of the Montagues and the Capulets.

I still dearly miss those weddings. Looking back, it seems the old-time working class handled high occasions better than their financial betters. Weddings, wakes, and baptisms (christenings, we called them) were marvelous bashes. The weddings, because of their sprawling nature, were called "football affairs." The caterer was a stranger to our culture (or lack of it). Long tables would wheeze under the weight of the food prepared by the couple's friends. Every woman contributed her own specialty, so there was a glut of hams, turkeys, salads, and Italian dishes. My mother had the lock on the Irish soda bread. To this day she maintains superstar status in that field in the old neighborhood. The booze was always first-rate, either because we appreciated it so much or, like most of the poor, because we were defensive about our standing among our neighbors. Thank God, we had not yet reached that middle-class mecca of pawning off Macy's scotch on our friends.

As a boy most of the wakes I attended were in homes. The corpse was laid out in the living room with the women in attendance. The departed seemed always to take up the space under the windows, presumably the best vantage point for the launching of a soul. The men held forth in the kitchen, eating and drinking, telling arcane union plots, and heaping monstrosities of virtue on the deceased. The latter always helped to ease the pain, since in most cases you felt you were burying a stranger.

Now I hate to attend an old friend's wedding or wake or his child's baptism. God forgive us, the caterer now takes care of our beginnings, middles, and endings. Weddings are conducted by a leering MC whom one could easily associate with a singles' weekend in the Catskills. The food is plastic, the booze is "Clan" something or other, and the music is Tin Pan Alley Irish. Cloying cuteness abounds. The newlyweds must kiss when the guests tap their spoons on the water glasses—Pavlovian fornication. Wakes are no better. The main man here seems to be a Mafia reject with gray hair and a blue rinse. Indeed, at one wake I was informed that the corpse was laid out in the "Mustard Room" (I had dire thoughts of what the cover charge would be).

So there was much to be loved "back then," but there also was a bleaker side. The feeling that your life was programmed from cradle to crypt. Your education would stop by some common consent; college was never mentioned. Of about thirty friends only one obtained a degree, and that was at night school. Civil service was in the wings, or, failing that, your father or a friend of your father's would provide a job.

Your sexual appetites had to be satisfied within the perimeter of your existence. Marriage would be made not with an exotic stranger but with the most familiar of faces. Death would have no drama; you would be the recipient of one more mass card in a continuous collection of mass cards. It was then you realized continuity can be choking. Like Wolfe with his Chapel Hill and Anderson with his Winesboro, the melancholy moment hit you—your Brooklyn would be hard as hell to escape, even if you *really* wanted to.

But if daydreaming is a magic carpet, I guess I always wanted to take it on the lam. I received good marks in grade school but was the worst of scholars. Discipline wasn't my strong suit. I applied myself to what I adored and gave everything that bored me the back of my hand. And when on my first day of school, a nun spied my colossus of a dome and said, "I'll call this one Big Head with Nothing in It," I realized my tenure would be more slugging than spiritual.

My father died a violent death when I was seven, and the already tight purse strings of our family life became a noose. It was through the tough-ness of my mother, Maggie (O'Casey would be at home with her matri-archal strength), that we held together. My two older brothers and I chipped in whatever small coins we earned from after-school jobs as de-livery boys and paper sellers. The last of the brothers, Eugene, was but nine months old.

Because of my age, my father (or my memories of him) became mythic rather than real. It wasn't until nearly thirty years later, when I wrote a novel titled *Fogarty & Co.,* that I realized the damage and the loss. The novel took a turn of its own and began to abound with father and son re-lationships.

My two older brothers, Doc and Billy, managed to carry the Flaherty flag to the field of honor by winning scholarships to Catholic high schools. When my turn came, I was gross under pressure. Even though my marks were always among the top five in my class in grade school, I failed to win a tuition-free scholarship to a diocesan school. This is blackly known in the family as the Catholic choke.

But they would be damned if they would relinquish my soul to those heathens in the public school system. (I would be lost soon enough with-out early impetus, they rightly reasoned.) So I was packed off to St. John's Prep at the heavenly cost of $30 a month. I argued against it, since I had already had a bellyful of Catholic schools, but to no avail. After eight years of dropping decisions to the nuns, the thought of tackling the Vincentian fathers for another four (I was being moved up to the heavyweight divi-sion before my time!) offered little solace. I presumed that upon my graduation I would look and talk like Jake LaMotta after he hung them up.

Thankfully for both sides, St. John's demanded academic standards I couldn't or wouldn't approach. To this day the thought of solving an algebra problem or conjugating a French verb is enough to send me to a saloon for a week. So with the delicacy of governmental change in a banana republic (they ordered, I fled), the good fathers and I parted company.

My next stop was William E. Grady Vocational High School, which was known for its production of esthetic zip guns. With my conniving tongue I convinced my mother I was destined for higher things in the future with Con Edison and should pursue courses in electrical wiring. It was a con so base that it still makes me blush, since I still advocate re-pairing a fuse by putting a penny behind it. But like those who defend a good dose of the clap as a manly experience, my days at Grady are not to be dismissed.

It was there that a boyhood friend and I became the foremost juvenile critics-at-large of American cinema. School was rarely attended, and if it was, it was for a class or two before we "cut out." Our days were spent in those wondrous dark balconies of New York movie houses, to be followed by a gourmet lunch at Grant's on Forty-second Street of hot dogs (still the best in the city) and a cherry smash (instant diabetes).

The expense for the day was marginal, since we rarely paid for the movie. Under the tutelage of O'D's brother Tommy (aka "Bimbo" and "Broadway Sam"), a tactical genius on the scale of Rommel, and my brother Billy (aka "Hollywood Harry"—he was a bit of a dandy), we learned to crash every major movie house on the Great White Way. The plans for these capers were so bizarre that they shall be saved for a surrealistic novel, but for a teaser the Old Globe was partially negotiated by sliding down a forty-foot laundry chute. Some days went badly, and we were caught and beaten by ushers and movie managers; others, we had Ruthian success, crashing the Mayfair, Criterion, and Paramount (regular picture plus a preview) in one day. A blinding headache aside, it is a campaign ribbon to be cherished.

Indeed, we became so adept at it there was a day of fulfillment when we had to opt for the Ace Poolroom, because we had seen every movie playing on the main stem. We also attained a certain cachet on our home turf. As many of today's moviegoers slavishly consult Pauline Kael before they make their "cherce," neighborhood devotees of the silver screen searched out O'Donnell's and Flaherty's exalted opinions. Our respective mothers got wise to our shenanigans when Pete, the local deli man, after watching us go off to school for several months with our hands in our pockets, queried them incredulously in his heavy German accent: "Mein Gott, what kind of a school has no books?"

I gleaned three other things from my days at Grady: an encounter with a marvelous teacher, my first unassigned reading experience, and my first foray into writing. Mickey Spillane was the national rage, and I devoured his books. (What other writer would have the gall—or the balls, as Mickey would put it—to claim such a mentor?) The teacher, Mr. Liebler, conducted an exciting, unorthodox class. It was one of the few I attended. He allowed us to write our versions of current newspaper stories, and since the *Daily News* was our Bible, the class usually split their artistic endeavors between whatever rape or murder (rape, I believe, held the horny edge) cases that were sizzling on the back pages (this said, because the sports pages, even though numerically higher, were the front of the paper). It was a clever move to gain our attention, since in our thuggish minds these were "current events." I was so zealous about my attempts I went on to write detective stories, à la Spillane. Not parodies, mind you, but adorations for the select circle of between class smokers in the bathroom. My heroines always had "brazen nipples," and my hero was more interested in laying them to rest with his .45 than simply laying them with that object whose function still baffled me. If nothing else, I learned a little along the way.

But all this only shortly forestalled the doom and disgrace I was about to heap upon my mother. She was advised that I should be removed from school (her disgrace, my reprieve). It was a teary scene. My mother cried, when my Irish guidance counselor said I had shamed her, my dead father, and—most important—the Irish, a charge that has chased me through the years. I believe his conclusion was that I was acting like an Italian.

So with my mother weeping, and me following suit because my Jiminy Cricket was manhandling me between two stand-up file cabinets, my conscription in the hells of ivy came to an end.

"Throw the bum out to work," the conscience of the Celts shouted, "work the ungrateful bastard to death." With this blessing a Brooklyn Lemuel Pitkin swaggered out of the room and into the sunset to make his Cool Million.

My visitation into the world of commerce drew place money to 1929. A cousin of mine obtained me a position as a squad boy on the floor of the New York Stock Exchange. My job was to take the recorded sales and place them into a cylinder, then send them up a pneumatic tube, where they would be shot upstairs to a teletypist, who would then send them out over the large ticker that was visible to all brokers on the floor. Did not Wernher von Braun start so meekly?

Every morning I flew up the subway stairs at the Wall Street stop, sporting my Billy Eckstine-collared shirt and looking like a Dow-Jones Dumbo. Everything went quietly at first—tragically, too quietly. There were a couple of minor skirmishes with summer-working college boys who made remarks about my shirt or one of my ever present pocketbooks (they dared put the knock on Mike Hammer!). The latter worked to my advantage, since one of my critics goaded me into reading James Jones' *From Here to Eternity,* and a new world opened for me. But alas, enough was not going on. Even employing the fantasy of a wing commander sending endless bombers airborne ("Did Forrester get back yet?") didn't stem the ennui. So games had to be devised. The favorite was to write a bogus sale on a piece of paper—usually 2,000,000 shares of GM at 60¾—and pass it to the new squad boy to skyrocket up the tube. Nobody ever fell for it till one day I found a true believer who sent GM soaring. I was fired immediately and walked to the subway hugging the building to avoid being flattened by the leapers.

Wall Street was to have one more shot at my errant genius. I went to work as a mimeograph operator for a small stock house. This was in the fall of the year, and I solemnly swore I would stick it out at least until I attended my first carnal Christmas party. But the Lord works in strange ways and decided to intercede to protect my most unwanted luxury, my virginity. One day while I was Walter Mittying the mimeograph machine, I forgot to screw the cap on the cylinder holding the ink. When I flipped the switch, shrieks arose from neighboring desks. A Transylvanian nightmare was in full motion. Black-winged globs were flying about and coming to rest on people and furniture, walls and floors. Even secretaries bedecked with crosses and chains were not safe. Needless to say, I spent that Christmas unemployed and as untouched as the new fallen snow.

It went on like that for another two years. I worked as a helper on a laundry truck and fell in love with every tanned Bermuda-shorted housewife I encountered on my suburban route (yes, Scott, they are different from you and me). I spent one full day in a factory that manufactured airplane parts. My job was to check if a certain part was balanced by measuring with an instrument so small it was like trying to put leggings on a Lilliputian. The trick was to balance a bubble in the instrument (the emperor's bubble), thus indicating the part was precise. My co-workers all walked around with purple hollows under their eyes in a zombielike trance. They gave me such advice as: "Kid, when you're watching TV, make it as dark as possible. It will save the peepers for the next day." At the end of the day, when I saw the men and women file out and grope for their time cards, like an Esalen encounter group, I took my baby blues home and never returned.

But, I found out, life is sweet. I landed a job as a candy packer in an A&P factory. The variety was stunning. In the spring I packed chocolate Easter bunnies, in the fall chocolate turkeys, in the winter chocolate Santa Clauses, and was laid off in the summer. Praise be to the one who divines such things that there was a summer solstice. Could chocolate groundhogs be far behind?

I frolicked with my saccharin friends from 4 P.M. until midnight and then drank beer in the local pub till 4 A.M. It wasn't debauchery but self-defense. If I went home sober and tried to sleep, endless legions of these acne-giving little bastards would parade before my eyes. I was suffering the first recorded case of DT's from dextrose. So in 1955, in a fit of preservation, not patriotism, Flaherty traded his chocolate browns for GI khaki.

I'm afraid my military career owed more to Beatle Bailey than Von Clausewitz. For some reason known only to God and those who devise the Army IQ tests, I was slotted to be a tanker. This spurred fantasies in me of dispensing Hershey bars from the top of my panzer to Corinne Calvet in a plunging peasant blouse. Far from it. I was shipped to Fort Riley, Kansas, for three months, where I did battle with battalions of ticks. From there it was six weeks in Death Valley, California, for exercises in desert fighting. (Could the Afrika Corps be far behind?) The Army with improvisational genius then doublebanked me from 137 degrees in the

California shade to the Fatherland, where it was 30 degrees below in the sun (the coldest winter in Europe in fifty years).

But there were bonuses. A new continent to explore and the acquaintance of an Irish genius with the Joycean moniker of Richard Solomon Delaney. Delaney, years my senior, became my intellectual, spiritual, and sexual mentor. Tutelage in all three were sorely needed. Delaney was born in Dublin and had reached the highest strata of Celtic mythology when he secured a position as a cook in Guinness' Brewery. He came to the states and opened a café in New Orleans and, as the saying goes, was happy for a time. But the Irishman's siren call for the ould sod wafted across the waters, and he joined the Army for a European tour that would bring him closer to his birthplace.

He stood no more than five feet seven inches, was pudgy, and cut his few remaining hairs defiantly short. The whole ensemble rendered up an aging Celtic Casper the Ghost. But this said, he was still one of the best wooers of women I have ever met. His knack, as in everything he approached, was that he dissected it to its essence: women, God, and literature. His theories were endless. He smoked C-ration Camels (obtained from the battalion kitchen where he was company cook), because he believed they were so raunchy they warded off the clap. He was also below knavery. He would dry out coffee grounds on his windowsill in the sun and that night present them downtown to his lastest *Schatz* as pure ground roast. When on one of our overnight passes, I failed to bed a woman, the next day I would receive a two-hour critique on my ineptitude. Of course, it was never considered that perhaps I was just damn homely. No, there were always subterranean reasons. As a tactician he claimed I rivaled the Italian chiefs of staff.

There was validity in this. As a Wagnerian wooer I suffered from a double fault: I was a verbal dandy and a romantic. My Brooklyn imitation of George Sanders just didn't cut through their ice. Delaney constantly accused me of chasing the best-looking women in the dance halls, which was true and, I thought, eminently tasteful and healthy. Not so, according to my Dublin Don Juan.

In his broad Irish accent he used to explain: "Look, son, first you talk too much. Touch is the thing. Get up and grab them by the hand and drag them out on the dance floor.

"Worse, you want to 'fook' who you want to 'fook.' The secret of love is to get the one who wants to 'fook' you, regardless of what she looks like."

He firmly believed in the Tin Pan Alley catechism that for every man there is a woman—that is, as long as you had the staying power of a long-distance runner and, as the night wore on, your taste whizzed downward as quickly as corduroy knickers on a banister.

"At ten in the evening we all want Rita Hayworth," he would say. "At midnight you settle for a costar, and at closing time love is to be found among the extras."

His theory on my verbal veronicas was right on the deutschmark. On an evening out with a blonde, with legs the length of stilts, I was once again stymied. To add frost to frigidity, her car got stuck in heavy snow, and I got out to push. Well, this frolicsome *Fräulein* thought it would be just *wunderbar* to hit me in the kisser with a handful of snow while I was huffing and puffing against the rear fender. After suffering months of indignities without indiscretion, I attacked back, maliciously and manifold, when out of the snow rose such a clatter I didn't know what was the matter. Squeals of sexual titillation punctuated the Bavarian night. The next thing I knew, I was prostrate, wondering if I had missed the message in *The Student Prince*. Let it be recorded for history that neither Neville Chamberlain nor Flaherty could ever fathom the Germanic mind.

On a higher plane Delaney was a strict supervisor of my reading. He instructed me what books to read and then proceeded to tell me I didn't understand any of them. (The Irish I missed totally, of course, but I was a little better on the limeys—they were most simplistic to grasp.) But when I told him I would like to try my hand at writing, he kindly encouraged me. He thought his future vocation (after another decade or two of tomcatting) was to be found in the priesthood.

"Jesus," he explained, "what can those celibates tell anyone? I'd be the most sympathetic of priests. You couldn't shock me with anything new, and the pulpit is a hell of a place to expound your ideas."

I saw him only once after we were discharged, an afternoon at Suffolk Downs racetrack in Boston, and then we lost touch. One prays he is a corpulent bishop in the wilds of County Kerry.

When I was discharged from the Army, I went into an extended period of R&R (rest and recuperation). I found myself standing at bars woefully telling a woman (Jake Barnes to Lady Brett) that I was recovering from a shadowy military trauma. After eight months this shtick became ludicrous (even to me). Besides, the vessels of my outpouring began to wonder what in the hell could have happened to a clown in a peacetime army.

During the killing of the clock, though, I did manage to continue reading. There was no doubt about it—I wanted to become a writer. The plays of Eugene O'Neill piqued my Irish gloom, and I wrote boozy tragedies of dinosaur proportions. Needless to say, they are as extinct as the aforementioned beast.

But it was Fitzgerald who haunted me, especially *The Great Gatsby*. The delicacy of the blue lawns of Long Island was a three-sewer clout away from my Brooklyn streets, but he was my main man. After Gatsby, I just had to be a writer. But much to my dismay I discovered (as usual) that I lacked discipline, and my style was not dashing and new but bowed to the secondhand shops of literature. In short, I had no voice of my own.

When this discouraging news hit home, I left home. The Army had instilled in me wanderlust, so I split for that curious land I had previously visited for a while—California. There I followed my true star, marginalia. I went from selling my blood for cash to selling shoes for cash. (Knowledge accrued: Many English women don't wear panties.) Ever onward and upward, I became a female placement counselor in an unemployment agency, a job that combined the spiritual qualities of a father confessor and the horniness of a Freudian counselor.

There was one more fling at academe. I entered Los Angeles City College (having obtained my high school diploma in the Army) to study English and creative writing. It seems clichés have the nasty habit of popping up in one's life (perhaps they are the only realities), and my teacher turned out to be a dowager in tweeds and Red Cross shoes, Margaret Rutherford without the charm. We reached a civilized détente for a while until she asked me to write an essay, titled "What Does English Mean to You?" (Was this how Scott got started?) In what I assumed was a brilliant tour de force, I wrote that to me, coming from an Irish home, English was always a hyphenated word, English-bastard. Well, my tour was taken for a turkey—exit laughing.

But California was not without its moments. After many hectic furlongs in New York, the leisurely pace suited for a while. I got happily married (many years later, sadly divorced). I found new friends. What one thought were philosophies on reexamination were discovered to be merely attitudes. Short stories were written. Publishers: "Please submit through an agent." Agents: "We handle only published writers." In the classic Mailer canon, a circle jerk. Short poems were submitted to a Texas magazine; from the usually verbose Texans short notes saying no came back. The metabolism passed the tranquil stage and segued into sleep. Like the hillbilly song says, it was time to be movin' on.

Back in New York, I entered the family business (my father and brother before me) and became a grain trimmer on the waterfront. It was the best job I had ever had. The work was hard in the best *macho* sense, the pay high, and the men I worked with the funniest and lustiest I had encountered. I settled into a life, and though the dock wasn't Daisy's, I was reasonably content.

An interest in local politics offered me a chance for publication. I wrote various news releases and political opinion for the neighborhood paper, the *Park Slope News* in Brooklyn. A metaphor petted at a local social gathering is not to be denied. Men have got by on less.

It was in 1966 during John Lindsay's first term as mayor that Mother Muse, or Lady Luck, flashed me a wink. One summer evening, exiting from my subway stop, I encountered a mob. John Lindsay, I was told, was to arrive in minutes to promote his referendum for a Civilian Review Board of the police. The crowd sounded like those mobs that gather for lynchings or necktie parties in stock Westerns: "Argh, argh, who got a rope? Argh, argh, string 'im up." Diversion was always my sport, so I watched.

Lindsay arrived as touted, and his vaunted charisma was evidently a clunker in Brooklyn. He wasn't allowed to speak. Taunts and litanies of "nigger lover" fractured his every sentence. One fat guy was the biggest offender, and I told him to shut the fuck up and let the mayor speak. The loudmouth weighed my strange makeup, a beard (he could cream such a fairy), and my longshore rig (maybe not). He acquiesced, and the mayor of New York gave me a grateful nod. Already I was recognized in high places.

I was so upset by the filth and vituperation that came from the mouths of my fellow citizens over such a gratuitous but civilized issue that I went home and wrote a piece for the local paper trying to fathom what was happening to New Yorkers. In truth, during my discourse in a style that was florid even by my standards, I attacked the Irish, the Italians, the American Legion, the Knights of Columbus, the Holy Mother Church, and anything else I had been dying to kick for years.

The paper, then conservative (now liberal), was aghast. There was much talk of a heavy blue pencil on my blue language. But in the end they decided the sacrilege couldn't be salvaged. Unbeknownst to me, two young staff members, Bob Townes and Jack Deacy, admired the piece and sent it off to Dan Wolf at the *Village Voice* with a covering letter presumably signed by me. For my part, I presumed the piece had died at the local level.

Two weeks later, when I was working on the docks, I received a phone call from my lifelong saddle tramp Ace Gillen, telling me what a wonderful piece I had written for the *Village Voice*. I informed him that his sense of humor was sick, but he then went on to read from the piece. I still didn't believe him (even though he hadn't seen what I'd written before), because I had that week's issue of the *Voice* at home, and surely I would have seen my own piece. But this didn't stop me from charging to the nearest newsstand.

Not only was it my own deathless prose, but I had the flag of the paper, titled "Why Has the Fun Fled Fun City?" I scooped up all the papers I could carry and retired to the nearest bar, where I read each copy in disbelief, accompanying each reading with a shot of Irish whiskey, while tears the size of the dome in Houston rolled down my cheeks. That night I floated home on a sea of glory—among other things.

The following Monday after work I appeared at the offices of the *Voice* and asked to see Dan Wolf. The receptionist took one look at my getup and informed me that Mr. Wolf was off on an extended sabbatical in the Far East or some such. Would I like to leave my name? I did, and there was a flash of recognition. Was I the one? Yes, I was. Mr. Wolf, like Phileas Fogg, it appeared, had miraculously just floated in the window from parts unknown.

Immediately, I realized Wolf was a man to be dealt with: a graying, handsome cosmopolite who smoked a corncob pipe. I checked my wallet. He asked me if I liked to write, and I endlessly gushed out my heart. If he had had the sense to tape that session, he would have me as an indentured servant forever. With a bemused, puckish quality, he asked me if I would like to cover the PBA's victory party, since the rejection of the Review Board was a *fait accompli* according to the polls. Reasonable enough, I thought. My wallet was fine; it was my brain that needed checking.

I arrived for the festivities at the Commodore Hotel with sidekick Gillen. Everything looked fine; we were among winners. The booze was flowing, and there were nice touches of cop culture: 1950 ID bracelets galore, Tony Curtis hairdos, and the ever-present lumberjack shirt under the unbuttoned police tunic. Cops just getting off duty jammed the ballroom by ten o'clock. Everything was fine until I began looking for interviews. My *Voice* credentials placed me a notch below an agent from the shoofly squad. I asked an off-duty cop his thoughts on this victorious evening, and instead, he gave me his thoughts on my sexual proclivities. Now I had seen *Front Page* fifteen times and knew well no hard-boiled reporter takes that shit. I coolly grabbed him by his shirt collar and bow tie and dragged him toward me, practicing my Bogey snarl. But this hip *pas de deux* ended up Buster instead of Bogey. It seems his bow tie was a clip-on affair, and like the bewildered Keaton, I stood staring at the strange, disembodied apparition in my hand, while the cop promptly clocked me an overhand right, driving me to my knees.

I scuffled to my feet, and we did a violent polka across the room, landing on top of a makeshift bar and sending endless jugs and hundreds of glasses crashing to the floor. (So you didn't believe those old Herbert Yates Westerns?) In the din I heard an unmistakable Kerry accent shout: "Jesus, a beatnik is killing a cop!" This was followed by the pitter-patter of a hundred flat feet. I felt a hand snatch me by the seat of my pants. It was Gillen, and we fled down the marble stairway of the Commodore out into the night and safety.

My third assignment was in a way a breakthrough. I covered Joe Shaw, a welterweight fighter owned in part by George Plimpton, Norman Mailer, and Pete Hamill. I didn't like the smell of the evening and proceeded to cuff it about in print. Pete took umbrage and in turn cuffed me back in print. The *New York Times Magazine* loved the whole donnybrook and assigned me to write an article on a bookmaker. So within six weeks (after years of *nada*) I was in the *Voice* and the *Times* and being bandied about as "one of the bright New Journalists." A lesson for young journalists: In your early rounds forget the body and go for the head.

The "new journalism" tag, though it pleased me, also baffled me. Not that I hadn't read journalists avidly. I had. Like most New Yorkers, I was a newspaper maven. Over the years I had respected the daily baseball writing of Dick Young (still the best in the field), the columns of Cannon, Breslin, Wicker, Hamill, and the new think tank genre of Mailer and Tom Wolfe. There are many more who arrived in the sixties who qualify. But my most revered were Red Smith and Murray Kempton. Especially Kempton. His column had the intrigue of watching the puff of smoke rise from the Vatican. You knew history was being made in the inner chambers of his head, and if you had the layman's patience to mull over his quixotic metaphors, you, too, might be blessed. He was and is the best reporter who ever worked this town in my time.

So if the original dream was deferred, I was proud of the company I kept. I still hate the solitude of writing, and I suppose this comes from merry years of working in the company of men. (I'd trade a blank page for an afternoon in the snug of a pub every time.) But no remorse. Writing has enabled me to travel to many places and to meet men and women who were once but magical distant names. If you're slipped a ticket to ride this merry-go-round, it's always a treat to latch onto a horse that goes up and down.

It has come to that time when the reader awaits the answers to those "do you sleep in the nude?" questions. For my personal life I'll give a little but, I'm sure, not enough. I have fathered to me (nothing unique in this boast) both a fine son and daughter and revel in the company of an exquisite woman.

My work ethic is simple: Never give a blind quote, and never withhold a fact that will hurt a public figure, regardless of your political leanings. Also, I don't believe in so-called objective journalism. My byline appears on my work; thus, the reader knows that it is my head on the platter. (Opinion, not distorting the facts, is what I'm talking about.)

For my philosophy, I'll borrow Auden's, that man has ever had only two things—prayer and laughter. Sadly, I'm a flop at the former and an apostle of the latter. For the future, I'll be content to be a shade less than Shakespeare, but only since I was reared with a profound respect for the dead.

Would I be happy in another profession? Absolutely. As the trainer of great thoroughbred horses. Better yet, I would like to *be* a great racehorse. Endless Saturdays of standing the toughest of critics, punters, on their ears; then a graceful career at stud, where the most magnificent mares would be brought to my court. This bestial dream is considered only because no one ever offered me the position of God. The only ambition for a truly serious man.

Enough. An epitaph should be considered. Though I be undeserving, the only one I have ever wanted was Prospero's Epilogue in *The Tempest*. And since I'll sulkily hold my breath for an eternity for it, it might as well be granted here.

> Now my charms are all o'erthrown,
> And what strength I have's mine own,
> Which is most faint: now, 'tis true,
> I must be here confined by you,
> Or sent to Naples. Let me not,
> Since I have my dukedom got,
> And pardon'd the deceiver, dwell
> In this bare island by your spell;
> But release me from my bands
> With the help of your good hands.
> Gentle breath of yours my sails
> Must fill, or else my project fails,
> Which was to please. Now I want
> Spirits to enforce, art to enchant;
> And my ending is despair
> Unless I be relieved by prayer,
> Which pierces so that it assaults
> Mercy itself, and frees all faults.
> As you from crimes would pardon'd be,
> Let your indulgence set me free.

JOE FLAHERTY

New York City
April, 1973

One: Clocking This Race

Why Has the Fun Fled Fun City?

They all stood there waiting for the helicopter to come down. You had the feeling some of them wouldn't have minded if it didn't make it on its own power. Up in the sky was the mayor of New York, John V. Lindsay. He was coming to the corner of Plaza Street and Flatbush Avenue to speak to his fellow New Yorkers about the Civilian Review Board.

His welcoming committee was there in strength, passing out "Stop the Civilian Review Board" posters. Wherever you find Lindsay, you find the Conservative Party. An Irish guy in a tweed sport jacket was instructing the crowd that a "yes" vote on the referendum was a vote for Lindsay. In a sentence he told what the Conservative Party in this city is all about.

He was a big kid but not like his ancestors who worked the docks or the ones who wore shamrock-embroidered trunks under the Garden lights on long ago Friday nights. He had the weight, but it was going nowhere. His backside looked like a giant teardrop, probably from sitting too long on stools in the Knights of Columbus drinking 10-cent beer with his own kind to the tune of "The Ballad of the Green Beret." Working with him was a short Italian in a windbreaker who was using the hard sell. He was insulting anyone who wouldn't accept the Conservative Party-PBA literature. One woman complained to the Irish guy that his partner was hurting their cause with his rudeness, but with his collar turned up around his neck, street corner style, he moved through the crowd keeping up his attack. He said the Review Board was another offspring of Earl Warren's court and hadn't Warren "banned school prayer"?

Looking at this guy's action, you couldn't help thinking that the last time he saw the inside of a church was when he rifled the poor box when he was sixteen.

Two Negro kids crowded near the platform from which the mayor was going to speak. A great inspiration struck the two patriots. They scotch-

3

taped two anti-Review Board stickers to the black kids' leather jackets and smiled triumphantly at the nastiness of their joke.

The helicopter came down in the Sheep Meadow of Prospect Park, and Lindsay arrived by car at Plaza Street minutes later. The first thing that strikes you about Lindsay is that he doesn't look like a politician. Bob Wagner's sad eyes make him look like a beleaguered basset hound; Frank O'Connor's face has the decency of a guy who heads the Holy Name Society; and if you put Mario Procaccino in a white apron, he could hawk mackerel at the Fulton Fish Market. Lindsay's good looks are theatrical, not handsome enough for Broadway, but one could picture him signing autographs at a matinee in Bucks County.

A nice-looking kid in a blazer spotted Lindsay coming through the crowd and began to shout, "Here comes the guy who's for social security raises, welfare, and unions." Here is this kid who never said "en garde" to his chin with a Wilkinson sword blade sounding like an honest-to-God John Paul Getty, crying creeping socialism and the whole lot.

As the mayor mounted the platform, you heard everything from a bravo to a Bronx cheer. He tried to speak, but the teardrop wrapped in tweed started to chant, "Stop the Civilian Review Board." A guy wearing work clothes and sporting a beard turned to him and told him to shut up and give the mayor a chance to speak. The guy in tweeds muttered something, and the beard told him that there should be an ethical review board to examine his lack of manners. The tweed eyed the size of the guy and decided to shut up. Right away you knew this was one Hibernian who wouldn't have gone one round in the Garden. Lindsay looked gratefully at his ally and began to speak again. He explained how the Review Board has been in effect since July and that New York City had peacefully passed through a summer that had plagued other cities throughout the nation. He spoke about how traditionally in a democratic system we have always reviewed the conduct of our various agencies. A woman in the rear of the crowd contorted her face into an anguished prune and began to recite a litany of hate at the mayor. "You are for niggers, taxes, and filth, and you are through in this city."

Lindsay stared unseeing above her head and continued speaking. He explained that the majority of the complaints received by the board came from whites, and that 85 percent of all complaints were dismissed as frivolous. A slight woman in her fifties held a "Stop the Review Board" sign; she constantly kept her head down so that she wouldn't have to look at the mayor. Not once during his entire speech did she raise her head to look at him. In memory, only Bela Lugosi showed that kind of dedication in his aversion to crucifixes.

Much sport has been made of Lindsay's reference to New York as a "fun city"; not enough attention has been paid to the validity of his statement. He's right; we have all the trappings of joy. We have a skyline that sends foreign visitors back to their homes with tales of a storied kingdom. Stand outside any office building in midtown, and the most gorgeous women in the world spin through revolving doors. On a summer afternoon you can go to the Big A and see Kelso and Gun Bow go head and head for a mile and a quarter in a rhymed couplet. Sit in the grass with a can of beer and watch the grace of two Puerto Rican teams playing softball. Their delight is expressed in their language, as quick and exciting as a young Ray Robinson's left jab. You can drink German beer in Luchow's on Sunday afternoon or belt boilermakers in Ireland's 32, or sip brandy after the theater in Shor's next to Gleason, Arcaro, and Graziano. You can put on a tie on Sunday and go to a museum and see anything from a brown and gold Rembrandt to a red and white Campbell's soup can. When the wife's lumpy mashed potatoes and overdone steak get you down, with a subway token and five bucks you can sample anything from flaming shish kebab to Indian curried lamb. And if you are looking for music, you just have to move up and down the scale of the city's streets. From the Met to Arthur to Roseland to a dime-a-dance joint, from the Clancy Brothers lamenting about "The Troubles" to Miriam Makeba clicking her African magic.

And if the whole world is a stage, we straddle the globe itself. We have Garland at the Palace and Hamlet in Central Park. Melissa Hayden will show you a beautiful arabesque at Lincoln Center, and Ann Corio will show you practically anything on Forty-third Street. You can be baffled by a happening in the Village or sentimentally reminded of Fanny Brice at the Winter Garden or be astounded by Zero Mostel as he becomes a rhinoceros onstage. And when the dark night of the soul comes and you feel like the most hopeless human on the face of the earth, you can go to Shea Stadium and watch the futility of the Mets and come home feeling like Norman Vincent Peale after he authored his book on positive thinking.

In a city that traditionally loved to see Jimmy Walker and the Little Flower hit the streets we can read about Lindsay playing touch football in the park or walking the city streets in shirt sleeves.

What the hell has happened to us? New Yorkers have lost their sense of style. Without style, life is reduced to arteries pumping blood, kidneys doing what they should, and hearts functioning as used car engines. To hear the critics of this city you would think we were something out of a Hogarth drawing. Nothing but rape, drunkenness, and violence.

How can our women be loving and generous when their mates are hysterical and fear-ridden? In the history of broaddom, from caveman to Bogey, women have always liked their men to be brave and cool.

We have all the intrigue of the Casbah, yet our souls are somewhere in Levittown. Once our streets exploded with the sounds of kids playing stickball, ring-a-levio, and kick-the-can. Now Grimm women spin themselves into their lace curtains and hang by their windows, and at the first sound of laughter and play they tap, hiss, and wave the kids away with their wandlike fingers.

Where can we begin? How can you bring music into the hearts of people who think John Gambling plays pretty groovy stuff? How can you get people to walk into Central Park to see *Hamlet,* when they're out of town visiting Peyton Place? How can you explain the Big A to a city of bingo players? What can be done for people who think that when Puerto Ricans speak they just jabber? How in the hell can you explain Toots Shor's to a guy who does his boozing at the Knights of Columbus or the American Legion? How can you sell shish kebab to a bunch of guys whose bellies are molded like mushy mashed potatoes? Even our cop-outs, the Mets, have sent their leprechaun manager back to Glendale and hired solid Wes Westrum, who turned them into a respectable ninth-place team. When Lindsay plays football on Sunday, we declare he's squandering the taxpayer's time and money.

The truth of it all is that we have the most magnificent playpen in the world, but we are childless. New Yorkers have become crotchety childless people living within a barren gray womb. Our lady in the harbor is without husband or lover; her maternal existence is a lie.

We would rather have the fatigue of Wagner than the vitality of Lindsay. Jack Kennedy is adored in bars with a James Dean reverence. We love him better in death, because the truth is that his ideas and his enthusiasm scared the hell out of us. We are a people of Wagners and Eisenhowers and Johnsons; we are more comfortable with a waspish nanny than with virile young men.

The sadness that shrouds Lindsay is that he thinks he is fighting for a Civilian Review Board. This is only the preliminary—the main bout is to restore some generosity and fun to this dreary city.

October 27, 1966

The Hawks in May: A Day to Remember

On Saturday afternoon past, with the war gods supplying sunshine to heat their passions, the Legions of Decency and Death paraded down Fifth Avenue. Like all war machines, they moved smoothly and with good reason. Their oil, in the form of thousands of empty beer cans and whiskey bottles, littered the side streets of the assembly areas off Fifth Avenue.

The day belonged to the "good Americans." If your hair was slightly

6

too long, your chin foliated, your dress too hippy, or your heritage Asian, you were best off south of the Sixty-second Street parallel of New York City. And as the day got blurrier, the patriots found it harder to distinguish friend from foe. Any intelligent chop suey joint proprietor had a padlock on his door. Even Jewish women in their wedgies sporting too much yellow from the Miami sun were suspect that their politics were more slanted than straight.

The parade organizer, Raymond W. Gimmler, a fire captain, demonstrated he was a master of incendiary happenings. Not only was the parade labeled under the baptism of fire "Support Our Boys in Vietnam," but it also was publicized by posters of demonstrators burning the American flag. In bold black type the posters stated: "If this makes you mad, march in support of Our Boys." So in one imaginative swoop everybody from the New Left to Senators Fulbright and Kennedy, to the Reverend Martin Luther King and Dr. Spock, to Pope Paul VI (who was shilling for the Reds in Fatima), fell under the totalitarian mushroom of long-haired, bearded, draft-card-burning, pro-Vietcong Communist.

To quote Harry Golden, such a coup could happen "only in America." And our fifty-year-old boys defending "Our Boys" ate it all up. There were the American Legion and the Veterans of Foreign Wars with their asses and their bellies sagging like our foreign policy in their khakis of yesteryear. Pathetically, they counted cadence with the rhythmic knowledge of a mother visiting Planned Parenthood for the eighth time.

As in all such national endeavors, God was much in evidence. Priests (ignoring their Pope's simultaneous pleas for peace in Fatima) marched with longshoremen bearing signs to drop a little sanctifying grace on Haiphong and Hanoi. Nuns acting out their roles as fraudulent mothers led a contingent of lay mothers who offered "an alternative instead of a criticism." Conceptually, you could remain a pill and insist on bombing Hanoi, or alternatively, you could fight Communism by "Praying the Rosary to Convert Russia," as one banner suggested. There were other such spiritual pleas as "Draft Martin Luther King" and "Kill a Commie for Christ."

One of the first labor unions to march was the ILA. Leading the group was a grinning, thin-lipped, skinny fourteen-year-old girl dressed in silver sequins, looking like a straight razor. As the group turned on to Fifth Avenue, a Negro woman held a sign stating "No Vietnamese Ever Called Me Nigger." As the marchers began to shout at her: "There's no home relief over there," a man in his thirties, dressed in an American Legion uniform, yanked the sign from her hands and punched her in the face. The marchers broke ranks and rushed toward the skirmish. To come to the aid of a lady? Not quite. About twenty started to throw punches and kicks at the woman. Finally, six policemen formed a circle around the

7

fallen woman and drove off her attackers. Another honest day's work done by American labor. No arrests were made.

Also there were the Teamsters, who seem to have a history of backing Presidents with strange policies. According to the Sunday *Times,* they didn't go to work till Seventy-eighth Street, where they beat and tarred and feathered a youth named Lance Grady for the subversive act of having long hair and sandals. Two of these patriots were interviewed on the late night news by an NBC reporter. One lamented that by the time he reached the scene he couldn't find room to "get in a good punch or kick." His partner's complaint was that Mr. Grady got off so easy. When queried by the reporter on whether this was the American way, our boy blandly stated, "I would like to have left him for dead."

The floats in the parade were monuments of black humor. One group had a Volkswagen bus draped in black cloth (windshield included); strapped to the roof was a coffin that must have been made for Primo Carnera. There was a Cuban group riding on a flatbed truck with a sign stating "If you want to know what Communism is about, ask this mother who lost her son to Castro." And sure enough, sitting in a chair on the truck was a woman wrapped from head to toe in black mourning lace.

The John Birch Society had a flowered float of the Pasadena Rose Bowl genre with a gold lamé statue of Paul Revere on horseback. And Martha Raye was a spectacle unto herself. Dressed in the battle garb of the Green Berets, with her mouth open as wide as the Maginot Line, she counted cadence for a group of children in battle garb marching behind her.

Everywhere you looked American flags were on display. And to demonstrate that free enterprise and patriotism go hand in hand the zealots were hustling flags at a premium price with all the patriotic fervor of a camp follower on payday. The two other flags much on display were the Cuban and the Irish. And, of course, the bars along the assembly area shook with songs of the Irish Rebellion. The rebels from Rockaway, Breezy Point, Brooklyn, and Queens liquidly stoked their fires and struck a blow for freedom by depositing quarters in the IRA collection jars on the back bars.

Their day was complete when they passed the reviewing stand. There stood their Cardinal—in flight training to become a hawk—waving his blessing at them. But the bonus of the day was Mayor Lindsay's absence. "Where's the mayor?" they shouted. "He don't give a shit about our boys," another answered back. And to document their reddest suspicions Lindsay was down at Gracie Mansion delving in the nefarious business of accepting a book of poems from Russian poet Andrei Voznesensky. May God have mercy on his political soul.

In this turbulent climate of booze and bravado on Ninety-ninth Street formed a gentle band of people known as the Flower Brigade. The group was headed by Jim Fouratt, who had been instrumental in staging the

8

Easter Be-In. The group was given permission to march, because Fouratt told the parade officials that they supported our troops but were against our foreign policy. Fouratt, who is against flag burning and the destruction of draft cards, wanted to meet these people on the grounds that "hippies are not un-American." Fouratt stated that he didn't want to anger them but to demonstrate there was ground for respected differences.

The Flower Brigade was composed mostly of young boys and girls gaily dressed, carrying bunches of daisies and dandelions. A police sergeant tried to persuade the group not to march, because "this is the most dangerous crowd I have ever seen in my nineteen years on the job." The sergeant went on to explain some of the ugly incidents that had happened on the parade route. "My God, we have a cordon of cops around the Russian Embassy, we're afraid these people might storm it."

Fouratt asked the police for protection for his group along the parade route. After much discussion and many phone calls, a police captain announced that there would be no special protection because the Flower Brigade was "like everyone else in the parade." It's amazing how you can achieve equality in this country when you're not looking for it.

Fouratt explained the situation to his group and told them nobody had to put his safety in jeopardy. He called for a vote. The brigade decided to march. Before they kicked off, Abbie Hoffman, a former SNCC worker dressed in a dayglo-colored cape, explained what to do in the event of trouble. He asked all the girls to "remove your earrings and any other sharp objects before we start." He then said: "If we are attacked, stay together and cover up your head and your genitals." A young middle-class-looking girl began to tremble and cry. Nonetheless, she marched. This kind of courage would never be understood in these settings: It came from neither numbers nor a bottle.

The group lined up at Ninety-third Street and Lexington Avenue behind a Boy Scout troop from Queens. They all bought American flags and stood in formation. Some guys drinking beer chatted with the girls, and for a while it looked as if everything would be all right. The presence of the Boy Scouts seemed reassuring. Across Lexington near Park, chapters of the Conservative Party stood waiting to march. They congregated under banners stating John Paul Jones, Flatbush, and Babylon Conservative Club. Their jackets sported orange and black "Buckley for Senator" buttons. The only son of God who ever attended Yale.

A woman began to scream at Fouratt and asked him what he was doing there. Fouratt gently tried to explain his group's position. The woman whispered something to the scoutmaster and walked toward the Conservative encampment. Ominously, the Boy Scouts moved away from the group. The eighteen of them stood alone. Then it happened.

The street exploded. Shouts of "Kill them," "Murder the bastards,"

9

split the air. Grown men lustily punched and kicked girls no older than their daughters. American flags were ripped from their hands and torn in bits, seemingly because they were contaminated. The men in the group were bashed into cement walls. A young child fell in the path of the attackers and was nearly trampled. Housewives cheered their hubbies on to destruction. Red paint was thrown in the hair and faces of two screaming girls. Finally, the police surrounded the group, and they fought through the mob.

As they headed east, more cops joined the protective circle. The attackers chased the group across Lexington Avenue and ripped the remaining flags and "Love" signs from their hands. People in cars and on stoops shouted, "Die" and "Take a bath." The door of an Irish bar on Third Avenue swung open, and a fat man in a T-shirt shouted, "Bring them in here, and we'll bend them over and stick it in their queer asses." The young middle-class-looking girl was near collapse. Finally, the cops got the group to First Avenue and boarded them on a downtown bus. A sergeant summoned a patrol car to trail the bus all the way to the Village.

Perhaps the most significant counterpoint of the day was when four Hell's Angels (the clean-shaven variety) pulled up on their bikes at Eighty-sixth Street. They had American flags embroidered on their jackets and carried a large flag. They wore German helmets with swastikas decaled on the sides. They were warmly cheered as they joined the parade.

Perhaps it was prophetic.

May 18, 1967

The Love Ethic on 125th Street

In times of national tragedy the barometer of the mood of the people can best be researched in saloons or cathedrals. Being more comfortable in the former, Friday afternoon I stopped into a pub in the Wall Street area. Besides the normal Friday fare of melted cheese and fish, the main offering seemed to be paranoia.

A rumor was circulating that at the Dr. King memorial in Central Park a militant had suggested the group march on Wall Street and "get the money." Negro waiters were eyed suspiciously as they served platters of shrimp and scallops. Dun and Brad could have sold a premium on food tasters.

The bulls and bears drank in conclaves. The collective courage of the place was about as thin as a strip of ticker tape.

10

Any horror about the murder was tempered with selectivity. A middle-aged man in a gray suit who was holding forth at the end of the bar summed up the establishment theory about the assassination: "It's a shame it had to be him instead of that son of a bitch LeRoi Jones."

The mood in Village bars was its usual mixture of compassion and cynicism. The eulogies for King were secondary to anti-American dissertations. Local social critics who have been theorizing about our national shame for years seemed to find some justification in King's death, since it proved their thesis. The euphoric mood of a week ago when President Johnson withdrew was nowhere in evidence. Then again, there are those people who can only understand withdrawal.

Saturday night all the civility of the city seemed to be located on 125th Street in Harlem. On the subway uptown, white passengers stared vacantly at advertisements, not daring to glance right or left at their fellow black passengers.

An old Jewish couple entered the train at Ninety-sixth Street and sat down with the resignation that history was about to repeat itself. But in actuality the train ride was more serene than on a normal Saturday night.

The extreme west end of 125th Street was virtually deserted. A small restaurant owner snobbishly stated that this end of the block was always quiet. "All that noise and trouble takes place over by Seventh Avenue." True, the street below was noisier, but trouble seemed nonexistent.

A tour of the street is always an education to the white outsider. Butcher shops advertise strange wares such as hogmaws, chicken necks, and slabs of salty pork that the downtowners usually relegate to the garbage pail instead of the stewpot. Nationally owned shoe chains display styles that never would see daylight on Fifth Avenue. A young man pointed to a pair of green suede shoes trimmed with alligator: "You see what I mean, man. That crap is straight out of Sportin' Life."

Some of these stores were looted Thursday night when news of King's murder reached the community. And when one looked at the twisted steel gates still lying in the street, he was struck by the anger of the destruction. The network of steel was mangled and bent as if the looters were pulling the white man's veins out of their street.

The cops, displaying their usual sensitivity, gathered in clusters in doorways, wearing orange plastic helmets with all the tactical intelligence of waving a red flag in front of a wounded animal.

But it was the people who were the city's finest. Women shyly nodded greetings to the white face. Men who usually pass each other by lent their smiles and hellos as if they were passports to safety. The militants and the Mau Mau who usually deliver racial harangues on the corner of Seventh Avenue were absent; the word was that they were out trying to cool the kids who caused most of the damage on the preceding nights. A record

11

shop was playing the words of King over a loudspeaker in the street. A cop car pulled to the curb and asked the woman inside to stop playing the record. A Negro cop with a white Ho Chi Minh beard called me over to his car. His black partner shook my hand, and they asked me politely to leave the area. "Things aren't as safe as it looks for a white man up here tonight," the bearded one advised.

A group of young militants who were gathered around the record store watched the action. When the cop car pulled away, one of them stepped from the crowd. "Hey, baby," he called, "what did the man tell you?" I smiled and said, "He told me my white ass wasn't safe up here." "Don't listen to that bullshit—tonight we're all brothers." With that he put his arm around me and escorted me to a bar. "That's the trouble with this place," he said. "The only white cat who has the balls to walk up here is John Lindsay."

The long bar was covered in leatherette, and every five feet it curved inward, like a woman's hip. A go-go girl in a bikini on a platform absentmindedly humped pillows of cigarette smoke. The men at the bar were engrossed in conversation and boozing, and the go-go girl was left to entice phantoms. Men came up and shook hands, and we all talked of the sadness of it. I was told to keep my money in my pocket, that the drinks were on my newfound brother. "Tonight we have to obey the memory of that man and all be brothers."

When I finally said I had to leave, the young man tried to sum up Dr. King's love ethic. Perhaps it wasn't exactly what the Baptist minister was striving for, but when the words of saints descend into the streets, one can't grumble about translations. Putting his arm around me, the young man offered me one of the last things that remain the domain of the poor, "I love you so much tonight, brother, if you stick with me, I'll see if I can set you up with a good piece of ass."

April 11, 1968

The Legions of Fear Huddle Against the Night

About 13,000 of the folks showed up at Madison Square Garden last Thursday evening to stomp, hoot, and holler for the man who holds the key to their hearts. The Garden was a perfect setting. On other nights, below in the dressing rooms, young fighters' legs have grown old and aging pugs' stomachs have turned sour with fear when it was their turn to walk through the dark chilled tunnel that leads to the main arena. And fear was what this evening was all about.

Fear that was so diverse it came in legions. Black fear, hair fear, press card fear, busing fear, guideline fear, and endless other fears that make up the litany of right in America today. And the little man behind his bulletproof podium epitomized their anxieties.

Before they had a chance to hear him, they had to run a gauntlet of about 5,000 demonstrators who thronged the streets surrounding the Garden. A coalition of young whites and blacks and those foreboding ladies from Women Strike for Peace must have resembled the residents of Hades from the way the believers scampered for the safety of the Garden. Inside, they were afforded police protection (both on and off duty) that is usually reserved for Mafia funerals.

The whole affair was something of a cross between the Grand Ole Opry and an Oral Roberts redemption meeting. We were treated to the Lord's Prayer, the national anthem, "God Bless America," and strains of "Yankee Doodle Dandy." Red, white, and blue boaters (what else?) crowned every head. Wallace's running mate, Curtis LeMay, was allowed a few words, and this was indeed a surprise. After his initial speeches on nuclear weapons, the general is now exposed rather selectively—like French postcards.

As the general spoke about accepting a spot on the ticket as his "duty," a strange feeling came over me. The face was familiar, but I couldn't place it. The chubby cheeks, the small eyes, the glasses sloping down on the nose. Then it hit me. My God, put a shawl on him and he was Jonathan Winters' Maude Frickett!

His wife, who looks like his sister, talked about how she was going to make Central Park safe to walk in at night. This had to be the joke of the evening. For in this crowd of thousands from Brooklyn, Queens, and Staten Island and those who chartered buses from the suburbs, it was doubtful whether more than a handful had ever ventured into Central Park during the day, never mind at night. But the general and his lady stood there grinning at the cheers like two slightly dotty sisters who had just won first prize for preserves at the county fair for their apricot napalm.

Then they brought in Wallace. For about fifteen minutes the Garden exploded with clapping, whistling, foot stamping, and shouting. Since they weren't strangers, you walked among them to see what had brought them to this. There were the Italians who had left their sanctuaries in Bay Ridge and Staten Island with the Blessed Mother standing sentry on their lawns. There were the young Irish kids who shot baskets at netless hoops on the blacktop schoolyards of Our Lady of Something or Another. These were the same kids who drank flat pitcher beer at Coney and Rockaway

13

and lived by the credo of a "fair fight"—one on one. And now a nickel and dime demagogue had turned them into an ugly lynch mob. Their wives stood cheering with them, and whether it be at a prizefight or a rally like this, there is nothing more ugly than a broad cheering for blood.

And these were the innocent, untouchable girls of our boyhood. Their faces now prematurely old with hate and their legs grown heavy with too many children. The same girls you tried to maneuver against banisters with their mothers a flight away, trying to negotiate the impossible through bulky winter coats till you reached the détente of a white-gloved hand decorated with the ever-present imitation pearl that has served as the Irish sexual surrogate for decades. The others were strangers, and they didn't matter. These were the ones bused in from the antiseptic suburbs. Impeccably groomed, smelling of toothpaste, talcs, lotions, and deodorants. When people stop smelling like people, they don't count anymore.

But there was some beauty to the evening. And this belonged to the young black kids who sat in the balcony. They were not the militants who so often parade before the TV cameras, but kids with souls as black and tough as coal. Even their signs had spunk: "George Is LBJ's Sister" and "Welcome to New York, You Racist Bastard." The Wallaceites, who outnumbered them beyond count, were intimidated by them. Oh, they called them niggers and screamed to have them ejected from the arena, but they made it clear that the cops should do the ejecting. It was Saigon against the Vietcong all over again.

Wallace tried to deliver a prepared text, but when the heckling began, he happily abandoned it. The speech was going nowhere, and the hecklers were a blessing. It afforded Wallace a chance to go into his standard repertory. To hecklers: "All you need is a good haircut." Or "I'll autograph your sandals." To the cops: "I'll stand with the police and firemen in the land." To his civil libertarians: "I'll repeal the open housing law," or "The Kerner Report is the most asinine document in America." And his trump card: "Rid the nation of pseudointellectuals" (the largest orgasm of them all).

"They don't have any faith in people," Wallace says of liberals and intellectuals. "Lots of them don't really like people when you get right down to it."

This tragic charge is the foundation of the Wallace movement. It is tragic because the left is vulnerable to it. For the Wallace movement is leagues away from the fat cat Goldwater movement. What he has perceptively achieved is to reach out to the dangling man in America—the white worker who earns between $6,000 and $9,000 a year, whose paranoia has more than a touch of reality to it. In a political year worthy of Beckett absurdity, George Wallace has stolen a page from the "black is beautiful"

14

syndrome. He has taken a classless majority without sufficient economic and social power and told them they were the true soul of America.

The shame of it is that he encourages their fears instead of putting them in perspective. The Olympian left has relegated their anxieties to a Neanderthal mentality. But the truth of the matter is that life in American cities is a dangerous proposition. Neighborhoods in racial transition and the specter of busing their children and the rising cost of welfare are issues of concern for all—not just the domain of screaming racists. The situation has arisen where the left has cavalierly dismissed these people as the lumpen products of such hinterlands as Brooklyn and Queens. So the essence of the Wallace campaign is "mediocrity is beautiful."

At the end you pitied them more than you hated them. For surely once upon a time there was a humanity in these faces, and as a nation we failed to preserve it. Now they are sick, frightened, lost souls. As they left the Garden, they performed the most primitive ritual of the evening. They gathered in groups, as they made their way toward their homes, like men in a time when fire was not yet discovered, gathered to protect themselves against the eternal black night they live in.

October 31, 1968

Requiem for the Payday Patriots

It seems we have underrated Richard Nixon. Not only does he play the dummy admirably, but in the last weeks he has shown a flair for ventriloquism by finding a voice for his Silent Majority. But it's a damn shame that it was the workingmen who were wooden-headed or hard-hatted enough to climb upon his knee.

At first glance it seems incongruous that the working class would gravitate toward Nixon. His style is not theirs. Wallace, yes. A face in the crowd, a small, lonesome road that runs through dirt farmers' country and pauses in the early-morning hours at truck stops. But Nixon's odyssey isn't even on a workingman's map. The class debater, bench warmer for the football team at good old Whittier College, a man who sees Knott's Berry as America's happy farm, the master of the cheap shot (or a "shy rap artist," to use a laborer's term), a whiner in defeat, and a paranoic by profession.

Then why the recent alliance between Nixon and the workers? It is a wedding of his pomposity and, sadly, their circumstances. The key word is "majority."

15

If you came out of a working-class family, you always wanted to belong. Only aristocratic politicians long for "humble beginnings." Anyone who was born there doesn't want to go home again.

It isn't that this class has suffered the abject poverty of blacks that either deadens or ignites the soul. The working class always has lived financially, ethnically, and culturally from hand to mouth. There was sufficient, but not enough. Were you Irish or Irish-American? Italian or Italian-American? You've come a long way, baby, from a "harp" or a "wop," but would you ever be honest-to-God American in your breast or in your brain?

The schools were as half-assed as everything else. You knew your catechism, could read all the books that didn't mean anything, and had learned the one fundamental lesson. When you graduated, the odds were 8 to 5 you would work for a smart Jew. Or perhaps a Protestant, if any of them except Henry Cabot Lodge could be identified.

So you wanted in. An identity, but more a nonidentity to blend in with those who moved around without disturbance. Not the top. You knew better than that. "Just a small piece of change," as Brando said in *On the Waterfront,* but surely a small piece of the pieces you'd never had. "To be liked, well liked," as Willy Loman said. "The majority," as Nixon says. Or a "regular guy," the canonization members of the working class themselves devoutly wish.

But one thought there was a limit on the dues they would pay to belong. It seems wreaking havoc at a memorial for four dead kids is a stiff tariff to pay for such limp company as Nixon and Agnew, though in retrospect it had been coming for a long time.

The kids are scattering that "small piece of change" by demanding that blacks and Puerto Ricans receive equal employment in restricted unions. Worse, they are sacrilegious to such "regular" relics as the draft, the American Legion, and dying for someone else's notion of their country. So the stomping, the skull cracking with tools, the five on one beatings (whatever happened to the saloon society ethic of one on one?) were only a matter of time. And, of course, some of McLuhan's Marauders ("I'm pissing on the flag up here, CBS") and those purveyors of love who oink-oink behind their daisies have helped speed up the action, get the cameras rolling, and put out the lights in many peaceful demonstrations.

So now the more zealous workers, along with their exotic opposites, pose, parade, and pontificate for posterity nightly at six. It's a shame David Merrick doesn't move in and take the stripe and starstruck on the right and the bombs bursting in air segment of the left and move them up to New Haven for the summer to get the kinks out of their act.

But the workers would have struck without provocation anyway. Their street smarts told them they finally had the credentials for the All-America

16

Club that nobody else on the scene possesses—muscle and the nastiness to use it. It came as no surprise that the most rampant brutality happened on a Friday—payday, which means early boozing and 90-proof patriotism. And the Wall Street workers cheered them on, showering them with capitalism's sperm, ticker tape.

The working class finally had made it—grimy John Glenns and Tom Seavers, not only being accepted but adored by those they viewed as their betters. In a fine article in the New York *Post*, Tim Lee quoted the feeling of one of the ironworkers: ". . . I was Jesus Christ walking among them, and people in the crowd shouted, 'God bless you,' and patted me on the back. That was the proudest day of my life." The need and subservience in that quote stuck with me.

I knew these men when they were better than that. Over the years I've admired their penchant for tough work and their strong sense of family, and on many bleak nights I've been warmed by their humor. Moreover, I have been the recipient of their kindness time and again. The working-class community has that generous quality of the early settlers' barn raisings. One helped his neighbor paint his new apartment or move his furniture. The small stores had an intimacy and standards that the plastic Prussian supermarkets never can achieve. Then there are the moments of happiness and sadness. The men gathered around a Formica table in the kitchen drinking a toast to the newborn and the women in the living room offering condolences for the dead. It seems odd that these robust people (both in body and spirit) seek the approval of a bunch of white-collar lackeys.

The office workers and clerks who had any spirit quit the Street when their Republican masters told them to remove their FDR buttons or lose their jobs. The ones who remained now tell you how democratic their company is, because on their annual outing "the old man himself joined the softball game. Singled to right in the fifth, and when it was over sat right down with us and drank canned beer. The old so-and-so is a regular Joe at heart." Meanwhile, the regular Joe's wife was bitching at him for acting so common, until he told her to stop being a cunt, because all such bullshit counts a lot to these boobs when he has to negotiate salary.

And of course, there is the new breed on the Street—with his first snap brim hat, his attaché case, and his tightly wound umbrella, trying like hell to forget his father cleaned out the holds of ships or emptied trash cans to put him through a course in business administration, so now he can walk into the Bull and Bear on Friday nights and order a Beefeater up, instead of a beer or a rye and ginger. So he roots for the ghosts of his violent past to keep his newfound world secure. And who knows? If he gets lucky, he just might meet someone like Julie on *Dating Game*.

Then, too, there is the workers' much-needed image of *macho*. I suppose the thinking goes Tough on the Job, Dynamite in the Sack. So the word most frequently heard during the demonstrations (excepting U.S.A.) was faggot—Lindsay was one; the protesters had no fear of being drafted, because they all were faggots; and bystanders who made peace signs also were included. The specter of homosexuality seems to haunt many of these men. It seems ludicrous and illogical to make these charges of a generation that probably has been with more women in fifteen years than mine and the workers has seen in thirty.

The phenomenon of growing up in the fifties was that when someone asked you how many times you had scored that week, he was talking about masturbation, not fornication. Old men ought to admit their envy. As a class, we rubbed our groins up against more bars and shuffleboards than we ever did against women. And when you saw the hard hats carrying a scantily dressed "Miss Liberty" on their shoulders, you knew she was "the Flying None" of their movement.

But the real sadness is that the working class has allowed their unions to rob them of their pride and manhood in their work. Like the socialist sob sisters of the Telephone Company, they have opted for "security" (a guarantee of pensions, medical care, and thirty-seven toasters and waffle irons when they became engaged), and the integrity of their work be damned. The only evil they've ever seen in automation is the loss of jobs, not the demeaning of their lifeblood—work.

As a class, they have reneged on their standard of acceptance—achievement in a decent job. When the blacks and Puerto Ricans took the same route out of oblivion they did (as laborers and civil servants), they still were looked on as "spades and spics." A class cannot discard the foundation of their lives without madness resulting.

But the most tragic placard in sight at these demonstrations was one proclaiming "God Bless the Establishment." It's pathetic to think that the workers really believe they're a part of the power structure, the same structure that indiscriminately uses their sons as cannon fodder in a war they don't really understand, a war that has driven up the unemployment rate among their own to the highest level in a decade. The same beloved Establishment that rapes the quality of their daily lives by channeling their tax dollars into *Terry and the Pirates* adventures, building highways they'll never use, and granting tax exemptions to fat cats who sneer at them. Whatever happened to their built-in shit detectors that told them the only way to win the Congressional Medal was to come home in a box. Last week Nixon handed out a dozen at a White House ceremony as if they were crackerjack prizes to add some glitter to this gory war. To be shilled by the powerful is expected, but to join them in the dupe is disgusting.

These men weren't raised to hit boys and girls in the street and to spit

18

on grown women who disagree with them. At their best, they are as generous a group as I have ever met. Easy terms like "Neanderthal" or "Fascist" should be left to the granite-tongued Maoists. Johnson and Nixon have sent their sons and relatives off to die, and it's hard for any man to admit his issue died for a crock of shit. But it's harder still when the message comes from draft-deferred college students who, in the workers' minds, have it made. But understanding their exploitation goes only so far. They still are men with singular minds and souls who consciously are selling both for acceptance to a dismal dream of "respectability."

Hamlet's tragedy was "to be or not to be." A choice of the cosmos— all or nothing at all. Most agree Willy Loman's odyssey was less profound, since he conspired with forces that were destroying him. But was it less profound? Hamlet was; Loman populated that neuter terrain of the never-beens and the could-have-beens.

So the working class, like the country in which they labor, have to be relegated to an unfulfilled potential. Not quite failing but also not adventurous enough to attempt real fulfillment. Their souls and the soul of their country resides neither in heaven nor in hell.

So the Silent Majority's tragedy will come full circle. In the end no one weeps for the citizens of Limbo.

May 21, 1970

Give Me Anything But Love, Baby

Once upon a happy time, one spent a month in the country to get away from newspapers infested with death, destruction and racism, all, one believed, provinces of "the right." This summer, a time was spent at Saratoga Racetrack reading that civilized chronicle the *Morning Telegraph* ("America's Oldest Authority on Theatre and Turf") and thinking how blissful it was to escape the love tyranny of the left. An interlude during which one was spared those ever so heavy, humorless tracts about the love bombers for peace, the love of Gay Power and the love of Women's Liberation. All commandments not to be challenged (never mind shattered) unless one wished for a baptism of blood by the "ists:" fascist, racist, sexist, chauvinist, and whatever other "ists" now being created to cover positions, political or sexual, not yet discovered. So, as a spiritual man who doesn't mind a double dunking, I will stick my head into the fount once more.

19

It is repulsive that movements which start out on such fine basic premises are allowed to be perverted by fools because, in the grand liberal tradition, the given movement must encompass all who believe in the final objective. The lack of criticism (not to be mistaken for inside fighting for power) by members of certain movements not only has attracted open hostility to the left, but at present has brought about a counterrevolution that has rendered the left (aside from its splashy headlines) for all practical purposes, such as power, impotent.

In the mind of the populace today, the peace movement rings a Pavlovian bomb. Those gentle days in New Hampshire are now a fairy tale, while the carnage of universities, public buildings, and some mangled bodies is the reality. In a grand gesture, those who pulled off the University of Wisconsin caper tell us how deeply sorrowful they are about inflicting death; however, we should rejoice in their grand blow against imperialism. No one bothered to ask the corpse how he felt about his dubious contribution for love, justice, and peace. And of course, most of the members of the left press tell us, with their usual sophistry, that death is to be decried, but one cat in Wisconsin really is small potatoes to what we're doing in Vietnam. Don't blame children for playing with fire when their national daddy is playing with napalm.

Or how do you morally indict someone for shooting cops? After all, these are just the deaths of pigs, and even some highly religious people disdain pork. And, as every true revolutionary knows, these men even in their playpens cherished a dark Disney Fantasia of pounding the skulls of niggers and children. The enlightened purveyors of love *know* that cops were conceived in gnarled wombs destined for dirty business. They are not men capable of love and family feeling who mainly came to their jobs because it was a step up the ladder in their economic circle.

So the shooting incidents in Philly draw silence, instead of the castigation the murder of Fred Hampton rightly received from the left press. One suspects this stems from the guilt of those scribes who have dehumanized these men in print. Is the love revolution that is going to change our minds and save our souls one which condones selective murder? One feels the line "The death of any man diminishes me" still is a nobler sentiment than "the death of *some* man. . . ."

But what is most abhorrent is that the machinations of the left always are cloaked in the word "love," a hypocrisy with which the villains on the right at least don't perfume their shit. Ask any love child, and he will tell you he is oozing love and peace except for "the pigs, the straights, the white middle class, those Southern peckerwoods, Middle Amerika, and those fucking weeping liberals who are holding back the revolution." I begin to get the dark suspicion that Woodstock would be too large to house the privileged leftovers; any broom closet would do.

If anyone wants to contrast vividly the difference between life and death, love and hate, he should read Don McNeill's beautiful coverage of the first Central Park Be-In; then listen to Jerry and Abbie circa 1970 (between contractual meetings with their publishers, lawyers, and agents) telling kids to get guns—all in the name of love, of course.

The latest "love" movements have been the Gay Liberation and Women's Liberation, both justly conceived, both now sadly developing vicious asides. I must admit the first delighted me, since it best exposed the Play-Dough consistency of the movement-oriented mind which is tyrannized by any cause that, naturally, espouses love. To watch hetero-sexual writers painfully theorize (perhaps thinking of their first gay date) in print that possibly bisexuality is the salvation of oneself (a thought that never entered their heads prior to their assignments) pro-vided some dark hilarity. It had never occurred to them that salvation through sex as offered by Lawrence, Hemingway, and Mailer was now under vigorous attack for confusing the soul with the libido. But then, vogue is the hare that outruns us all, and these were innocent deviations.

What has become disturbing about the Gay Movement is that the con-temptible bullying the homosexuals are fighting against is the same in which they are engaging daily at Sheridan Square. The Young Turks, now liberated, shout "Cunties" at passing women, run up in a group behind young girls, and make obscene sounds and gestures while they goose and pinch. Well, you see, they have been brutalized all their lives, and now the revolution is swinging the other way, so. . . . Love.

I have saved the last waltz for the women. The love movement which would liberate not only them, but also us. On their day, one had to be impressed by such loving kisses of death on placards as "Tell him what to do with the broom" and "Don't Cook Dinner—Starve a Rat Today." Pig. Rat. Ah, you've come a long way, baby. And for a little more hypocrisy, Gloria Steinem on the tube informing us that the movement is loaded with blacks and construction workers' wives; Gloria, ever so demurely, telling Dick Cavett that she regards herself as "a house nigger" (good Jesus!) as opposed to a field nigger. House niggers, we were told, were the pretty variety. Don't look at me for my sex, but twat an object am I. Now I have fond feelings and respect for Steinem, with whom I worked during the Mailer campaign, and it saddened me to hear her using the old political shill of the blacks and the working class. Are we really to believe that black women from Harlem and Irish housewives from Bay Ridge made up the guest list for the Sculls' $25-a-head bash where the *Voice*'s own Jill Johnston buoyed her boobies? I'll have to reread Charlotte Curtis to see if Molly Kelly in a Pucci housecoat was drinking canned beer at poolside.

Then there were those loving feminists who declared that their husbands could only cure their complaint via Portnoy on Lib Day. A ploy which made them sisters under the sheets with those pinnacles of humanity who used to "cut off" (an apt term, that one) their hubbies if they staggered home from a Saturday night on the town with the boys.

One black in the movement, Flo Kennedy, a lawyer and the Paladin of the left ("Have Cause, Will Travel"), stated in the New York *Times* that alimony was a woman's due, because men should pay for the pleasures they received from women's bodies. You talk about sexism! Just imagine, say, that a male spokesman said he didn't believe in alimony because of all the great dicking he had given his woman. My God, Lucy Komisar and her ilk would level the Washington Monument and anything else that sticks straight up in the land.

Perhaps the problem is that one should learn how to love on an individual basis before he tries to preach it in a collective situation. Group speech and group passion, along with group guilt, seem to me a strange way to foster love. I find my fellowman's puppytail hopelessly hanging these days, because his every life action has branded him a chauvinist. One argument is that religion is patriarchal—thus chauvinistic, because God is portrayed as a man. I ask you, what closet John Wayne among us would identify with a thirty-three-year-old virgin who presumably was conceived without sin and passively allowed the Romans to do him in while they shot crap for his robes? Come now, let's have a little Marquis (or a Marquise) of Queensberry rules in this game.

What of those poor boobs of men who go out daily to work the docks, carry furniture, climb the high iron, and drive trucks, who mistakenly think they are doing it with the age-old hope that their sons and daughters won't be subjected to such drudgery, only to learn they have been exercising their chauvinism while they jailed their mates at home with the brooms and the kids? For shame, brothers, for not liberating your women for such higher purposes as liberating McSorley's and the men's bar at the Biltmore or picketing the Miss America contest or whistling at construction workers, all issues of profound interest to the women of Harlem and Bay Ridge. Like most juntas in this country, this one has begun at the top, and one wishes the women would have the honesty to say so.

Women rightfully want power, but what they fail to see is that most men are powerless. They are making the mistake of using the blanket term "male" much the same way segments of the Black Movement use "power structure" when dealing with anyone who is white. The fact of the matter is that in America the top of the pyramid where the pointy heads gather is much more weighty than its broad base. If housework is a drudgery, it is no more so than the majority of work offered in this country, a fact that Kate Millett profoundly and passionately expounds. The problem with collective mentality is that there is a shadow belief that if the yoke of oppression were lifted, like cream we would all surface. All of us would be transformed into corporate heads, political leaders, artists, doctors, lawyers, and daily drudgery would disappear. Plumbers, longshoremen, waitresses, secretaries and hackies would be passé. Sadly, life is not that fair. This is not to say that as men and women we should shorten our vision, but it is to say that we shouldn't heap life's and our own woes on the shoulders of the nearest group and species. If the way to the mountaintop is over the carcasses of other human beings, I'll pass on the new version of the Promised Land.

What woman who has ever engaged in the battle of the sexes can sanely go along with Ingrid Bengis' ("Heavy Combat in the Erogenous Zones," *Voice,* August 13, 1970) pronouncement that women have to go through all sorts of aphrodisiac exercises to be attractive to men, while men merely must be "capable of having an erection!" Dear reader, as Humbert Humbert was wont to say, in what society has this woman been living? Since true confessions seem to be in order, what lonesome man has not suffered at the hands of women who haven't given his soul a wink while they batted their lids at muscular, blond volleyball champions whose brains were as full of holes as the nets they had mastered?

Dear Lord, how many times has flat-footed me lost out to some nimble nincompoop who had mastered the Savoy or the Lindy while my heart, skipping with the agility and grace of Fred Astaire, went unnoticed? Am I to take pen in hand and indict all womanhood for such conduct? Never mind the sneers my acne received, a tragedy that would take novella length to explore.

Nor do I find Miss Bengis' alternatives of chastity and teddy bear impotence attractive; since I believe in the revolution, at least the love gun should be loaded. Instead of indicting all men as hip, coldhearted studs, should not Miss Bengis' examine the company she keeps? And while changing shrinks, could it be possible she should switch venue—a summer in Coney rather than Fire Island might be productive.

Perhaps a moratorium on the collective use of the word "love" is in order, since we seem to have lost all understanding of the word and the emotion. Better we explore this emotion that makes life endurable on a one-on-one basis, rather than defile it in the public arena. Because it seems that the measure of our national grief is that when one is presented the flower of love, the scent of the midnight mushroom is not far behind. So, better in our privacy, like all good men and women down the ages, we find our hearts and cherish what is good, spit on what is vile, and leave a legacy of fineness for those who follow. For one still feels that love in private, though difficult, is possible while in public it has become a political perversion.

So to all men and women, black and white, hetero and homo, I wish you the just power you deserve, the freedom which should be yours, and the peace essential to your growth. But my song to you has one dark refrain: Collectively, you can give me anything *but* love, baby.

September 24, 1970

Willowbrook's Children: Our Final Shame

One wishes statistics would move us to passion, but they don't. Numbers are abstractions, lifeless equations that suffer, die, that are unemployed and unfed.

The bureaucrats know this, and that is why they take refuge in numbers. The war is better, because the body count is lower. Unemployment is measured in percentage points, not in the loss of human dignity or distended stomachs.

There are no tears recorded on a Bell curve, only the sly wrinkles of those who are trying to pacify us. Unless a digit is a subtraction from the sum total of our lives, we just chalk it up, like an insomniac counting sheep. The only people I know who take statistics to heart are baseball buffs.

After all, we can argue, in the dead circle of our emotional zero aren't other places on earth worse than America? In a list of hits and misses isn't it judicious to say that America is among the Top Ten in human endeavor? Sure, we blow a few, but even the Beatles had a couple of clinkers. It's all so soothing, but then to be twice removed is a safeguard we cherish.

But at Willowbrook State School the numbers are horribly animated: children with faces like twisted 8's, children with legs like rickety I's, children with eyes poked out, producing a light and a dark zero, bodies scattered over the floors like spilled bingo pills—all adding up to a hopeless naught. And the bureaucrats there want to blame it all on the cash register in Albany.

This seems too simple. Director Jack Hammond, who has supervised this seventh circle for seven and a half years, was quoted by Howard Blum in *The Village Voice* as having said the conditions were "intolerable and inhuman," but he explained, "You can only do so much without money."

True, Albany has cut more than $37,000,000 from the Mental Hygiene Department's budget, but why did Mr. Hammond not call our attention to the horrors at Willowbrook? (One shudders at the quasi-English

24

country manor name of this dungeon.) Mr. Hammond was silent until Jane Kurtin of the Staten Island *Advance* and Geraldo Rivera of ABC's *Eyewitness News*, with the aid of Dr. Michael Wilkins and social worker Liz Lee, broke the story. For being the prick to Mr. Hammond's conscience and for trying to organize the patients' parents, both Wilkins and Lee have been fired from the institution. Bureaucrats don't fancy numbers that don't stay in neat columns. The question is why Mr. Hammond himself didn't open the doors to the media to arouse the public to the "intolerable and inhuman" conditions that so plagued his soul. It seems one dons the cloak of redemption only when he gets caught with his pants down.

Then, too, there is our own conscience to be dealt with. Since civilization yawned, retardation has been a condition we shook from our connubial sheets into some closet. After all, it is a product of sex, and that is an activity in which we invest so much. Salvation has been sought more often between a pair of legs than between the pages of the Bible.

The proper tit was probably what Ponce de León was after all along, and nowadays we have Lewis and Clark expeditions paddling their way through our organs to find where the river of the orgasm begins. There are those who say it isn't in the mainstream at all, that the true course lies in tributaries, and oral sex sometimes seems to be described as mouth-to-mouth resuscitation. We invest too much in a fickle bank.

Sex is where we are most vulnerable. Accuse an adult of mental shallowness or lack of social grace, and the odds are that the insult will be temporary, not permanent. But assaults on sexuality have cluttered more couches than an aunt with a throw pillow fetish. And, in the language of Houston Control, a retarded child is a "malfunction" of our ego—the child is a dark report card from God. This is no mean indictment to a society obsessed with perfection, in which even our own body odors are considered offensive.

So we pretend the retarded children are not there, and we bill and coo over the "perfect" replicas we reproduce. After all retardation is not a chic cause. Who would want to throw a fund-raising party on the blue lawns of Long Island or the Upper East Side for retarded kids? No revolutionary berets present, no kicky ethnic costumes, darling—nobody who is anybody would attend. Supposing someone brought some of the children? My God, one of them might stick his hand in the pâté. So the "real" revolution goes on, while suffer the little children, for isn't theirs the kingdom of heaven? A tour of Willowbrook will tell you, like hell there is.

I was shaken out of my role as a sheltered parent when Malachy McCourt, who has a stepdaughter in the institution, asked me to tour Willowbrook with him. McCourt is one of the leaders of the parent group who had stormed the doors at Willowbrook the week before. Needless to say, he is not a welcome sight on the grounds, so we arrived unannounced.

As we entered the first ward, our noses were greeted by the perfume of the consigned damned, piss and shit. The walls were cracked with age and plaster-scabbed, much like the faces of many of the patients. The room was about seventy yards long. On the cold marble floor lay the patients, some dressed, others nude, like some strange flora. The ward had about seventy patients and two attendants, contrary to the national guideline of one attendant for every four patients.

There wasn't one item of diversion (books, toys, etc.) in the room. Open pipes ran overhead, marking a perimeter for the bare light bulbs. The bathroom reeked of stale excretions, and many of the stalls were without toilet paper. This condition, according to Dr. Wilkins, results in a 100 percent rate of hepatitis among patients. The sole diversion in the ward was a TV set blaring, "Everything's Better with Blue Bonnet on It."

By the time we reached the next ward the word was out that we were on the grounds, and as we entered, attendants were hustling clothes and sneakers in to the patients. This is not meant as an indictment of the many dedicated attendants our group encountered at Willowbrook. The institution is so understaffed that the attendants in most wards have all they can do to keep the patients clothed and fed and to clean up the excretions.

A retarded child should require about fifteen to twenty minutes to feed; but because of the understaffing, each child is fed in about four minutes. This forced, birdlike feeding (virtually shoveling food down the gullet) has resulted in deaths, because the food goes into the lungs and causes chemical pneumonia.

As you look at these tragic victims, you have to fight back the impulse that death is not a blessing. I suppose another reason one doesn't like to look at retards is that it assaults one's faith. After a couple of hours at Willowbrook, your curses are leveled at heaven as well as earth.

But man shaking his fist at God is an old and futile exercise. Things can be done for these children. They respond to attention and play like any other children, and there is no reason they shouldn't be granted the basic accouterments of humanity in warm clothes and food. Also, we must find those who shouldn't be relegated to limbo. Many at Willowbrook have the potential to work outside the institution in structured situations. Five thousand dollars a year is spent on each patient, and the money shouldn't be used to maintain human beings in a zombielike existence. Love has never been the exclusive province of the perfectly formed.

The sickest sight we encountered was in a ward with about fifty retards. We found two children of perfectly normal intelligence sentenced there because both were paralyzed from the waist down. The nurse in attendance said that they had been there for years and that both had parents of means. Michael, age nine, and John, age eleven, talked to us, as they sat in wooden carriages that resembled Porgy's vehicle on Catfish Row. We talked about baseball, television, and other subjects, carefully avoiding any mention of their parents.

The nurse later told us that Michael had been turned down for adoption, because the couple who wanted him was "too old." So some bureaucrat has taken two perfectly healthy minds and, because they had the misfortune to be born with twisted legs, consigned them to a peer group who can do no more than grunt. This was enough to make you curse the unholy trinity of parents, bureaucrats, and God.

Oddly, you blessed the television set in this ward. It was the boys' only articulate company here, even though Magilla Gorilla was the spokesman.

As we were leaving, the boys asked us to return and bring them some baseball picture cards. McCourt, a big, shaggy panda of a man, was weeping openly. "You never get used to it," he said. "You come a thousand times, and you never fucking get used to it."

As we drove away from Willowbrook, we passed the trustees' housing high on the hill with manicured lawns (many attended in slave labor fashion by the patients), all prime propriety. It was like driving through the officers' compound on an Army base. The scum was kept downwind so it wouldn't contaminate the aroma of their meals, their fine sensibilities, and their locked-up women.

This is an issue we can't let die. Governmental pressure must be brought on every level until funds are restored and creative programs instituted. In the meantime Willowbrook accepts unpaid volunteers. All you have to bring to the job is a human touch. Also, clothes and toys can be dropped at any local firehouse, and they will be delivered to the institution.

Here is a challenge to the age of consciousness raising: Go look at the slaughter of the lambs. My words can't evoke the stench, the vacuous existence, the garbled cries, the spastic bodies, or the program that allows these marred innocents to be designated as human disposables.

Our time has dulled us with a thugs' war, with the murders of those we had anointed as hope. Our country has donned the harlequin costume of black and white. But unless we are men of stone, Willowbrook must move us to weeping because our final shame has come. The curse of Herod is upon the land.

February 3, 1972

A Terrible Blather Is Born

This piece is dedicated to Frank McCourt, who, with the wisdom of Solomon, spent the day lying on his bloody Irish arse.

Sweet sufferin' Jesus, thank be it is over for another year.

I'm no good at these occasions of calendared merriment. I go mad with depression on holidays, and for good reason. At Christmas it is demanded I be gentle beyond my means, on New Year's I'm called upon to be a lunatic with a monkey's hat on my head, at Easter there is a suit to be bought I can't afford, and on St. Patrick's Day my consumption is expected to equal the reserves of the Grand Coulee Dam. As a man grows older, he longs to pass his life away in a rosary of innocuous Wednesdays.

Now, as a race the Irish are no more mediocre than any other group in large numbers, but this year they were enraptured with their own purity. Since Northern Ireland began to dominate the headlines, there has been flap about an Irish Renaissance or what-have-you, and every paddy in sight has bored me with the beauty of us all.

In point of fact every non-Irishman I met also mumbled leprechaun lyrics in my ear. Greeks quoted Yeats, Jews sang ballads, and Croatians gave me clenched fist salutes. Irishmen who had developed their biceps by throwing bricks at peace and civil rights marchers compared themselves to the Vietnamese and the blacks. A terrible blather had been born.

The whole experience kept me in a maudlin drunk for two weeks. The only green I sported was what I was hacking out of my lungs every morning, and by the end of it you could have written "Goodyear" across my liver. My mailbox was stuffed with pleas for every Irish cause from Derry to Harrisburg, and the Irish-American Cultural Society (that must be an elite group) demanded a contribution of $50, $100, or $150 from me, which was an insult beyond repair. I rationalized that if I were a trophy of their culture, they should have been sending me checks.

Total strangers elbowed their way to the bar to discuss our "literary tradition." I said fine, let's talk about the *Daily News* and the Brooklyn *Tablet* and the *Baltimore Catechism*. But this didn't seem to satisfy them, so I had to recite how we had starved O'Casey to death and turned Shaw and Wilde into the best bogus limeys since Douglas Fairbanks, Jr., how Joyce, soused in Paris, trembled over nightmares of hell for sins of self-abuse, and how Samuel Beckett has adopted a foreign tongue. But there was no stopping them. They mistook all this bile for vaunted Irish wit and hugged me, pronouncing I was a regular ould sod brother.

Radio and television shows beckoned me to take on the airways to extoll my heritage. What in the name of hell did these people want to know? I had cauliflower ears courtesy of the nuns. Every time I get acid indigestion I check into a hospital for a biopsy, fall on my knees, and say an act of contrition because of my esthetic concern over which band of angels I will end up singing with.

Certainly they didn't want to know about my early sex life because if they did, all they would have had to do was air a minute of silence on their networks. I was terrified to leave my home in the morning for fear there would be a group of sociologists on my doorstep waiting to kidnap me off to the Smithsonian: "Authentic Ethnic Found in Wilds of Village."

But when the day finally came, sanity returned. There was the parade in all its glory, with Jack McCarthy narrating on TV in a borrowed accent so heavy St. Christopher couldn't have shouldered it. McCarthy was adorned in a white fireman's hat, presented to him by one Raymond Gimmler (best remembered for staging the prowar march of 1965).

As one women's college group passed, Jack cooed, "Their proudest claim to fame is that they produce Catholic mothers," a curriculum, one presumed, that started with a drop of holy water and ended with a splash of sperm.

But one has to admit Jack knows the nature of every Irishman's dreams —to make a fortune in the new country and spend it in the old. He spouted blessings on Irish Airlines and various hotels and resorts in Ireland, and you knew old Jack was in for a grand summer.

They came in legions: the sons of every county, those out-of-step high school bands (we reserve our rhythm for the sheets, not the streets), the good nurses, the good clergy, the good civil servants all paunches and pensions, and the grand marshal himself, proudly stating that that very evening 2,500 Friendly Sons of St. Patrick would be attending a dinner at which Spiro would be the guest speaker. Agnew was to repeat his triumph on Sunday morning at a breakfast of the Holy Name Society of the Police Department before 3,500 wildly cheering guests.

When our Renaissance came marching by, wearing black armbands and chanting at the pols in the grandstand, they were told to keep their arses moving, or else it was time for a commercial interruption. Jack put a final benediction on the whole affair with his patented tagline: "May ye be a half hour dead before the divil knows it."

As I walked into a saloon that night in my beret and shaggy locks, a fireman with the face of an uncooked roast beef looked up and snarled, "Hello, Pierre." It was the first honest comment I had heard in weeks, and I was tempted to say it was grand to be back among my own.

I have lived as Irish-American for thirty-five years. I have endured it, and it is too late in the march for me to believe we are going to become champions of humanity. Which is not an insult, since I don't believe any other race has a franchise on that claim either.

So I hope that by next year all the blather fades, and the cynical gilders of humanity spend their day in church with the saints and let the people have the street. If not, look for me to be marching in the middle of the parade, carrying a red, white, and blue banner and loudly proclaiming: "Ireland, Get Out of America."

March 23, 1972

The Tale of the Dilettante Donkey

I tell you this election is a steamfitters' number. They should put up George and George.

—JOHN BERGEN, the local commissar of Lion's Head politics

Just what kind of an election was this to be? I wondered as I prepared to leave for Miami. Already I was in a quandary. Earlier in the year I had testified with my money that McGovern would never see the light of nomination. One down. How many more to go?

More confusion. I was supposed to fly to the convention with the New York delegation on National Airlines—that is, until the women of that delegation forced the group to denounce "sexist" National and fly Eastern to the sun (daughter also, I presumed). Then my flight was delayed for forty minutes for "mechanical reasons." Now what the hell did that mean? Had some vaginal vigilante placed a ticking box on the plane? Such pondering could be done only with the aid of gin.

What kind of minds did these people have anyway? How could some silly ass Madison Avenue slogan such as "Fly Barbara" be transformed into "Fuck Barbara"? Like the FBI, did they see perversion in the innocuous? With such thoughts I boarded "Phyllis." I ran down my erotic roll call for a Phyllis to no avail. The closest a Phyllis had ever come to my bed was in the shape of the lovely light verse of Miss McGinley. I relaxed till "Phyllis" taxied onto runway 13—such symbolism this early in the sojourn was unbearable. This plane would never get up.

Paranoia proved paranoia. My taxi passed by numerous hotels with façades of wedding cake icing before I arrived at the Diplomat, the home of the New York delegation. The surrogates of the "People" roamed the lobby, reminding one more of Bloomingdale's than Bloomington, Biloxi, or Bakersfield. The smaller lobby that led to my room was bedecked with two bogus Rembrandts and one Renoir, and I trembled with expectation when I turned the key in my room lock: Would the bellboy be Lautrec? It was now a question of whether it would be steamfitters or stylists.

There was a marvelous scam afloat. At the bars there were whining declarations that there would be massive walkouts if McGovern were defeated. After all, he was, in the Flatbush lexicon, the "people's cherce." The left is stupendous at such self-chicanery. For years they have been spouting mythical coalitions—blacks, Chicanos, respectable radicals, and the poor whites of Steinbeck and James Agee. This failing, they sported this year a new coat of many colors, and "populism" was the hook on which they were going to hang it.

Three essential patches were to be added: the red of the Indian, the purple passion of the students, and, lo and behold, the yellow of "Joe's" hard hat. Dear old "Joe," with his Seagram 7 & 7, his phone order Chinese food, his ketchup on meat loaf, his bowling ball, and his frumpy wife with her dumpy rump encased in a bourgeois botanical garden of a housedress was to be stitched on arbitrarily to create the new Frankenstein that was going to trample the Establishment. My bile began to rise.

But early in the primaries it was found that Dylan's guitar fell mute on "Joe's" ears, that he was off to Alabama with a banjo on his knee. So the left, the masters of riff, broke into "Good-bye, Joe." Still, the "Man of the People" myth prevailed, even though William V. Shannon pointed out in a *New York Times Magazine* article that the total popular vote in the primaries showed Humphrey first with 4,051,134, McGovern second with 3,950,394, Wallace third with 3,612,650, the corresponding percentages being 26.5 percent, 25.8 percent, and 23.6 percent. Also, as Mr. Shannon asked, "Is the man who was defeated in New Hampshire, Illinois, Pennsylvania, Ohio, Florida, Maryland, and Michigan *really* the choice of the people?" But purist snowballs have a way of building into avalanches, so this mental slush went unchallenged at Miami.

Too, the "populist" balloon was found to be floating more on hot air than wings of the dove when the Washington *Post* did an income survey of the "proletariat" on the convention floor. The study's findings were as follows: The national percentage of those under $5,000 income is 18 percent, delegates in this bracket 6 percent; 32 percent of Americans make between $5,000 and $9,999 (thus, this is the heartland of our economics), the delegates in this range numbered 10 percent. The next income group includes those earning between $10,000 and $14,999—27 percent of the national income, delegate income 20 percent.

But it is the last two income brackets that tweak the "populist" tail: 18 percent of Americans make between $15,000 and $25,000, and the delegate income in this category was 31 percent. Those in the country who make over $25,000 are listed at 5 percent, delegates in this income group were listed at 31 percent! One began to wonder whether the "new populism" bespoke Getty or ghetto.

A look at the educational statistics was no more favorable: 39 percent of the delegates had done postgraduate work, compared to 4 percent of the nation; 12 percent of Americans have some college education compared to 27 percent of the delegates; and slightly more than 6 percent of the total population hold college degrees, compared to 20 percent of the delegates.

Now, since I was instrumental in the Mailer-Breslin run for City Hall, I am not averse to blatant snobbery—as long as one doesn't couch it in "people pieties." We offered a midnight witchbroom of a philosophy, hoping that the hip and the bored might hop a ride. But the McGovern forces trying to con off this conglomerate as a combo of the Joads, Bigger Thomas, Studs Lonigan, and Sacco and Vanzetti were as tough to swallow as a raw oyster on the morning after. The dusty "prairie populism" began to smell "posh."

It soon became clear what was at stake here was not what kind of election it would be, but rather something more fundamental, something more indigenous—power, the ownership of America. When the Turks canned the Daley delegation on Monday night in favor of the Singer delegation, it was a case of David declaring his moxie. Not that one can muster tears for the cowardly lion (I can't), but some basic law and, moreover, some basic street smarts can't be ignored.

Daley's delegation trounced many of the challengers in an open elector primary, 900,000 votes recorded. Second, the Singer delegation was less representative of the Chicago populace than Daley's. As Mike Royko, author of the anti-Daley tract *Boss* pointed out, the Singer delegation had one Italian and three Poles on it, and besides, the Reverend Jesse Jackson, one of the honchos of the challenge, didn't even vote for himself in the primary. Indeed, he has never bothered to vote in a Democratic primary! Also, one should realize that vengeance will be taken when there is no shot at retribution. Daley now has the pleasure of November nastiness.

As Gene McCarthy said in a 3 A.M. phone call, "My God, I used to think the Papal saints were dangerous, but now I know it's the Methodists we have to be terrified of."

After the California win and the Daley defeat, the drama went out of the "open convention." The nine women who challenged the South Carolina delegation were sacrificed to expediency, so that the merits of McGovern's California bloc would not come under challenge. This offered the small drama of Bella Abzug chasing Shirley MacLaine's falling star among the feminists around the floor, accusing her of selling out her sisters.

32

Indeed, this most "sexless" of all conventions was to prove rather raunchy. Male prattlers for Women's Lib had quail stashed high in the aviaries of the hotels, while their domestic hens sat on the nests at home. Liberated hussies, housewives on the lam, and Collins Avenue hookers simmered on their seats at the Fontainebleau's Poodle Lounge. It was at this site Ms. Germaine Greer engaged in a dialogue with a Bambi-eyed hooker on the merits of the working feminist. The hooker took umbrage that Ms. Greer was selling her talents to a corporate magazine, while she, in the true spirit of populism, was attending to the needs of the masses. Ms. Greer tried the "sister" line, only to have the hooker turn away and proclaim she was "no fuckin' sister." For her half-truth I bought the lady in question a drink.

When it became evident McGovern had a lock, a joint bender took place. The purists who won started to caucus with the sexual frequency of goats, and those who had lost got drunk with despair. The press (of which I am a proud member) needed no excuse except our bile, and our boredom outdid all. While the New York delegation was calling for "loyalty oaths" from its leaders (it seems it's a short route from Gene to Joe), the Chicago delegation ("the fighting 17th C.D." as they billed themselves) waged war on anything that was corked. And if you wanted to graze mentally, there was enough grass to satisfy Man o' War.

Madness began to abound. The Honorable James Breslin, delegate from Queens, having had enough of Mickey Mouse caucuses, kicked a fellow delegate in the ankle. Matty Troy was game for anything from fighting "the mayor of Chicago" to calling for "a united Ireland." Whiskey and cigarettes closed reporters' stomachs to the size of keyholes; days passed without food. Doug Ireland, the missing link between rogue and reform, in a Herculean feat, ordered two triple vodka screwdrivers (six shots): "Fuck lettuce, I got a ban on solids," drinking these fishbowls within ten minutes. Old labor leaders and regular Democrats and reporters were at sea. What was happening?

It was as if one were inhabiting a spaceship on his own planet. Where were the farmers, the mechanics, the workingmen with the kids and the mortgages? Had some strange suction machine lifted them off the face of the land? Was the America I had twice driven across gone? Were the McDonald's all head shops, the farms communes, the black neighborhoods African states in exile, the factories dormitories? Was there a pair of overalls out there without a daisy implanted on its seat?

And yet to come were platform planks to abolish income tax, on abortion, gay rights, a $6,500 guaranteed annual income, returning federal lands to the Indians, and, sweet Jesus, yes, school prayer! Was Fellini en route to shoot this meshugginer Satyricon? Would the Lord turn this city to salt?

Gin and tobacco had me on edge. I needed an old anchor. A priest wouldn't do, but a philosophical prince of the church was at hand. I decided to journey to the Americana Hotel and simply ask Gene McCarthy: "Who owns America?"

July 20, 1972

McCarthy: Displaced Godfather

En route to McCarthy I tried to fathom the strength of McGovern. Was he tough, wishy-washy, or pragmatic? I considered the comment of one observer: "His charm to the kids is that he's a permissive father whom they feel they can bully around."

But one wondered how accurate that assessment was? After all, Mc-Govern had hinted at promising diverse minority groups everything and, in fact, delivered them nothing. He commanded his floor troops to defeat the minority planks on abortion, homosexual rights, and the $6,500 income, and his stance on amnesty was fudged with a clause to examine each case on its individual merits, a far cry from Gene McCarthy's call for all-out absolution during his 1968 campaign. But then it might be harder for a draft resister to pass through the eye of a Methodist than a Catholic.

The most pertinent testimony to McGovern's fiber was that in a despotic coup he had laid the guidelines that ensured his victory. Such blatant banditry made me recall my stickball days on Vanderbilt Street. We would change the ground rules arbitrarily late in the game, depending on the situation (the California challenge was the voice of the people, Chicago was the groan of the machine). So the consensus was that Mc-Govern was not the cupcake he was first assessed to be but very possibly a tough cookie.

But a primary is a parlor game played with familiar pieces in safe isolation, generally away from the roar of the crowd. What would the bleacher bums do to McGovern when he was forced to open up his game? Or, if one is allowed to mix his sports metaphors, as McGovern walks the fairways of national life, how many Bunkers are awaiting him? If the 1968 Wallace voters' figures are an apt indication, McGovern is in for rough going.

The McGovern forces, though, seem to be basing his November strategy in yet another parlor. Instead of a broad-based appeal, they talk of the "youth vote." That is, they claim they will register 18,500,000 kids and

34

receive 70 percent of that vote, which would make McGovern not the President but our first Lord of the Flies. This, of course, is based on the romantic assumption that all youths are pure of heart, which works well in a Charles Reich fairy tale but not in a Gallup Poll. The latest poll shows that there are 9,000,000 unregistered noncollege students, compared to 2,500,000 unregistered college students, and that the choice of the un-tutored is Nixon by 48 percent to 44 percent. Who owns America?

How about that, Mr. McCarthy? The tanned, relaxed McCarthy replied: "Well, it reminds me of the French Revolution, in the middle period without the violence." (Oh, that head that haunts him. What mysterious seas would he have sailed with us as passengers?)

But since the McGovern phenomenon is a new experience, McCarthy was more intrigued than affronted. On the question of McGovern's Sherwood Forest economics: "This is the first time in history that 70 per-cent of the people are being asked to vote themselves a private gift at the expense of 30 percent." And with a smile that has clocked the greed of man he added: "You know, it could prove to be an intriguing proposition."

McCarthy feels that the current chaos is directly attributable to Johnson. "It was Lyndon who wrecked the party, and I don't see anyone around who has the power to reunite it. I think only Bobby had the power to do that. I remember the old days when the national committee was still powerful, and we relied on them for contributions. Bill Proxmire used to come out of the committee room, holding his hand over his chest where the envelope was and looking toward heaven, and I was outside waiting in line as if I was going to confession."

Since McCarthy was the godfather of this movement and is now ignored (indeed, insulted only four years later), it was pleasant to find him in such good humor. As usual, he was anxious for zany gossip, and stories were swapped: the New York delegation standing en masse and shouting, "Right on," when Reuben Askew quoted Cochise in his speech, funnier yet when you realized that the only image of the old warrior they probably had was Jeff Chandler in *Broken Arrow,* or the saga of the gay who pulled out his prick in the gallery during the debate on the homo-sexual plank, an incident I said I thought McGovern could finesse by simply stating that it wasn't the first time a prick had been seen at a Democratic convention. That comment moved McCarthy to ad-lib: "Some-times we've even nominated them."

Then there was the tale of Doug Ireland watching the convention in his room with his ever-present veep, a jug of vodka. Ireland retired to the bathroom for a sobering shower, and in his absence the convention went off the air, and the film *Mr. Smith Goes to Washington* followed it. The slightly chastened Ireland returned to the room to see Jimmy Stewart leading the Boy Rangers onto a convention floor. "The way they've been conducting this fuckin' circus," said Ireland, "it took me ten minutes to figure out I wasn't still watching the convention."

We talked of the choice of a Vice President. "The consensus seems to be that they need a Catholic on the ticket," McCarthy commented. "I was talking to a delegate who felt Abe Ribicoff could fit that demand perfectly."

McCarthy's was to have been the first name put in nomination till he withdrew that evening. "I drew the pole position for tonight," he said. "Do you think you could sell it at the Diplomat in exchange for the cost of my hotel bill?" Then, with perverse candor he added: "I guess I'll have to find something to fake around with for three months, so that everyone will mistake me for a national voice."

I was with fellow Voicer Phil Tracy, and as we rose to leave, McCarthy bestowed this enigmatic benediction: "Mamie used to say that Ike's last prayer at night was that God should take over the country while he slept. So, like Ike, I'll leave it in your hands."

Perhaps the division of ages and ideology is best summed up in the following vignette. Sid Zion was standing in the Fontainbleau lobby when an old Jewish man walked up to him and asked: "Did they pick a Vice President?" Zion replied: "Eagleton." The old man shook his head in disbelief and said: "My God, they picked an Indian."

Whether McGovern can convince America's middle that he is not some starry-eyed evangelist remains to be seen. His biggest strengths now are two negatives: the hope that Wallace will run and splinter the South and Nixon's strength among the blue-collar workers and, second, Nixon's own sleazy makeup. McGovern and his people have to realize that wooing the Humphrey and Muskie vote is not a sellout to red-necks. These people have traditionally voted for progressive, liberal Democrats, and to force them to the right would be a tragedy. Fringe issues must have their airing in a society that prides itself on individual rights but not at the expense of discourse on jobs, housing, and the cities. One suspects McGovern has a little bit too much of the rube in him and feels more at home in cornfields than on concrete.

But it has been a perverse year politically, and one wonders if McGovern has some hip plan to put the snatch on America. Will the election mark the advent of a new sociology or business as usual? Is the prophecy that a child shall lead us coming to fruition? Will November bring us Georgie-Porgie with his promises of puddin' and pie, or did he simply kiss us to make us cry?

Who owns America?

July 27, 1972

36

Let George Undo It: A Sorrow and a Pity

Well, with the election over and the inevitable results in, the inevitable has happened—the pogrom has begun. Not, however, the one that was expected. In a perverse end-around that only Allie Sherman could admire, the winners are being sent to Coventry by the losers.

In reams of purple prose and mauve mouthings we are being told that the American electorate has lost its conscience and that the nation is off on a brownshirt bender. The members of the perishable set are once again packing their bags (was that a thunderstorm that followed the election or the sound of suitcases slamming?) for democratic bastions in Majorca and Ibiza. All is lost because the majority of people rejected George Mc-Govern for the most base of reasons: warmongering, racism, and a titillation with totalitarianism. Or did they?

As a McGovern voter, I'm afraid I must, in this instance, defend the elect rather than the select or, to put it differently, defend the dragon against the legions of St. George.

Examining the results outside the Presidential arena, one comes up with the unmistakable conclusion that if the country didn't exactly choose Nirvana, it didn't opt for Nazism either. The Democrats picked up two seats in the Senate, one statehouse, and maintained their superiority in the House. The Black Caucus was expanded. Daniel Walker, who indicted the Chicago police as the "rioters" in 1968, won the Illinois governorship, and Edward Hanrahan, who was linked with the slaying of Fred Hampton, was defeated. A disciple of Martin Luther King was elected to Congress in Atlanta, and special targets of a Rockefeller purge, Otis Pike and Ogden Reid, were reelected. California in its quixotic madness opted for capital punishment (too many good movies about the Big House) and rejected a referendum to stifle the power of Cesar Chavez's union.

Indeed, most of the liberal Senators and Congressmen survived the Nixon landslide. And according to the New York *Times* (no, it hasn't yet been taken over by the CIA, sweetie), the projection is that the two houses, if anything, will be slightly more "left" this time around. Which brings us to a handcuffed logic even Houdini couldn't have escaped: We shouldn't have let George do it.

Not so, those who know better tell us. Harriet Van Horne wrote in the *Post* the morning after that the people voted "their meanest prejudices" and followed with: "Those of us who believe in honest government and civil liberties are now passengers on the Titanic." As one of the cruise organizers for McGovern, Mrs. Van Horne seems in a moment of passion to have slipped her compass.

37

The other standard line is that McGovern was "too decent to become President, too good to become President." In other words, we were undeserving of his eminence. I admit I have a prejudice here since the good nuns tried for years to prove my unworthiness, but in a fit of spectacular rationalization I figured the Lord must be as much a sucker for good company as I, so I was safe.

I'm not trying to demean "decency." I admire it as much as the next man. My butcher and baker are amply decent, and the guy who sells me my racing form seems infected with that grace, but at last look none of them was seeking to lead me. One has to believe that future leaders require more than that. Besides, a quick perusal of his record leaves McGovern many electoral votes removed from canonization. But Nixon was the issue—right?

To many of us, he was, but this fact seemed to escape many of the Senator's adherents at Miami Beach. If one has a singular objective, the basic ground rule has always been discipline, the revolutionary religion from Che to Malcolm. The McGovern supporters at the convention were like a convocation at Lourdes—everybody had a crutch to chuck.

Some of the loudest spokeswomen for women were chi-chi Ms.eries who have been quoted as seeing marriage as the equivalent of prostitution. Anyone who dared question the validity of abortion was a vagina from the Vatican. The very thought that the beginning of life is a delicate hair trigger in the brain and soul was not to be considered. But then, subtlety was not their strong suit. Like their candidate, they were divinely anointed to lead.

Why, if McGovern, the man of decency, was such a superior choice to Nixon, did the women, the gays, the disenfranchised engage in wild exhortations which gave the enemy ammunition (surely, they realized it) instead of biding their time and allowing President McGovern's "decency" to manifest itself? It seems to me that their ardor for McGovern was based less on his being a mind to lead than that he was an upturned top hat into which they could throw their ideas as one throws his gloves.

All this doesn't excuse McGovern. If a man is responsible for his face when he's over thirty, a candidate is responsible for his supporters.

We learn from Tom Wicker that McGovern was opposed to Muskie's candidacy (the most logical one, if Nixon was the issue) because Muskie was a Johnny-come-lately on the war. It seems the spouter of Isaiah has missed a couple of verses in the Bible—namely, those on forgiveness.

Indeed, checking the facts, McGovern's candidacy was based on purge. Only the young, the Wonder Women, the minorities, and the antiwar movement would be allowed to stand under the heavenly umbrella of his banner. The fact that in 1964 a great swath of this country voted for peace

38

escaped his doctrinaire disciples. Morally, such a stand was corrupt; politically, it was stupid.

Of course, there is the argument that his candidacy was crucified on the old rugged cross of radicalism. This also is boobery. His positions in mid-campaign were no more progressive than the average ADA member. By taking positions that weren't thought out and then abandoning them, he dealt radicalism a blow from which it won't soon recover. If one is out to foster a brave new world, he'd damn better have a firm axis to spin it on. McGovern's earlier positions on wealth distribution, tax reform, and welfare reform were as heated as a dockside departure. It was when they came under scrutiny (sex over love) that the nation received his Dear John.

When it became apparent that his Mouseketeers weren't going to materialize (what was it—25,000,000 new voters?), McGovern and his staff discovered there were other people out there. Ethnic groups were set up; rent-a-hard-hat was the clarion call. If it wasn't so sad, it would be damned funny.

I received a call two days before the election to convert the Irish in Queens from a sound truck. Even St. Patrick was given more time to purge the snakes. Another caller asked me to recruit a brewery worker friend to speak for McGovern. One began to think his New York staff had a central casting committee: "Hey, chickie, get me a rough-hewn type." In that sense the campaign remained morally constant—positions and people went under more conversions than the rollers at a tent revival.

On election night the high priests and priestesses lamented the nation's undeserving heathen. Gabe Pressman interviewed Nora Ephron and Dan Greenburg who, gee willikers, didn't know *anyone* who hadn't voted for McGovern (food for thought?). Actress Anne Jackson told Gabe she felt like Anne Frank before the storm troopers came to the door (God, what a delicious feeling!). I realize thespians have a tradition of killing Presidents, but this was a little much. One felt the last pogrom Miss Jackson suffered from a uniform and brass buttons was a snub from her doorman.

Mary McGrory tells us that for a while George even thought about leaving the country. (Did he hold his breath and kick the floor, too?) I missed Saul Alinsky election night.

So we've got four more years, and I'm sorry about that. But I'm not about to indict the American people for fascism. They were offered one of the most inept candidates of modern times. Vacillation and moral arrogance is not a gentleman's idea of a parlay. The war, to most people, was ending, since their own troops were coming home. It's sad that the bombing of innocent Asians didn't move them to remove Nixon, but their guilt was not singular. It was a tragic collaboration—thus, a sorrow and a pity. But I won't chime in with the avenging angels cursing the populace for their moral decay. In the tenor of the campaign I take my leave with a quote from Scripture:

"They shall not cast the first stone who themselves are rockheads."

—FLAHERTY, Ch. 1, V. 1

November 23, 1972

'Tis the Season to Be Churlish

The trouble with Christmas is that it's a wee bit like moral rearmament. I mean that it forces one to think "profound." Every year when the season arrives, I find myself thinking in Capital Letters: Peace on Earth to Men of Good Will, Bring the Boys Home for Christmas (why not on January 14? the same mind begs).

It's just that the pressures of the season encourage such nonsense. A message must be delivered. Mankind is up for grabs. Christ is on the hoof. Let's put loincloths on the savages, etc. Meshugginers became messiahs. It's all so damned ludicrous.

I know when December has arrived each year. I get the flu which will last through January 2. Besides that, I don't seem to speak in English but rather sound like a 3 A.M. message on television from Oral Roberts. Humankind is just not good enough for me. The next step is my Hansel and Gretel annual drunk—that is, instead of leaving crumbs for a trail, I leave my hat, my coat, my umbrella, my change, and most often my brainpan in various saloons throughout the Village.

If you doubt my premise, just check the output of newspaper columnists. Talk about "Miss Lonelyhearts"! Nobody, just nobody, will let the race wallow in their splendid squalor. Contrary to popular opinion, Christmas is the most antihuman season in existence.

Even this diatribe is a message. It is meant as balm for all of us who have to endure the year-end madness. And make no mistake about it—we are legion.

During my monthly carousing I, like George McGovern, have met ethnic despair. The Irish I have encountered tell me tales of bygone Christmases, when their fathers failed to arrive home till four in the morning on Christmas Eve, bearing three pine sprigs, because all the trees had been sold. Tragedy to be sure. Imagine trying to string four sets of lights around a bush!

40

In rightful paranoia my Jewish friends see the season as one large Passover Plot. Only the Italians, in their wink-at-life fashion, seem to have conquered the holy time—Bleecker Street has more cows and donkeys on it than there are in central Ohio.

The sound argument is that one should blank all this out of his mind and endure. But is it possible? Daily I receive Christmas cards (for the tenth year) picturing friendly lions lying in pastures with benign lambs. These usually come from zoologists whose husbandry relates to platers who can do six furlongs in 1:11⅖. The distaff side of my household also goes mad whenever she receives trendy greetings addressed to "Ms." "I will not be called by that damnable asexual label," she explodes.

And as the times dictate, we are bombarded by those cards shilling ecology (one is reminded of Jerome Kretchmer's monumental remark that his family uses only white toilet paper to preserve the cosmos). The only foul breath of fresh air came from my kid brother, who sent me a card featuring three camels in the desert running a hump-to-hump dead heat which he titled "The Stretch at the Big A."

Every year I promise myself I won't be sucked into the Santa insanity. But at the age of thirty-six one doesn't qualify for such gung-ho boasts. When one's own death has visited too often, it is hard enough to manage any holiday. I have just worked up to handling Groundhog Day, but Arbor Day looms like Good Friday.

Last year I went on a cyclonic toot with my good friend Fantail Murphy in search of a piece of Waterford glass that looked like a chalice—to space out his old man when he nipped. In the course of our mad meanderings I (as usual) became sentimental. We were doing a half hour on in Bloomingdale's and an hour off in a bar. Naturally, I thought of my mother. Maggie has conned me into "Christmas dinner" for the last decade by saying, "You might as well come, it will probably be my last." Damn foolishness on my part. Unlike Lazarus, the woman can be resurrected on the promise of cooking a turkey and yelling at her grandchildren.

Anyway, in a fit of boozy love I bought her a Belleek china plate (which I could ill afford), embossed with a seventeenth-century cross. I presented her with my munificence in her kitchen on Christmas Day while she was cooking dinner. As usual she was got up in Irish mod, a dish towel over her shoulder. When I gave her the gift, she perfunctorily looked at the plate (so delicate you could read the racing form through it) and wiped it "clean" with the towel she was using to baste the turkey! So much for the seventeenth century.

But all this sounds like so much unintelligible carping. Credentials must be established. Is it only me? Not so. Dear friend and fine writer Wilfrid Sheed delineated the whole syndrome in his witty novel *The Hack*. The hero, Bert Flax, goes mad trying to write a "Christmas Poem" (Capitals again) for a church magazine. A novelistic device, you say? Like hell, I say. Sheed and I have shared a few Christmases. Usually they wind up with both of us alternately staring at the bottom of our glasses and the half-time activities of the Blue Bonnet Bowl. (Sheed wins the home field advantage every year, because he has a 23-inch color set against my 16-inch black and white.)

So steel yourself, here comes the message. All you Christmas freaks, leave humanity alone. Don't gear everyone up to be better than he is. We are at best a tolerable mediocrity. The only moral message I have found in man's odyssey that was acceptable to all is the gospel "That's my round."

I promise that next year you won't have to tolerate this despair. I plan to spend the month of December in the Fontainebleau in Miami Beach. Think of the glories of a magenta Christmas tree! The temperature soaring into the seventies. Poolside drinks the like Jon Hall never envisioned. Excitement, of course: Nikon classes during the day and cha-cha lessons at night.

Until the day that Babe in the manger explains why His Father doesn't like us, my soul will ship south on His birthday. Or, in other words, "Merry Christmas. 1-2-3, Cha-Cha-Cha."

December 28, 1972

Two: Under Olympus

Shaw-Hinton at Sunnyside:
Even the Winner Lost

The literati took their fighter off Broadway last Wednesday night in hopes of shaping him up for a future performance on the main stem. Producers Norman Mailer, George Plimpton, Charles Addams, and Pete Hamill showcased their fighter, welterweight Joe Shaw, in Sunnyside Garden in Queens, the last stop on the pugilistic straw hat circuit.

The idea was that Shaw was to make it big against a local kid named Junius Hinton. Shaw was formerly in Cus D'Amato's stable, and the Garden matchmaker Teddy Brenner seized the occasion to take a cheap shot at Cus at the expense of Shaw. Shaw, who has never fought a rated fighter, was promised an unprecedented shot at Curtis Cokes, the 147-pound champion, in a nontitle bout at the Garden in March. Brenner was quoted as saying, "I want to show how smart D'Amato was. The amateurs —the writers—got Shaw more fights than he did." Like literature, the plot began to thicken.

The ringside was packed with Shaw's followers. They arrived by chartered bus, and a rented limousine transported his Village rooters. There was a cluster of *Vogue*ish young girls whose backbones protruded more than their boobies; their knees turned fashionably inward, meeting as they walked like knobby cymbals. There was Larry Merchant from the *Post,* Sid Zion from the *Times,* and Jack Newfield, the political writer from the *Voice.* Missing was Norman Mailer, who is battling his play *The Deer Park,* or maybe he just decided to hang them up after his preliminary with the Garden's cops the night of the Torres-Tiger fight. The rest of the ringside seats were populated by Village poets and jock-strap intellectuals. There had not been so many beards on display at a brawl since Christ decisioned the moneylenders at the temple.

Standing at the bar there was a terribly British-looking chap frocked in houndstooth, a bird swaddled in raccoon, barbarically drinking beer from paper cups. George Plimpton, who edits the *Paris Review,* was quoting Hemingway on the miseries of owning a fighter. One always quotes Papa at affairs such as this. There was a blond girl, the type who looks eternally collegiate, wearing a mini-skirt. Her long white legs stood out like goalposts against the green of her skirt, to be cleared only by the guys who make touchdowns in this life.

Shaw and Hinton came on around ten. Immediately you knew Hinton had nothing going for him. His nickname is Nice Guy. It lacks originality and creativity. Hinton's opponent fights under the name of Joe "Buzz" Shaw—Jesus, the poetic imagery almost takes your breath away. Hinton lost his first decision of the night to the literati.

The bell tolled, and the fight began. Two rounds passed with a lot of shuffling, light jabbing, and missed punches. Ringside looked worried; things weren't going according to the script. If Shaw was going to make it to the Garden, he had to win big. By this time Hinton was supposed to be a dangling participle.

At the end of five dull rounds Hinton was unhurt and still on his feet. In the sixth round Hinton started to attack Shaw's body. Shaw couldn't take the punishment and began to backpedal. (As the ringsiders would have it, he went into his *Rabbit, Run* phase.) Shaw had only two rounds left to take Hinton out. But the ringsiders didn't despair. They were sure Joe would end it with a *Prophetic Left*. In the seventh Hinton kept up the body attack. Swinging a right hand low, Hinton hit Shaw below the belt line. Shaw grimaced at the dastardly blow to his *MacBird*.

The judge and the referee gave it to Shaw 6–2 and 7–1. I saw it much closer than that, more like 5–3 in favor of Shaw. Apparently, Teddy Brenner also saw it that way. He canceled Shaw's appearance at the Garden.

Downstairs the gloom of Shaw's dressing room was matched by his backers' mood. Shaw stood sad and weary in the timeless dreary cement landscape. A naked light bulb illuminated the despair. A urine-stained bowl documented the tale of battered kidneys and dreams. Plimpton was saying only a lack of work made Shaw rusty. "He's so good we can't get anyone to spar with him. I guess we writers will have to spar with him." If you can afford human toys, you should be entitled to play with them.

February 2, 1967

Ali-Terrell: The Marquis in the Astrodome

Last night I sat among the other inmates in the Albee Theater in Brooklyn and witnessed the Persecution of Ernie Terrell directed by the Marquis de Sade as played by Muhammad Ali.

46

The house began to fill early with Ali rooters. There were cats with sunglasses, living in their cool, eternal nights. There were hundreds of guys in Sherlock Holmes' hats suggesting that Baker Street might be eligible for urban renewal. In the lobby the more energetic were bopping to the Ali Shuffle. The phrase of the night was "soul brother." It was even reported that the cigarette machine was dispensing Camels three to one over all other brands.

The opening shot on the screen was of the roof of the Astrodome rising like a giant pregnant belly sheltering 40,000 Lone Star children. The ring announcer appeared, wearing a Liberace sequined tailcoat, and introduced the fighters. Terrell was first to be introduced. The audience in the movie house booed, hooted, and jeered the challenger. It wasn't clear what Terrell represented to them—the Establishment, the White Negro, or a pugilistic Uncle Remus. The adopted son of Allah came bouncing down the aisle with evangelical fervor; the crowd heard the word—they cheered loudly.

The opening round suggested that Ali might be in for a fight. The bigger Terrell hit Ali with left jabs and seemed his equal in strength. This was to be the only round Terrell won. In the second round Ali seemed like an effusive kid; he did a funny imitation of Terrell's awkward style. This was the last humorous thing Muhammad Ali did all evening.

From here on Ali hit Terrell at will. Terrell, who has ugly scar tissue above his left eye, became vulnerable to the champion's jab. By the seventh both of Terrell's eyes were bleeding and closing. At this point it stopped being a fistfight.

All during the training period before the fight Ali would ask Terrell, "What is my name?" Terrell would answer, "Cassius Clay." Ali promised to avenge that insult to Allah and Elijah Muhammad by "torturing" Terrell for referring to him by his "slave name." In the eighth round the black avenging angel decided to fulfill his prophecy.

Ali speaks of a mother ship, a Muslim satellite that lies in the outer reaches of space. According to the champion, the mother ship holds 5,000 planes manned with the most deadly weapons, flown by black men who never smile. The champion demonstrated that he was an apostle of an ebony Bondian philosophy of mechanical destruction.

Terrell, nearly blind, moved around the ring like the stupe who was trying to master the two-step in dancing class. Ali would ask Ernie his name, and when the challenger didn't respond, he would bang right and left hands into the torn eyes while the blood flowed freely. Again the question, again no response, again more blood. Terrell's only salvation was to pay homage to the East in the Western state of Texas.

Cut, slash, and humiliate the helpless, and the crowd loved it. It is one thing to watch a man work out his personal madness, but it is quite another when he has cheerleaders. "Blind him, Ali"; "Cripple the mother"; "Make him say your name, baby," the theater crowd shouted. There hasn't been such a pageant of brotherhood since Sheriff Jim Clark and his dogs graced our national scene.

It was inconceivable that this magnificent fighter would demean his art in such a way. It was comparable to watching a man capable of beautiful poetry scrawling filth on shithouse walls.

Ali dragged and cut and humiliated his opponent across fifteen rounds. The sick audience never tired of the spectacle. But once again the champion couldn't bring his fight to a climax. Liston quit with a sore shoulder, Chuvalo was a battered stump at the end of fifteen, Patterson quit with a sore back, bullet-ridden Cleveland Williams was stopped on cuts, and a blind Terrell, waving his left hand like a tin cup, managed to be on his feet at the final bell.

He never can bring his fights to a swift, violent conclusion. People like Ali can't climax.

There is no one around who can beat him—but he is not the greatest. He is not even great. To be great, one has to approach his work with love and sexuality. You see it in Arnold Palmer when he hitches up his pants and attacks the Augusta National Golf Course as if it were some sprawling bawd. Watch Jim Taylor fight a lineman for extra yardage like a guy wrestling his old lady for beer money on a Saturday night. Arcaro, married to his mount, held fragile horses together by the gentleness of his ride. Ray Robinson, defending a crown he loved, unleashed beautiful fury when he was challenging pretenders to his throne. Muhammad Ali is an onanist; his style is that of the bullwhip.

When Cassius Clay was in search of a new name, they should never have looked in the holy books of the East. Just flip any page in Krafft-Ebing, and you have a baptism.

February 9, 1967

Slow Bus to Bushville

They sat waiting in the bus, looking like the products of a clandestine affair between a box of cereal and a jar of wheat germ. Their dress: blazers, glen plaid slacks, loafers. Their speech: correct, flat, devoted to the nobilities of Teamwork and Dedication. Their physiognomies: bland and handsome. Except for their size, one would never guess there were football players under the insurance-agent surface.

48

These are the Westchester Bulls, members of a farm team of the New York Giants and one of the six pro-connected teams of the Atlantic Coast Football League. The bus was standing in Memorial Field in Mount Vernon, the Bulls' home pasture. Next Saturday the field will be the scene of a clash between the Bulls (champions of the North) and the Virginia Sailors (champions of the South) for the league title. But on the bright, fall Sunday afternoon here under consideration, the club was about to take a four-hour junket to Scranton, Pennsylvania, where it would meet the Wilmington Clippers (an affiliate of the Philadelphia Eagles).

Tom Scott, a former Giant linebacker and now the Bulls' general manager, gave the signal, and the bus pulled out. There were no cheers.

John Lium, a huge, 200-pound tackle from Notre Dame, didn't bother to look up from his book: *Cases and Materials on Torts*. Lium is studying tax law at St. John's University, and he intends to give "this life" one more year. "I plan to come to camp next year in the best shape of my life," he said. "I feel I owe it one more shot—but after that I've got a career to think out." "It" is, freely translated, "making it with the Giants." Tom Scott defines the Atlantic Coast League as "a place where young talent can develop for the pro leagues." Lium and his colleagues look at it the same way. They don't play for money, which averages from $50 to $100 a game and which includes three two-hour practice sessions a week. Exceptions to this money rule are the eleven members of the Giants' taxi squad, who are paid directly by the parent club and include some bonus babies. The rest are paid directly by the Bulls' owner, industrialist Cosmo Iacovazzi (an uncle of the former Princeton fullback of the same name).

Tackle Lium with his lawbook and plans for the future is typical of the Bulls. These are not a bunch of hungry kids from the proverbial spinach patch, their only hope of success represented by the big leagues. They are educated (all but one attended college), and they have a fair idea of their moneymaking potential in business. Ken Luciani, for example, a defensive halfback who operates a travel agency with his brother in New Haven, spoke of the value his ballplaying has to his agency. "You'd be surprised at the amount of business it brings in," he said. "I'll stick with it as long as I still get a kick out of it and it's valuable to the agency." Beneath every jersey there is a gray flannel suit.

The bus moved through the Pennsylvania countryside passing Wyeth wheatfields and multicolored trees spread out like bright parasols. Most of the players were engrossed in the Sunday sports pages. Robert Higgans, a graduate of C. W. Post and evidently the team wit, turned to a huge tackle: "Hey, Herzing, your picture is in the New York *Times*." Herzing, caught off guard, jumped from his seat to look. Higgans, with a small grin on his face, held up an advertisement of a naked young child with the

Fruit of the Loom trademark displayed on her bare backside. As the other players howled, Herzing flushed and hit Higgans over the head with his paper.

Higgans, an end who can run the 100 in 9:6, had a tryout last year with the Atlanta Falcons. "I was doing real well," he said. "Then I came down with an intestinal virus, and that put me so behind in training I was cut." Higgans is about to embark on a career as a market representative with Monsanto Chemical in its Astro Turf Division, and he expects this will be his last season unless he gets a call from the pros.

"This is fun to a point," he said, "and the guys are enjoyable to be with. They're college men and intelligent, and the relationships are fine—but how long does one stick it out? I'm twenty-three now, and I have to get moving. I have no intentions of ending up a bum in a small town with a pair of cleats over my shoulder."

The Bulls club also serves the Giants as a place where they can store some of their expendable players. At the start of the year the Giants, who are strong on runners and weak on defense, cut Chuck Mercein, a fullback (last year he was the Giants' leading rusher), to make room for linebacker Vince Costello. Mercein, oblivious to his surroundings, sat alone in the front of the bus, listening to the Giant game on a radio encased in a miniature Giant helmet. Holding it close to his ear, he looked like Hamlet holding Yorick's skull, a poignant old-timer recalling his past. A Yale graduate, Mercein lives with his wife and children in Scarsdale.

"When the Giants let me go," he said, "I could have tried to latch onto another team, but my roots are here." He paused to remove his tortoise-shell glasses. "I feel my stay here is only temporary. I could have stayed home and done some running to keep in shape, but I felt the need for contact is essential, so I came to the Bulls of my own accord. They hit pretty good here, but play execution is far superior in the NFL." Mercein, who ultimately expects to be a stockbroker, started to talk like one. "This is only an interim move for me. There was a lot of manipulation and ramifications connected with this. As I say, it's only interim."

But not all the Bulls are in an interim period; for some, it's the last stop. One such is Johnny Counts. For most of the trip Counts dozed lazily, his head against the bus window. "This might be it," he said. "It's no good when you start to dread practice sessions." Counts spent five years in professional ball, two years with the Giants as a punt return specialist, and three years in Canadian ball. In his last two seasons he suffered injuries— one year a broken collarbone, the next a broken arm. "I'm a little man (175 pounds), and they play some pretty rough ball up there."

Counts had left the University of Illinois to accept a pro offer; now he said, "I should have never quit school; I just messed up everything." He lives with his wife and three kids in a rented apartment in the Bronx, works at delivering packages on a United Parcel truck route. "It's honest, real work," he said. Counts had his two years in the limelight with the Giants, but he doesn't have that unexplainable "star quality" which inspires job offers from those businessmen who genuflect every time Frank Gifford enters Toots Shor's.

Hank Washington, the Bulls' second-string quarterback, is at the other end of the scale from Counts—a member of the taxi squad and bonus baby. (When asked the inevitable question, he demonstrated the quarterback art of deception: "Let's just say I signed for a considerable amount.") Washington is touted as the first Negro quarterback in pro football. There is a silent slur in sports that Negroes are great athletes but don't possess leadership qualities, yet Washington feels this is not a real barrier to him. "The only thing stopping me from getting to the pros is lack of experience," he says. "I don't drop back into the pocket fast enough, and it takes me too long to set up to throw."

The 6-foot-3, 212-pound Washington is a native of Los Angeles, but his philosophy of life seems more influenced by his years at West Texas State. "I don't care for New York," he said. "It's too close together, too many cars."

Washington lives in the Concourse Plaza in the Bronx with other Giant players. He works out two days a week with the parent club (as do all taxi-squad members) and three nights with the Bulls. He spends about fifteen hours a week studying his play book, which is written in pro football's own esoteric language, jockawobby. For entertainment he does some light reading, and, he added, "I dig goddess and Biblical movies like *Ben Hur.*"

He has no affiliation with any civil rights group. "My business isn't straightened out yet," he said. "How can I help someone else? When you don't know where you're going yourself, you stay out of those organizations or you just make a fool out of yourself." But like all twenty-two-year-olds, Washington has one special political interest. "I keep an eye on LBJ. I haven't been in the Army yet, and I want to know what he's doing in Vietnam." In a sad, country-boy way, he said, "John Kennedy had the answer—or why would they have killed him?"

The Bulls play a twelve-game schedule in a league that is reported to be financially healthy except for the Wilmington club, which ran into poor attendance at its home games. That was why the Bulls and Wilmington were to play this Sunday night game in Scranton, where the local Elks were promoting it and proceeds would be split between the Elks (for their charitable endeavors) and the sagging Wilmington franchise. But with the pro league saturating weekend television and stealing would-be game-goers, most observers feel that the infant clubs will eventually have to be supported by their rich, TV-subsidized parents.

The bus had been on the road for about three hours when the conversation turned to a common topic. The Bulls were hungry. The bus arrived at the Elks Club on the outskirts of Scranton where the Bulls were to have their pregame meal. Table conversation was less than sparkling; in fact, it was nonexistent. Mountains of toast disappeared; knives and forks flashed with surgical speed; steaks were gobbled up like so many anchovies. The performance would have warmed the heart of any Jewish mother.

Not all the Bulls traveled by bus. Randy Minniear, a Purdue graduate in physiology, arrived with his parents and his fiancée by car. Blond, even-toothed Minniear is what the back of Wheaties boxes are made for. Last year he was scheduled to start as a running back for the Giants in their first exhibition game, and two days before the game he broke his right leg in practice. Minniear has been frequently touted for the Giants. Meanwhile, though, he was entering a hearing-aid business with his prospective father-in-law.

While the rest of the Bulls were eating, Chuck Mercein, ignoring his stomach and heeding his heart, remained outside, listening to the Giant game. When the meal was about over, he entered the dining room and sat down. One of the Bulls shouted across the dining room, "Hey, Chuck, how did the Giants do?" Mercein, very pointedly, said, *"We* won." (Mercein's allegiance was temporarily rewarded the following week when the Giants recalled him. But shortly thereafter he was cut and put up for grabs around the pro league.)

Leaving behind the vivid colors of the autumn countryside, the bus made its way through the drab, deserted downtown area of Scranton. The multi-colored trees were replaced by billboards advertising beer companies and Pulaski Day Committees; a black mountain range of coal rose beyond the stadium. The terrain was timeless, the traditional setting for minor-league sports: Scranton, Harrisburg, Memphis—Bushville, U.S.A.

The field was littered with confetti, paper cups, and ice-cream wrappers left by the crowd that had watched two high school games earlier in the day. Patches of grass and dirt fought for equal yardage. Two rickety wooden goalposts were planted on the goal line (pro rules) while two steel posts stood permanently on the end zone stripe (amateur rules). The groundskeepers, having only two sets of protective pads, had covered the bottom section of the harmless wooden posts and left the steel ones menacingly naked. Three towers of arc lights stood on each side of the field. Like a panel of cross-eyed professors, their focus was helter-skelter. They brilliantly lighted some areas of the field while they left others (particularly the end zones) in shadowy darkness. The tops of the goal-posts (the kickers' guideline for field goal attempts) were painted dark blue—just right for a night game.

As the Bulls marched to their locker room with their duffel bags (holding their equipment) slung over their shoulders, a loudspeaker on a fire truck owned by a local insurance agency blared "The Yellow Rose of Texas." Wilmington players posed for local photographers with Elk members, with much switching of fire hats and football helmets. A Clipper trainer asked if the Bulls had brought any extra tape. This kind of bush slipup is not tolerated on the Bulls. Tom Scott muttered, "Extra tape! If we don't beat these guys, we should quit." The best the Bulls could offer was one roll (not nearly enough to tape all the Clippers' ankles and wrists). The Clipper trainer said sadly, "We would have had our own, but all the sports stores are closed, and it's so damned expensive in the local drugstore."

The Bulls' dressing room showed the gap between the minor leagues and the pros. The floor was cold, pockmarked gray cement—nowhere a remnant of Green Bay's much-publicized carpeting. Protective pads and cups hung from the institutional-green walls, mute testimony to the vulnerability of the human body. No TV commercials were ever filmed here. Nobody worries about what deodorant a Bulls player uses.

Watching pregame ceremonies in a dressing room, one marvels at the conformity of football players. Everything was done with assembly-line precision: ankles taped on one table, linemen's hands on another. Players seemed to lose their humanity; they became machines rolling into pit stops to service their particular needs. Then suddenly the machines ran down. It was nearly kickoff time. Very human fear filled the room, translated in terms of sweat and queasy stomachs. Players moved about dumbly, unseeing, gently patting each other on the rump. Robert Higgans, trying to maintain his reputation as the team's clown, weakly said to nobody in particular, "It's butterfly time, baby."

Alan Webb, a former defensive back for the Giants and now the Bulls' defensive coach, moved to the blackboard at the front of the room. "All right, defense," he said, "I know you're not ready, and I'll be goddamned if I'm going to beat any drums to get you up for this." Webb's speech was a tribute to the modern football player. No longer do you build the sentimental rube up to a pitch by pleading with him to "Win one for the Gipper." The urban sophisticate requires different treatment. Head coaches Harry Wright and Ed Kolman stood in front of their players as if they were conducting a shape-up. "You'd better want this game as much as we do!" screamed Wright. He added an existential exhortation: "Let's live every play." Kolman's approach was different. Like a hiring boss in the movie *On the Waterfront,* he simply said, "Let's go to work." The Bulls rushed through the dressing-room door with a roar.

With Washington at quarterback, the Bulls failed to move on their first series of downs. John De Noia, the Bulls' first-string quarterback, who was on the injured list, manned the field phones. A New Jersey tax lawyer who has no dreams of cracking the big leagues because of his height (5 feet 10 inches), he calls a more conservative game than Washington. While De Noia picks a defense apart, Washington relies on the bomb—which he can really toss. During the first quarter he threw the ball 55 yards while off-balance.

The first quarter was dominated by the Bulls' defense. When Wilmington was forced to kick from its own 36-yard line, the Bulls got their first score. Johnny Counts fumbled the punt (a problem he had with the Giants). And then, with Clippers rushing at him, he gathered up his own fumble and broke for the sidelines. Picking up his blocks, Counts sped 80 yards down the sideline for the touchdown. He trotted off the field with an embarrassed smile—and another memory to package away for those nine-to-five days on his parcel route.

The two key men on the Bulls' defense are middle linebacker Robert Fiorini and defensive tackle Dick Herzing. Fiorini prowls about the field with cyclone fury, doling out yards to the opposing offense as begrudgingly as a loan shark parts with his bankroll. He is obsessed with making the pros. "All I want is one shot," Fiorini says. "Just let them give me a try; I'll show them." Once Coach Kolman approached Fiorini after a game and told him he had just put in the best performance at linebacker he had ever seen anywhere. Fiorini roared, "Then why the hell am I down here?"

Herzing is equally intense. When his pass rush forced the Clippers' quarterback to throw an interception, he trotted off the field shouting, "Great rush, Herzing. Great rush." And when the game announcer failed to give him credit for a tackle, he glared at the press box and said, "Who the hell is working up there?"

The Bulls piled up a 21–0 lead. At half time they sat on wooden benches in the locker room, sucking Cokes and oranges. Club physician Alan Levy and trainer Mike Freehand applied more tape and massaged bruises. On the field a high school band blared patriotic marches, and young nymphets in scanty, sequined costumes strutted and shimmied. Only football half time shows offer this ambiguity—something for Jack Armstrong, something for Humbert Humbert.

The coaches drew plays on the blackboard, constantly offering adjustments in offense and defense. There was no praise for the first-half play. Harry Wright said, "We're doing all right, but we're not sharp. The second half is a new ball game. The score is nothing to nothing." Once again the Bulls charged through the door.

The second half was sloppily played. The Clippers scored on a long march, and the Bulls scored on a field goal. There were fumbles and penalties. The final score: Westchester 24, Wilmington 7.

The Bulls wearily boarded the bus for the long trip back home. Spirits were not soaring. On seeing cases of soda at the front of the bus, one player complained, "For chrissake, can't we ever have beer?" Another asked a teammate for a $2 loan to get in the blackjack game in the back of the bus. "I don't have it." "What did you do with your bonus money?" asked the would-be borrower. "I spent it all in a candy store," his comrade replied—no bonus baby, he. Lou Williams, a linebacker and a New York City welfare worker, groaned, "My God, I have to go to work tomorrow." And when the bus driver took a wrong turnoff, one youth sacrilegiously sang a variation of a tune once addressed to Giant coach Allie Sherman by disgruntled fans: "Good-bye, bussie; good-bye, bussie—we hate to see you go."

The bus arrived at Mount Vernon at 3:30 A.M. Monday. The Bulls' day was fifteen and a half hours old. How long will these ambitious young men work such long hours for short money? The bonus babies and the taxi-squad members will most certainly remain. But what about the others —those who study torts, the stock market, and the tax structure? As Eddie Cantor used to sing, "How 'ya gonna keep 'em down on the farm?"

November 19, 1967

Can the Mets Survive Respectability?

If in a moment of campy whimsy Susan Sontag and Salvador Dali decided to have a love affair and conceive a child without sin, he would be destined to grow up and become a New York Met. In a dastardly age when we are accused of genocide at home and abroad, the Mets remain as innocent as a feather boa or a Busby Berkeley musical.

Admittedly, baseball, in Red Smith's phrase, is still a game played by little boys, but it also is a serious business. One has only to remember the fabled exodus of Walter O'Malley's Dodgers from loving Brooklyn to lush Los Angeles. The shacks of Mexican peasants were torn down to erect (as the Hollywood press agents call it) O'Malley's Taj Mahal of sports arenas. And when his edifice was complete, it was discovered that there wasn't a water fountain in the place. O'Malley in his countinghouse realized soda pop cost money and water was for nothing. So those poor bronzed blond darlings of Southern California, those objects of adoration of all the Humbert Humberts among us, were being subjected in that land of wheat germ and blackstrap molasses to sugary cavities. But these devious machinations have nothing to do with the Mets.

In their six-year history (1968 is their seventh) the Mets not only gave away water but a torrent of ball games as well. Their pitching staff had the marksmanship of Sergeant York—they hit every damn bat in sight. Their batters were as aggressive as flower children, and their baserunners circled the pads as though Mack Sennett and Richard Lester were coaching on first and third. The Mets' defense was so feeble it could make Nasser feel like a Prussian general. Yet they were loved.

In six years they finished last in the National League standings five times and next to last once. Their unbelievable dramatic ninth-place finish in 1966 (28½ games behind the pennant-winning Dodgers) was relegated to a freak of nature when in 1967 they returned to form and finished last, 40½ games behind the World Champion St. Louis Cardinals.

But these were the innocent years. What could be expected of a club that paid $125,000 for Don Zimmer and Lee Walls and $75,000 for the likes of Ray Daviault and John De Merit? And who gave a hell about winning when their manager of three-and-one-half years, Casey Stengel, could combine jabberwocky and *Finnegans Wake* and convert tragedy into comedy? After Stengel's heady reign, the Mets went into their Eisenhower years. Under Wes Westrum, the ex-Giant catcher, the Met fans mistook boredom for serious stewardship. For nearly three seasons the Mets slept.

But precociousness is a fragile commodity. What is adorable in adolescence is contemptible in adults. 1968 was the year the Mets were supposed to grow up. And the reason for their maturity was the hiring of Gil Hodges as manager. The feeling was that Hodges, the gentle giant, the solid man who was adored as the Brooklyn Dodgers' first baseman for ten years, would bring stability to the Mets.

New York was always a National League town. The aristocratic Yankees are only tolerated here; the real action was always the Giants and the Dodgers. And Hodges was the embodiment of the golden years, the late forties and early fifties of the Dodgers. He was so unique as an individual he was never even jeered by the enemy Giant fans. In a borough that canonized the image of the "regular guy" Gil Hodges was a saint.

One remembers the elegance he brought to playing first base. His massive hands seemed to span the right side of the Dodger infield, making it impenetrable. And who could forget the 370 home runs—or, as Red Barber called them, "Old Goldies"? Then there was the human saga, the 1952 World Series in which Hodges batted 0 for 21, and on a Sunday every church in Brooklyn offered up prayers that Gil would end his slump. Indeed, Hodges always seemed to be a character in a morality play. One recalls the great confrontation between Hodges and Giant pitcher Sal "The Barber" Maglie. The blue-eyed Hodges at bat, who always had trouble hitting the curve ball, looking like Billy Budd facing the swarthy, unshaven Maglie as Claggart doing the unmentionable to the instrument of our national pastime—spitting on it—magnificently curving the hero to his death, while the faithful of Flatbush hissed the hairy villain. Even now

Hodges says with a self-deprecating smile: "Sal would have to make a terrible mistake for me just to hit the ball."

Hodges, who also was one of the original Mets, retired from active ball in 1963 because of a crippling knee injury. In 1963 he became manager of the last-place Washington Senators of the American League. Within five years as the Senators' manager Hodges raised the club from the cellar in 1963 to a respectable tie for sixth place in 1967. Then in '68 the Mets summoned Hodges home, though in a way he had never left since he has lived on Bedford Avenue with his wife and four children (a boy and three girls) since 1948.

But for those looking for the Met image to change drastically the spring season didn't offer much hope. The Mets compiled their worst loss record ever, and the zany stories were still getting into the press. Ron Swoboda, the team slugger and the sibling with the Chinese stepfather, was reported to heed a call from nature during an exhibition game and missed his turn at bat—once again, the Mets were caught with their pants down. Then there was the story of relief pitcher Hal Reniff urging Phil Linz, infielder and owner of the East Side swing spot Mr. Laffs, to come to spring training for a tryout. In typical Met fashion Reniff had a horrible spring and was cut, and Linz, playing brilliantly, made the team. In fact, Linz was so impressive that *Daily News* sportswriter Dick Young was moved to write that Linz was one of the best prospects in spring training. Linz, upon reading the accolade, was moved to comment: "I know that's not right."

But these stories, which were the substance of Stengel's existence, don't amuse Hodges. Sitting in his office at Shea Stadium, Hodges solemnly said: "I used to enjoy Met stories as much as anyone else, but I don't appreciate them anymore. We have to get away from the image of being a funny club." But the old image didn't have any major revision during the first two weeks of the season. The Mets blew their opening game to the Giants in the ninth inning and managed to lose six one-run ball games in their first twelve games through spotty relief pitching and horrendous fielding. In fact, if to err is human, to be a Met is divine. In the first seventeen games the Amazin' Ones made nineteen miscues.

But loving the Mets is not a rational thing; it's more like life with a drunken husband. He curses you, abuses you, beats you, and then every so often the lousy bastard does something so spectacular that passion overrules reason and your bed of nails once more becomes the arena of conjugal bliss. So it was with the Mets as they staggered home from their road trip, like Hickey the salesman, to their opener at Shea.

All the regular hoopla was present: marching bands, flags flapping everywhere, and a horseshoe wreath wishing Gil good luck. Then, in one loving swoop, all was forgiven. The current ace of Hodges' staff, twenty-five-year-old Jerry Koosman, not only struck out the Giants, but struck out Willie Mays with the bases loaded! But such treats are rare. The same weekend the Mets threw away a doubleheader to the Dodgers, and Hodges sat in his office, his massive hand shaking, holding a filter cigarette, unable to talk to the reporters. He seemed to be suffering the frustration of so many talented participants who are now relegated to the sidelines to manage the ineptitude of others. The best he could mutter was "We're beating ourselves, and that can be corrected." When one looked at the pale blue eyes vacuous and washy, the face from our boyhood now lined and looking prematurely haggard, one thought of John Lindsay after managing a couple of tough summer seasons in this city.

But after a day off, Hodges looked refreshed at a Tuesday morning batting practice. Here one catches the real essence of Hodges. Essentially, Gil Hodges is a father. Young ballplayers treat him with respect but not awe. His jokes are mild—not clever, not cutting, just a touch of chastisement in them. He was hitting ground balls to first baseman Art Shamsky, taking particular glee when he drove one by him. Shamsky sheepishly smiled at the past master of the position he was trying to conquer, and then Hodges, grinning broadly, would hit him an easy grounder to make him look good. Hodges' coach, Yogi Berra, was pitching batting practice. Berra is the only man alive who can make a baseball uniform look like a zoot suit. His low-slung pants seem pegged, his hat slouches over his eyes be-bop fashion, and his bouncy walk evokes the street corner. Tommie Agee stepped into the batting cage, and Hodges stopped smiling. Hodges traded away .300 hitter Tommy Davis and pitcher Jack Fisher to obtain the White Sox center fielder. Agee, who was suffering a terrific batting slump, couldn't even hit the ball in practice. Hodges eyed him intently, looking for some flaw in the swing that might bring Agee around. When asked about the wisdom of giving up the Mets' only .300 hitter for Agee (who later went on to tie the Mets' record for most hitless times at bat—0 for 34), Hodges in his usual gracious manner said: "Certainly I'll take credit for the trade. Tommie will come along just fine."

But all is not bleak for Hodges and his Mets this year. Relaxed in his office after practice, he talked about the positive side of the Mets. "Our pitching is our strong suit," he said. "These young boys are fine." Indeed, the Mets do have a fine young staff in Koosman, Tom Seaver, who won 16 games last year, and Nolan Ryan, whose speed has been compared to that of Koufax and Feller. And Ron Swoboda is off to the finest start of his career. But there are the others, the nameless mediocrities who fill out the roster. Hodges has set a goal of winning 70 games this year and perhaps playing .500 ball next year. "These boys have it in them. They're fine boys."

"Fine boys." The phrase is slightly square for a paid athlete. But then Hodges is slightly square. But then again baseball, like Hodges, is square

—but in a nice sort of way. It is a game that is meant to be played under God's sunshine, as Phil Wrigley used to say. Unlike football, it has no snob appeal. It's a game for kids, cabdrivers pulling long night shifts, and the old Jewish men who stand on Flatbush Avenue outside Garfield's Cafeteria. It's a beer drinker's game, where the fans do corny things like sing fight songs and take seventh-inning stretches. And Gil Hodges fits perfectly into this milieu.

For all his size (6 feet 2, 210 pounds), one could never picture Hodges in pro football where everyone uses war game parlance as if they were bastard sons of Robert McNamara. Or where the season ticket holders are the ad boys with their plaid-covered flasks holding their Ambassador Twelve, snobbishly talking about "Z-outs" and "zig-ins," as if they were talking about *Kama Sutra* positions instead of a ball game. Hodges seems content to settle for the glitter of Abner Doubleday's diamond.

But one wonders if his team should be the Mets. One remembers the hand shaking, the soft drink on the desk, the pale face, and the hesitant speech. Then one thinks of Stengel, booze in hand, regaling sportswriters with sidesplitting tales of his clowns' ineptitude. Hodges can't play the buffoon; he takes his "boys" seriously. This may be the sadness of his homecoming. The Mets still look like a team to be run by a tipsy Falstaff rather than a sober, brooding, fatherly Lear.

May 27, 1968

That Innocent America: You Can Go Home Again

As we have been told many times by those who have tried it, nostalgia is a dusty emotion that should best be kept locked in the attics of our minds —you just can't go home again.

But since prizefighting of late has all the vivid color of a Herbert Yates Western, I decided to row my boat against the current and revisit a sport (?) that intrigued me in my childhood—namely wrestling. Or as we children of that city across the river called it—rasslin'.

My interest in wrestling was at its peak in the early fifties. One should be sympathetic toward the taste of my generation since as one social critic said: "We were children bracketed by Dwight Eisenhower and 'Love Me Tender.' " I remember evenings with my boyhood friend Joe O'Donnell watching his seven-inch Admiral TV (it was the only television set on the block, and for months the family was considered Irish aristocracy). After

59

his father received a $5 raise from the Edison Company, the family got so brassy they bought a magnifier which transformed the gentle snow on the screen into a raging blizzard. But our eyes, like postmen trudged through the elements to watch the grunting and groaning of Lord Carlton, Gene Stanley, Antonino Rocca, and Gorgeous George. So, looking to recapture some of that innocent America, I went to Madison Square Garden last Saturday night.

Wrestling matches still maintain the best elements of Hollywood's old star system. The earlier bouts are all marred (deliberately?) with inadequate acting in order to build you up to the grandeur of the stars. And the stars all have a familiar repertory of holds and flips that the audience lovingly awaits as moviegoers did Cagney's strut, Grant's jauntiness, and Bogey's lispy snarl. Today's children are the fans of the ad lib, the storm trooper intrusion of the inventive. But what of the good old songs? The familiar old joke so dog-eared with use that it was guaranteed to produce a response not because it stealthily came through the cellar of your subconscious, but because, like any decent God-fearing American, it walked openfaced right into your living room. Ah, that's what the fifties and wrestling are all about.

And the audience themselves are unlike any other sporting crowd. Fight fans, fragmented by ethnic rooting, populate the reaches of arenas like Roman legions camping on various hills. The blacks, the whites, the Italians, the Irish. Only the money boys—the stale old cigar butts, as Norman Mailer calls them—remain constant at fights. The wrestling fan has only one canon: Regardless of race, color, or creed, the villain must lose. And in a time when John Wayne is no longer cleansing the sands of Iwo Jima but defoliating villages, and the magicians of Madison Avenue are telling us Nelson will lead us on the rocky road of evacuation, and Hubert is assuring us that to be a teammate is one thing but if we gave him the bat and ball we would have a new ball game, such absolute moral judgments are reassuring.

People who possess righteous wrath are not to be taken lightly. Ring announcer Johnny Addie warned at the beginning of the bouts that anyone throwing anything into the ring would be arrested, not just evicted from the arena. The heavenly hosts stoned him with a chorus of boos, and Addie, not wanting to be associated with the forces of evil, quickly added: "I can't help it—it's not my idea."

The evening began to take tone at the beginning of the second bout. It was between one Carlos Colon (hooray) and Butcher Boy (hiss). Carlos was the darling of the middle-aged ladies in housedresses who sat at ringside. Carlos wore red knit trunks with CARLOS emblazoned in gold across the front and COLON spanning his posterior. His popularity with the ladies seemed in no small way to be connected to the nonsupportive quality of his trunks. The trunks were of the Fire Island variety that mar one's sensual structure by allowing dangling participles. The Butcher Boy, Bunyonesque, with beard and plaid shirt, was loudly booed by all but one.

His one fan hung over the railing trying to touch this 300-pound man as he made his way through the crowd. Indeed, she was pound for pound as impressive as he. And in an era when most women are stacked about as thick as the magazines they adorn, she paraded her sexuality about the arena. She had that lost superiority of the fifties. Wearing a cheap white sweater, her chest, like the derby of the returning salesman, was flung into the room first. One could envision her on a summer street corner in a tight polo shirt with two divots of hair protruding from her armpits, her jaws two-timing Fleers Double Bubble, and the memory of her ankle circled by an ankle bracelet, while she tore a coupon out of a movie magazine for Frederick's of Hollywood harem pajamas. The Butcher Boy, a fine appraiser of flesh, gave her a covetous stare.

The gods in the higher reaches of the balcony didn't like the way the evening was going. Carlos had his moments of isolated splendor, but it just wasn't in the cue cards for him this evening. To make matters worse, the Butcher Boy arrogantly strutted about the ring after he dumped Carlos on his gold COLON. The mood began to get ugly. An old man dressed in a blue suit and a bow tie waved his cane in anger. A broad, her hair in rollers, like snails in a sea of peroxide, stood on her chair and gave Butcher Boy the classic thumbs-down Colosseum verdict. An elegant Negro woman dressed in basic black with a single strand of pearls delicately parted her lips and indelicately produced a Bronx cheer.

But wrestling promoters are men of genius. When the revelers get too boisterous, bring on the midgets. And on they came—FOUR OF THEM TO BOOT. It was a tag team match, pitting Irish Jackie and Little Beaver against Little Brutus and his partner, whose name I couldn't catch over the roar of the crowd. Irish Jackie looked like a smaller Mickey Rooney—sort of a chip off the old chip. Little Brutus sported a beard, and his partner with his balding head and sad, wrinkly face looked as if he should be selling seeded rolls in a Lilliputian version of a Malamud grocery store. But then there was Beaver with his Mohican haircut. Have no doubt about it—Little Beaver had star quality. If some people can light up a room when they enter it, granting Beaver the handicap of his size, he could do the same for a broom closet. And Beaver knew the center stage was his. What he looked and acted like (in proportion, of course) was the head of a large Italian family. He gave instructions to the referee, he theatened his opponents with gestures of slaps to the head (as one threatens unruly children), and fondly he rubbed his potbelly with the contentment of a well-satisfied man. The action was blatantly rehearsed and received the intended laughs, but it also was believed. This schizophrenia that affects wrestling fans is beyond my comprehension.

Take this scene, for instance. Little Beaver stands barefooted on the top strand of the ropes, posing like Cupid shooting slaps to his opponent's bare head every time he comes within range. Scene two: His partner, Irish Jackie, is being illegally pummeled by the other team in mid-ring. Little Brutus winds up to punch Jackie while his partner holds him. Jackie ducks, and Brutus flattens his partner. Beaver, showing great concern, descends from his perch, and he and Irish Jackie carry their battered opponent to his corner, where the worm turns and flattens Brutus. But then the great Fields' touch. Beaver pats the loser on his bald head, shakes his hand, then with a roundhouse right flattens him in the middle of the ring. When Beaver's team is declared the winner, an argument ensues, and the four midgets go into a Sennett chase around the referee. A standing ovation. No credibility gap here.

The fun is over. It's now time for the great moral confrontation. Budd against Claggart, Othello against Iago, St. Michael against Satan, tonight Champ Bruno Sammartino against Ernie Ladd. Ladd, the huge Negro tackle from the Kansas City Chiefs, is the villain. Black and white and Puerto Rican heap scorn on him. A Puerto Rican girl, pale with anger, has her insults muzzled by her boyfriend's hand. Sammartino enters the ring with his purple championship belt, displaying all the dignity of a cardinal. Ecumenical love drifts down from the rafters. Ladd is not only evil, but dastardly. He kicks Bruno in his unmentionables and sticks fingers in his eyes. Bruno, from the *Open City* school of acting, suffers in the center ring. Like the blinded Lear, he gropes in the darkness. Only the audience's mood is blacker. Then! If there is hope, there is light! Bruno sees. Justice throws off its blindfold. Bruno begins to batter Ladd. Ladd is now at his mercy. Bruno asks his audience if he should demolish him. The audience, devotees of the Old Testament school of an eye for an eye, rise in unison and deliver the verdict. Eight thousand thumbs, like divining rods, are spiritually pulled downward. Ladd has had it. The audience rises in a standing ovation to its own purity. The boulder has been rolled back again. Goodness has risen.

On the way out of the arena a little old Negro man summed up the feeling of the house. "I am so happy Sammartino won," he said. "He is the finest gentleman in sports. I'm seventy-five years old, and I still come out to see him wrestle. I've got to hurry home to Jersey to call my brother, he won't sleep till he finds out what Bruno did tonight. I've got to call some friends, too. I'll be calling till midnight." Sadly, he shook his head. "I don't know what's wrong with that Negro boy [Ladd], he was nice when he first came around here. Now he acts like an animal. Yes, sir, I'm glad Bruno won—he's the finest gentleman I know."

It was oddly touching to find something that resembled innocence even if it was only naïveté. And it was nice to think that the combatants were probably now having beers and sandwiches, and no one was suffering eye gashes or brain damage. The knock against wrestling is that "no one really gets hurt." For a sport that may be detrimental, but think what a marvelous national policy it would make.

But for those who need balls in their action, there is this vignette. As I passed by the dressing-room door, Butcher Boy and his single fan stood huddled in a corner. She stood, autograph book in hand, and their eyes were trying various holds on each other. Their faces smiled broadly while visions of body presses danced in their heads. One sadly reflected he was going to miss the best bout of the night.

July 18, 1968

Spring at Aqueduct: Lady in the Saddle

Sanity and love have returned to New York. The horses are back. Cab-drivers no longer deliver long harangues on John Lindsay; they now bitch about "that pig I bet on in the fourth." General racial slurs are now passé, qualitative ones are in order. "That spic Cordero stiffed the favorite in the feature." Children are once again impressed by their drunken fathers reading an esoteric paper full of figures they mistakenly think is the *Wall Street Journal*. But perhaps this phenomenon is best summed up by the husband who was studying the form at the breakfast table on opening day. His wife commented that she wished the sight of her could move him to the ecstasy he reserves for the horses. With the wisdom of Socrates he replied: "Then why don't *you* try leaving town for three months?"

The love of betting on horses is like all other perversions—no matter how hard you try to explain, the uninitiated will never understand. But I'll try. Poker playing is a lot of beery camaraderie till the end of the evening when some smirky bastard you despise walks out grinning with your money. Crap shooting is unmentionable; it's for dolts. How can anyone enjoy action that can be altered by a freakish bounce or a loose tile on a bathroom floor? Ah, but horse racing. It is here the gifted mind can measure such delightful shadings as pace, track conditions, weight shifts, and even the type of shoe your charge is wearing. It is so delightfully

63

snobbish that one assuredly thinks George Sanders must be a devotee.

Besides all this, the racetrack is a mother lode of folklore. I shall never forget six years ago on a Memorial Day when my brother Doc was approached by a rather tipsy lady who informed him she had "a lock in the eighth race," but had only 65 cents and needed $1.35 more to wager. If he was generous enough to contribute to her "lock," she informed him, he could have a piece of ass under the escalator. Think of the magnificence of her offer in light of today's nudity fad at off-Broadway theaters and art film houses which seat only a paltry few hundred. This was truly living theater. A piece of ass on Memorial Day in front of 70,000 spectators, and under the escalators no less!

And there is the tale of another boyhood friend, one Buddy Howell, who looked like a sinister Fulton Sheen. He solemnly swore he was at the track one day when a man dropped from a heart attack, and three patrons stood on his chest to get a better view of the finish. When his distraught wife screamed, "My husband is dead," a voice of Christian charity offered: "Somebody oughta frisk him and see if he had the winner."

Of course, there are the glorious superstitions of the individual players. I knew one, Danny Money, who after having a winner refused to move from the spot he was standing on when Dame Fortune struck. He wouldn't move until he lost a race, but since his chances of winning two in a row were as likely as Halley's Comet appearing three days running, this quirk was no problem. But the black thought that haunted all of us was: What if he hit a winner in the last race? Would he stoically hold his ground overnight, or would we have to drag him screaming to our car like a protester going to the paddy wagon?

I also knew a Cub Scout Mafioso (since then he has won his merit badges and is now an Eagle Scout) who upon hearing about the betting prowess of Orientals used to follow a Chinaman around the track to see what he was betting while the terrified Chinaman thought he was being tailed by a button man from Chairman Mao. But most disturbingly, there was a longshoreman friend, a man in his forties who was sane in any other milieu but that of the track. He would station himself by the rail in mid-stretch and when his horse appeared, he would race to the wire with the horse, beating *himself* on the ass. The tragic thing about this, of course, was that inevitably he would beat his horse to the finish. In fact, his performances were so scintillating rumor had it the stewards were thinking of giving him a urinalysis.

Opening day at Aqueduct I sensed the gods were with me. While making a phone call from a pay booth, I jiggled the receiver and 65 cents fell into the coin return slot. Already my bankroll had begun to multiply. I took the Aqueduct Special (75 cents) from Forty-second and passed through a horseshoe stating "Good Luck" that was so moldy it must have been constructed out of frozen manure. Obviously, the Transit Authority's idea of sporting class. The train makes concessions to the degenerates it serves—you may openly smoke without getting arrested. After twenty minutes of being underground, the train surfaced in Queens, and two men rushed to the window as if they were viewing the aurora borealis and lovingly said: "Jesus, there it is."

As the train pulled into the station, there were still thirty minutes left till post time for the first race. But logic had no place with such a passionate group. Coronary and cholesterol cases, diabetics, senior citizens and barbers (since Monday is their day off), and cats who never ran before in their lives except from cops sprinted down the ramp to the admission gates a good 200 yards away. It was a cold, windy day, but the track, ever conscious of the nature-loving souls of its patrons, had planted plastic tulips in the frozen ground to give us an antiseptic whiff of spring.

It was now approaching one thirty, and one and all were waiting for the lovely street-corner nasal tones of track announcer Fred Capossela. The climax finally came: "It is now post time" reverberated through the track like a fancy snooker shot. And then the nearest thing to communal love this side of the Haight-Ashbury happened. Thirty thousand people rose to their feet and cheered and applauded. Not the horses, not the jockeys, but that obscure thing called "action" that was back in town. One recalled Nick the Greek's comment on the need for it: "The next best thing to winning is losing."

In the first race I bet a gelding regally named High Chieftain, who ran with such humility he is probably now being considered by the College of Cardinals for canonization. While I was intellectually betting on four more losers for profound reasons that would go on longer than *Finnegans Wake* to explain, I bought a lottery ticket (keep the action going) and watched the airplanes circling Kennedy. The same threatening airplanes that prompted an assemblyman in Albany to comment that Belmont Park must be built, because if a jet crashed into Aqueduct, the state would have no plant for racing and lose millions of dollars in tax revenue. It's always nice to know what our rulers consider expendable.

By the sixth race my day picked up on two counts—I had a winner prophetically named Adrenalin and ran into two old friends, Noonan Taylor and his father, Big Joe. Noonan has the distinction of having been in more barroom brawls than any other male over thirty living in Brooklyn. His face carries his credentials. His nose is a thing of beauty, so grandly broken countless times it seems to be orbiting his head. His arena used to be the Caton Inn, a bar so civilized you weighed in at the door so you wouldn't get hit with a beer bottle by a guy who was out of your weight class. Noonan is now a retired gentleman who has taken to drinking Miller High Life—out of dainty nip bottles! Big Joe (all five feet two inches of him) is the only man who believes in more second chances than Adam Clayton Powell. When you ask him how he could bet on a horse that has lost twenty times in a row, with unshakable faith he answers, "Jesus, he's due to win one of them."

So it was a lovely day, having lost only $8, still having my $100,000 lottery ticket working for me, and most crucial, beating the Bell System out of 65 cents. But Friday was still to come.

On Friday, into the immortal world of Georgie Wolf, Earl Sande, Sonny Workman, and Eddie Arcaro was to ride Barbara Jo Rubin. And the male supremacists in attendance didn't like it one bit. But then again, Aqueduct is not exactly the Ascot scene in *My Fair Lady*. It's more Leo Gorcey than Cecil Beaton. It's not frock coats and derbies, but upturned collared, zippered windbreakers and gray peaked working man caps. The architecture is flat and uninspired but efficient—it is built to suit its clientele, good hard-nosed functional action. And that clientele is democratic to a point: If you're Puerto Rican, Panamanian, white, or black, it's okay if you can deliver. But Jesus, never a broad!

She entered the paddock for the third race in yellow silks with her braids daintily tucked under her cap, and it began. "Go home and cook," came a voice from the upper stands. A guy disgustedly puffing a cigarette said: "If I don't quit playing the goddamn horses now, I never will." And then calamity struck. She was lifted into the saddle. By God, she was going through with it! Now it really got nasty. A young Italian who looked like a Jilly's reject, who still believed the most essential asset to getting laid is a good barber, shouted to the male jocks: "Hey, fellas, you're all going to score tonight." And with this, Mrs. Portnoy on horseback rode out onto the main track.

An old harridan at railside whose sex looked as if it were reduced to sparring with her old man on weekends cackled: "She looks like a boy, you can't tell the difference. She has no chest, she's probably half and half." A sympathetic male challenged the ire of his brothers: "She's got guts. I hope she wins." And there I was, the complete feminist (I thought) succumbing to the smart money, refusing to back her with $2 worth of love. My artistry felt minor. Fellini would have bet her.

When the gate opened, Miss Rubin was in front; as they traveled down the backside, she was still in front; and as they hit the stretch, she had a length on the field. But the drive through the stretch was still to come, and here's where the smart money showed. After all, this wasn't some bush track, this was the Big Apple. But Oh Dad, Poor Dad, as they passed under the wire, Barbara Joe's pretty duff was bouncing like a cottontail two lengths in front.

When the $28.20 payoff went up on the board, many of the boos were converted to cheers. But many more remained adamant. A young stud who felt he lost more than his money shouted: "This phony fuckin' track, it was a fix." But a black cat saw the light. He screamed at the male jocks: "You guys stink—I'll never bet a man no more." Then, strangely, there was a young girl in her twenties looking like a sexy version of Grumpy of the Seven Dwarfs. "It's just against my philosophy," she said, "my day is ruined. The racetrack is one of the last places left that is sacrosanct for males, and it should remain so. I'm sorry, it's just against my philosophy." I was tempted to kneel on my discarded losing tickets and propose.

But perhaps the most interesting theory for Miss Rubin's success was rendered by Carmine Mele, who has been contributing to the betterment of the breed for more than twenty-five years. Mele's contention was that male horses never like to pass fillies in the spring, because of the aromatic delights released by the distaff members during the mating season. With a grin he said, "Maybe the same thing holds true for male jockeys. After all, she was out in front all the way, and her behind was nicely propped up in the air. It's nearly spring, you know."

Seasonal considerations aside, Miss Rubin seems here to stay. One wonders what consequences will be forthcoming. Will Norman Mailer finally read Jane Austen? Will docile wives now demand to ride on top once a week? Indeed, one is tempted to say that this might open a veritable Pandora's box.

March 20, 1969

The Day the Shoe Came Back

The little man sat there in unfamiliar garb: white raincoat, turtleneck sweater, striped slacks, and red hat—natty as usual, but unfamiliar. Down below, the horses were entering the gate, and the well-known litany, "It is now post time," reverberated across the track. The little man tensed in his seat, and you wondered why. He had been poised in similar gates 23,254 times before on cheap platers and champions, on lightning-fast tracks and deadened, muddy surfaces from Golden Gate Park to the opulent Long-champs racecourse outside Paris.

The gate exploded open in a kaleidoscope of colored silks and jockeys' mingled curses in English and Spanish. As the horses went into the first turn, the little man said with disgust, "God, he has the favorite four wide on the turn." Then you knew why the little man wanted to come back after a year's layoff from an injury that nearly ended his career. Because he, Willie Shoemaker, does this kind of work better than any other man alive.

On January 23, 1968, Shoemaker was aboard a horse named Bel Bush on a muddy track at Santa Anita when a horse in front of him fell. Unable to check his mount, Shoemaker went down, too—the premier jockey in America lay crumpled in the mud like a wadded rag. The result was a fractured right femur that is now held together by a pin extending from his hip through his thigh. In a society forever opting for the easy life, everyone expected the millionaire jockey to retire. Indeed, why should he continue? There was little else for him to accomplish on a racetrack. After nineteen years of riding, his mounts have earned a record $40,600,000; he has been national jockey champion five times; he has won more $100,000-plus races than any other man in the history of the sport; and he has worn the jewels of the Triple Crown: three Kentucky Derbys, two Preaknesses, and four Belmont Stakes. Only John Longden's record of all-time winners (6,032) eludes Shoemaker, who to date stands at 5,758, only 274 back.

But mainly because he was thirty-seven years old and in a sport where 105-pound men have to guide 1,200-pound, high-strung thoroughbreds through congested traffic, using only dainty slivers of leather, the prudent felt he should be thinking about Palm Springs or Kern City. Shoemaker, however, sees it differently: "Hell, it's been my life. What else would I do?"

It was Thursday, February 6, and because of the heavy rains drenching Southern California, Shoemaker's return to "his life" would have to be postponed for a while. So, for another day, he would have to sit in the stands as spectator and watch others do the work he so dearly loves, and he had no taste for it. "I don't like being a spectator," he commented. "You just sit here. I make a couple of small bets . . . what else is there to do? Everybody wants to know *why* I'm coming back. Well, I enjoy riding. The question is *why not?*"

But coming back wasn't a simple matter. After three weeks in the hospital under the care of Dr. Robert Kerlan (who also treated Dodger pitcher Sandy Koufax's arthritic elbow), the jockey was released. Then the dull, hard work began: painfully lifting weights with the leg and endless bicycle riding. "I began exercising about three months after my release from the hospital. I never had any doubts about coming back."

All this brought the rider of such speedballs as Swaps and Round Table to January 4, when he ignominiously took a leg up on a fat, safe, matronly stable pony. But ignominious or not, the talk in the backstretch had it: "The Shoe was back in the irons."

But if the rain was dampening his rebirth, it gave the little Texan a chance to reflect: "I think I have been around too long to have any fear about coming back. I know, I haven't broken any horses from a gate in a year, but that's something you don't forget. I just have to believe I haven't lost anything." Perhaps not. But the one fear nobody would speak of was silently descending from the heavens. The rain. The rain that turned hard racing surfaces into unnavigable swamps, that created the mud in which he

68

lay silently a year ago. Only his agent, Harry Silbert—a stocky, cigar-smoking man—would mention it, and that was in a whisper to the interlocutor: "He's not riding till we get a fast track."

A well-wisher approached the jockey and jested that colleague Bill Hartack was to be taken off a three-year-old colt of Kentucky Derby caliber named Majestic Prince, entered in today's eighth race, and Shoemaker would probably set a track record for changing clothes to get aboard the coveted mount, wouldn't he? Shoemaker laughed and replied: "The Derby is a long way off. Right now, I have to get up on the first one. That's the one I'm after."

The mention of the Derby spurred memories. "I've been on some great ones—Swaps and Gallant Man were about as fine as any runners you'll see. And I've ridden against great jocks, too. Hell, there must have been twenty great ones, but Arcaro was the most stylish rider I've ever seen."

Arcaro's name prompted him to reminisce about the great match race between Swaps with Shoemaker aboard and Nashua, Arcaro up. Arcaro, employing a totally unorthodox tactic for a distance race (1¼ miles), furiously whipped Nashua out of the gate to a five-length lead, and by the time the astonished Shoemaker recovered Arcaro had stolen the race. Paying reverence to the Old Master, Shoe grinned and said: "He really waxed my butt that day." Someone else recalled Arcaro's reply when he was asked what job he would like when he retired. With verbal style befitting his much-envied elegance on horseback, Eddie had answered: "To be a bookmaker in the jockeys' room." The Shoe broke into broad laughter and noted: "I'd retire for that position myself."

And on it went. Warm memories to ward off the chilling reality of the falling rain. The jockey and his agent sat there like children perched behind a window waiting for their chance to play . . . if only the rain would go away and come again another day.

The rain finally stopped over the weekend, and Monday is an off day at Santa Anita, so by Tuesday the track was rated fast. At 7:30 A.M. the jock arrived to work a couple of horses for trainer Charlie Whittingham. When Shoemaker moves through the gentle world of the stable area—green and white sheds, steaming hay and manure, cordial grooms and hot-walkers, yapping dogs and strutting roosters, all eyes turn toward him. Like DiMaggio and Sugar Ray, he has an aura about him, that indefinable element—class.

His appearance is a combination of impeccability and style: brown leather jacket and boots, fawn pants, and a deep-blue velvet hat. A groom gives him a leg up on the horse he is to work, and he allows himself an exaggerated groan and says, "It's a long way up. I must be getting old." As he moves the horse toward the main track, there are greetings every step of the way. Johnny Longden, who looks as if he should be sitting under a toadstool instead of on a horse, passes him on a gray pony and calls: "To-day's the big one." Shoemaker smiles at Longden, then looks at the threatening sky and is glum. The warm, pastoral mood is ruptured. With resignation he sighs, "I guess I'm not going to beat the rain."

The condensation is so heavy it's physical; it wetly licks you like a large, friendly dog. Outsiders, morning visitors to the workouts, mingle at rail-side with the backstretch regulars. The difference between the two groups is easily detectable. The regulars—little men with brown, creased faces like walnuts, gentle country boy blacks, and tough stable kids who seem to be trapped in a time capsule from the fifties with their pegged pants and slick hair brushed back like jet streams into that relic of hair dressing, the ducktail. And the outsiders—Richard Nixon's silent Americans from sur-rounding Arcadia, San Gabriel, and Huntington Park with their zippered windbreakers and close-cropped hair.

The voice on the loudspeaker announces that Shoemaker is on the track to work a horse. The coffee drinkers desert the refreshment stand and move to the rail. The horse is to work six furlongs, so Shoemaker breaks him on the backstretch at the three-quarter pole. Horse and rider move effortlessly around the turn, into the stretch, across the wire. He looks good, but it is only a workout—no gate, no real exertion, and most important, no traffic jams or rain.

Whittingham looks at his stopwatch and smiles. Another trainer ap-proaches him and asks: "How did he do?" "He took that horse in nearly even furlongs, every one of them twelve seconds or a shade better," Whit-tingham answers. The questioner shakes his head in awe: "He hasn't lost a thing, not a goddamn thing."

He works one more horse, and Whittingham expresses his appreciation in terms befitting the jock's stature: "Thank you, Sir William."

Shoemaker now seems confident, content. Passing a barn where grooms and hot-walkers are shooting craps in one of the stalls, he cautions, "You'd better get back to work. Here comes the boss." As the grooms scurry back to their duties, he smiles at one and says, "I hope you didn't quit a loser." A Mexican boy returns a stakes performer named Racing Room, which Shoemaker is scheduled to ride in today's feature race, to the barn. The jock asks, "Is she ready, Pop?" "He is ready." The jock smiles: "Now all we have to worry about is if I'm ready." The exercise boy won't tolerate such blasphemy: "I'm not worried about that; all you have to do is ride him."

The jock's work is done for the morning. He now returns to the jockey quarters for breakfast, a steam bath, a nap, and the long wait. That wait will not end until around 3:30 P.M., post time for the sixth race, when Sir William will be introduced to a sweet running filly, royally baptized Princess Endeavour.

The jock's luck was holding. Although the clouds were bullying the sun, the final confrontation never came—the racing surface remained fast. And even though the clouds and the smog were dense enough to obscure the San Gabriel Mountains that loom behind the backstretch, the crowd was in a sunny carnival mood.

But racing fans always are. Only prizefight crowds and devotees to the betterment of the breed bring high style to the sports they support and follow.

Baseball buffs are frolicking picnickers, beer drinkers spending an afternoon in the sun, as American as a Norman Rockwell cover. Football fans are snobs; they intellectually reduce violence to the Pentagonese that has made the game the love of Madison Avenue types across the nation.

But horse players are vulgar, sentimental, demanding, and bawdy. They are Elizabethan. They are kin to the hooters and roustabouts who populated the seats in the far reaches of Shakespeare's Globe Theatre.

Santa Anita itself blends with the personality of its fans. Unlike many new sports plants, it has none of that shopping-mart sterility. It is a perfect example of Southern California grab-bag architecture: touches of Spanish, Moorish, and glorious movie back lot *Citizen Kane* Xanadu. Pale green and ivory walls give way to floors of coral tile; gaudy gazebos stand like trollops in pastoral fields of yellow and purple pansies. On the refreshment stands All-American hamburgers and franks live in harmony with their more passionate south-of-the-border cousins, enchiladas and tacos.

It was now about twenty minutes before post time for the sixth race, and the only name on the lips of the bettors was Shoemaker. A Mexican woman confided that she had been secretly hoarding money from her husband for a month against this day. A child accompanied by his father peered through the four-foot fence that dwarfed him and asked: "Where is he, daddy? Where is he?"

A black radio and TV repairman named Willie Sanford stood with a handful of tickets on the jock's mount: "I'll bet him every time because he can do something to a horse no other jockey can do. He can beat these other guys just by sitting up on a horse." Patting his prospective fortune gently, he said, "He's my man. He either breaks me or makes me."

The maker and breaker now entered the paddock to a sentimental chorus: "Hi, Bill"; "Nice to have you home"; "Welcome back, champ." He was greeted by the attractive blond mistress of Llangollen Farm, Liz Tippett, owner of Princess Endeavour. Her arm circled the jock's shoulder with the protective custody mothers usually offer a child on his first day of school. Trainer Whittingham gave him brief riding instructions: "She's a nice filly to ride. Get a decent position, and do the best you can."

The jock stood there nervously, his small hands trembling. The call came for "Riders up," and trainer Whittingham, giving him a leg up, said the words he had waited a year to hear: "Come on, let's go to work."

As he made his way onto the track, the stands resembled a deck of cards slowly being flipped over. Section by section they rose in a standing ovation. Princess Endeavour had closed second choice in the betting. The race was to be run over seven furlongs, and Shoemaker was to break from post position 12—not an advantageous position in a sprint race, where the rail is so valuable. But this and other imponderables of racing luck were not of the moment—it was now "post time."

When the gate sprang open, the jockey exploded his filly into the lead and adroitly tucked her in on the rail. He then allowed her to settle into third place, while a long shot and the favorite vied for the lead. He held her there down the backstretch, saving ground along the rail. As they went into the turn for home, he swung her around the leaders and asked her to run. His little body stretched out on the mount—pumping, urging, cajoling —a perfect communion between horse and man, a union so wedded it was connubial. As they went over the finish line $2\frac{1}{4}$ lengths in front, the Princess and Sir William were a rhymed couplet. Time 1:22$\frac{4}{5}$ for seven furlongs.

He stood in the winners' circle that was so familiar to him, surrounded by the press, answering questions: "Yes, it's nice to ride a good one." The little legs were visibly shaky. He winked at the questioners and pointed to them: "Yes, the legs, a little bit . . ." and the words trailed off. He didn't bother to finish.

Now he walked back to the jockeys' room through rows of well-wishers and backslappers. Inside, he stripped off his silks, and for the first time he became ebullient: "I couldn't have written that any better." Turning to his smiling fellow jocks, he jokingly said, "I wrote the script, and all these other guys went along with me." The Brooklyn-born jockey, Walter "Mousey" Blum, shoulders slouched in the familiar Eastern street corner stance that resembles a fatigued question mark, said between drags on a cigarette: "It sure is nice to see something like that."

Shoemaker was scheduled to ride twice more that day, and he won them both (on Racing Room and Jay's Double). Three out of three—what later was to be described as a perfect Hollywood ending.

But the jock knows better than to think of life in terms of Hollywood endings. Later, over coffee, he summed up what it meant to him: "A week from now, nobody will talk about it. It will be just back to work as usual."

And this was the important thing to the jock, for he had not only won a horse race. For a while, William Lee Shoemaker had beaten what John Updike called "that small death that must come to all athletes . . . retirement."

April 13, 1969

72

Bagging Dick Tiger: The Mockery of Age

There was a small requiem for a light heavyweight at the Garden last Wednesday night. Then again, nobody really thought that Dick Tiger's end would be an occasion for anguished weeping and wailing. As a fighter, Tiger was never a wonder, but a worker, and dawn and midnight are the tragic hours, not nine to five.

Tiger was meeting his old adversary, Emile Griffith, but only the buffs were really concerned. Griffith was trying to regain a shot at his middleweight title, the one he lost to Nino Benvenuti, and Tiger was looking for a big evening to convince light heavyweight champ Bob Foster he was worthy of a return.

Yet both prospects seem unlikely. Griffith and Benvenuti have had at it three times (Nino winning the first and third bouts), and the turnstile magic is no longer there. And Foster knocked Tiger cold early in their only outing, and no one thought the script would be any different if there were a next time—only more abbreviated. Yet 8,000 came. It was not love that brought them, only memories of things past.

Both men have owned two crowns: Griffith the welter and the middle, and Tiger the middle and light heavyweight; and they have provided New Yorkers with some memorable nights.

But most of the crowd came to see Tiger simply because he is Dick Tiger, a man who has suffered both the blows of his profession and the slings and arrows of personal despair without a whimper. He has just witnessed the death of his homeland, Biafra. And on Wednesday night, he tugged the heartstrings of the mugs who still find something in the sport.

The portents for Tiger were bad. He is forty-one years old to Griffith's thirty-one. At the weigh-in, the old gentleman lost his usual aplomb and ranted at one of Griffith's entourage for taunting that Emile was going to knock him out. He told the heckler: "I am more of a man than you are." What he really was saying was that he had seen too much manhood. Dick Tiger, in crotchety fury, was announcing (or denouncing) his forty-one years.

Then there was the paltry gathering of pugdom who were introduced in the ring before the fight: a young and obscure heavyweight, light heavy Charlie "Devil" Green (boxing's boutique in his jump suit and lizard boots), and "television's own Rocky Graziano," now more famous for his Trendex than his ring rating.

And when Tiger was introduced, it was "Dick Tiger from Nigeria." The final blow. The valiant old man with his homeland a skeleton tied to a new ship of state.

The weight, like the age, was a decade apart: Tiger, 167—Griffith, 157.

In his latter years, Tiger has been a slow beginner. Sweat, to an old boxer's body, is a lubricant, an additive to grease his ring machinery, but one thought the nostrils only caught old man's must. And then his feet—always slow and flat, planted in position to give him leverage to counter. But now they were a parody, like those elongated, floppy-tongued shoes in Dr. Seuss' children's books slapping up and down, seeming to stick to the canvas when they landed.

And there was the startled flinching. Old men are brittle in anticipation in the early rounds, their bodies twigs waiting to be snapped by destructive younger playmates. Griffith sensed it.

He jabbed tippy-toed, trying sucker right-hand leads—bait for a flounder, not a shark. But you waited. Many fancy dans mistakenly have thought they had bagged Tiger early.

But by the third round the pattern was inexorably set. It would not change. Though Griffith wasn't throwing heavy leather, he had the boxer's gift of time—legs. He also had his ever-present mother caterwauling him on from ringside.

Tiger's usual tribal rooting section of Ibos with their beating drums was missing. There are no Ibos anymore. Slaughter has made everyone a Nigerian.

Only the rounds marched on. Tiger remained immobile. He stood squinting, looking for an opening as if it would appear in a lyrical, slow-motion frame waiting for him to enter in a violent *pas de deux*. He defied Joe Louis' admonition to old warriors—that when you can see the opening, instead of responding instinctively to it, you're through.

Then Griffith began to mock him. He dropped his hands, wriggled his shoulders, and did his version of the Ali Shuffle. It was a graceless interlude. You scorn another fighter for many reasons: psychological oneupmanship, for the bad blood between you. But what kind of man mocks age? Only a fool does bravado dances around a monument.

Griffith doesn't realize that perhaps the gods are marking him for a similar fate. As he bobbed his head, you caught a crescent of a bald spot, a potential dark side of the moon of age. And one hopes the day will come for Griffith when a youth will jab and sucker and keep on his wheels—a bicycle thief to rob him of his dignity.

At the end, the best Tiger could do on any card was to win three rounds out of ten.

One is tempted to write a eulogy for Dick Tiger, but that would insult the man. Tiger is too much of a stoic, a man who understands the rules. If the deck is stacked, he simply says, deal the cards. He should be remembered not as that dry twig of Wednesday night, but as the spreading chestnut he was during his career.

For sixty-one wins, seventeen losses, and three draws, for too many rounds to calculate and too many bells to distinguish, remember only that when his corner men snatched the stool out from under him and told him to go to work, Dick Tiger did just that.

July 23, 1970

Even in Victory, the End of the Line

It was a fight I shunned simply because it had no significance either to the real or the romantic. What magic is there in combat between a has-been and a never-will? Then, too, I didn't want to dampen the enthusiasm of my friends who still find mystique in Patterson.

To many of my contemporaries who came out of the hubcap sociological school of the fifties, Floyd Patterson holds a sacred place in the heart though I relegated him to limbo a long time ago. So, like the tonsils of our time, I didn't want to be the little white cloud that cried all over their sunny reverie. Too many good evenings are marred by uncivility these days.

Patterson chose his path to mediocrity years back, and sympathy is hard coming. Some blame his former manager, Cus D'Amato, for his downfall; but Svengalis never survive without willing accomplices, so at best Patterson has to be indicted for consorting. When he was young and had talent (a talent, I believe, vastly overrated), he let it lie fallow against the likes of Pete Rademacher and "Cut-and-Shoot" Roy Harris.

And now, after a two-year layoff, he was coming back against a third-rate performer named Charlie "Devil" Green, a fighter whom light heavyweight José Torres had knocked out in two rounds when Torres' once-formidable skills were near nonexistent. But if one followed the New York sportswriters, Patterson was about to improve on the second coming, since this was to be about his fifth revival.

Milton Gross in the *Post* gave us daily bulletins on Freud vs. Floyd, the connection being, one supposed, that one fought from a couch, the other from a crouch. Then Floyd was quoted as having said that if he got by Green, he wanted Liston again, and the head dissolved into mixed literary metaphors: Floyd, like Quilty in disguise, tracking the great black whale across a sea of states and finally shy-rapping an aging Liston in a men's room in some saloon with Patterson emerging purified. For such thoughts, call me Schlemiel.

Finally, I thought of Patterson being glorified for returning from exile to take on Green while Ali, after three and a half years, has to fight Quarry, the best heavyweight (outside Frazier) and the nonpareil of the white hopes. It tells the tale of the two men and, indeed, of boxing itself.

So I decided to keep my dark thoughts to myself and watch the tape of the fight on television the following night. In truth, I was rooting for Patterson, since during his career he had given me moments of pleasure while Green had never given me a glimmer.

Green, a local Greenwich Villager who has a penchant for mod clothes, works as a bouncer at the discothèque the Dom, a socially significant fact in that it might be a testimony to the passivity of the Dom's drinkers. Green is an unruly mauler who has bastardized the fighter's basic weapon, the left jab, to the ridiculous. He actually throws the jab upward from his knee. Also, aside from his mod midi-trunks embroidered with devil's heads, he is displeasing to watch at work, since his ringmanship is marred by awkwardness and lack of intelligence. But then, the Village is bigger on boutiques than brains these days.

When the fighters were introduced, one thought that Charlie really was the devil from the way he was booed. Floyd was afforded the loving spoonful as usual. It's a phenomenon that he is the only black fighter who constantly is the favorite of the crowd, even when his opponent is white. He seems to evoke sentimentality for a more "civilized" time when the spirit of Eleanor Roosevelt always seemed to be at ringside. It is such an overwhelming devotion that it even somewhat colored Norman Mailer's otherwise memorable piece on the first Patterson-Liston bout.

Green's announced strategy was that he was going to take Patterson early, a sound one since Patterson is vulnerable in the early going. But badmouthing and boxing are talents apart, and Charlie opened up timidly, a Shavian Satan all talk and no action.

And if Patterson were to eclipse past memories, he, too, would have to perform the dramatic early. He had his chance in the third when he had Green woozy from a left hook, but the devil stayed alive and weathered the round. Most of the fight was consumed by grappling, hugging, slipping, falling, and one authentic monkey flip. Indeed, it looked as if Masters and Johnson had staged the whole thing to show how inadequate the human body can be.

Green's big chance came in the fifth when he opened a deep cut above Patterson's left eye with either a right hand or a head butt. From then on, the devil employed such inglorious tactics as blatant butting, thumbing, and lacing, all spectacularly obvious. (What can be said for a man who can't even cheat properly?)

But Patterson's corner did a good job on the eye, and Patterson did just a fair job on Green, though if one was to believe announcer Don Dunphy, it was Louis-Schmeling all over again. The problem with old radio an-

76

nouncers is that when the action starts, they forget that now we also can see it.

By the tenth Patterson was way ahead on points, but this was slim solace to his legions—they had come for more. Luckily for his fans, devils die easier than legends. With a left hook to Green's stomach with 1:57 gone in the tenth, Floyd kept the eternal flame flickering. Charlie took the ten count, and Patterson's disciples gathered at ringside chanting, "Floyd, Floyd, Floyd," for their great harlequin hope.

This corner can't offer much encouragement for Patterson's future. He was far from impressive against a nontalent. And even when he was impressive earlier in his career, he wasn't in the same class as an Ali or a Joe Frazier, so even his victories signal the end of the line. As you watched him prancing in his antiquated peek-a-boo style with the gloves up around his ears, you realized just how fragile and vulnerable he is. He looked like the little boy playing the reindeer in the Christmas pageant.

In the end, the fight proved only two things: Floyd Patterson can always come home again, and if Charlie Green is the devil, not only Milton—but old ladies—will reign in hell.

September 24, 1970

Amen to Sonny

Will no one say amen? After reading and listening to the New York press, it seems that Charles "Sonny" Liston's soul will be politely consigned to damnation.

Milton Gross of the *Post,* the Eleanor Roosevelt of the sports pages, said in last Wednesday's column that he'd decided not to call his boy Floyd Patterson with the news of Sonny's death till the following day, knowing that Floyd would say: "Gee, that's terrible. I'm sorry." Then Miltie hypothetically buried Floyd (in St. Peter's Basilica, one presumes) and commented: "I know Liston wouldn't have said the same." So much for a séance in a wet afternoon daily.

Another Patterson acolyte of old, Howard Cosell, appeared on ABC's six o'clock news and, in his best Battle of Britain tones, told us that it would be "unethical and unprincipled" for him to praise Sonny, concluding that there would be "no requiem for this heavyweight." This, of course, is the same Cosell who "ethically" gloated over Pete Rozelle's muscling Joe Namath during the Bachelors III affair. Sonny would have understood —he always understood the smart money.

77

And on the late ABC news Jim Bouton, the icky iconoclast whose reporting is so giggly that—in the words of Dorothy Parker—it makes you want to "fwow up," dismissed Liston with a cute anecdote, proceeding to interview ex-footballer-author Dave Meggyesy (*Out of Their League*) about the comparisons between racism in football and everyday American life and the similarities between football and the military-industrial complex, blah, blah. . . . The interview led one to believe that the only thing out of Meggyesy's league is the English language.

But what about Floyd himself? The *Daily News* told us that Patterson, upon being informed of Liston's death, exclaimed: "No, no! I had told them I would fight Liston again." Such humanity! It would crack the vaults of heaven. Poor Sonny done went and died before Floyd could cure his psyche. The eternal truth is that even in his present condition Liston would be 8 to 5 over Patterson.

Well, the reader may justifiably say that the back of the hand is the only tribute a blackguard deserves. After all, the man was busted twenty times. He was a union goon, ran with the mob, cracked heads with the same niftiness a short-order cook prepares "two over light." True, so very true. But transgressions always are forgiven in boxing if the sinner prostrates himself in front of his better sinners—namely, promoters, managers, and boxing commissioners. But like Ali after him, Sonny was a psychic breakthrough in the sport and in the American (both black and white) mind. He was a blatant mother in a fucker's game.

He arrived at a time when hopes of integration were high in the air, and Patterson and Ralph Bunche were everybody's prototypical black men. I can't recall anyone I know (with the exception of the Philadelphia-based writer Jack McKinney) who publicly wanted Liston to beat Patterson for the heavyweight championship. In Patterson's corner were clustered Jimmy Baldwin, Norman Mailer, Pete Hamill, and the NAACP (which didn't even want Patterson to give Liston the fight, because of what Liston would do to the "Negro image"). As Ali murdered the myth of the sixties, so Liston was the pallbearer of the fifties' liberalism. He embodied what they didn't want to recognize—that our streets spawn a sea of Sonnys. Like the song, "Night Train," to which he jumped rope, he was that underground fear we wouldn't face—the menacing black man who invaded the subway of our souls at four in the morning. In short, Sonny was a badass nigger.

But Liston was only a minor-leaguer in evil compared to the sport at which he toiled, a crude crusher in the domain of charlatans. He wasn't allowed a license in New York State, and indeed, he wasn't even allowed to be introduced in the Garden ring before fights. This, while such erstwhile solid citizens as Rocky Graziano (who evaded the military before it became fashionable) and Jake LaMotta (a self-confessed dumper) were wildly applauded. Of course, this is the same New York that denied Ali a license for being unpatriotic until a $10,000,000 gate appeared on the horizon and transformed him from a traitor to a pugilistic Patton. Ah, what the green can do for the old red, white, and blue!

Promoters are blessed with more positions than either Nixon or the *Kama Sutra.* I remember when I was working on a piece about the late Frankie DePaula, an Italian fighter who used to fill the Garden as if it were a church on Palm Sunday. DePaula came under indictment for grand theft, and I called the Garden for his home phone number, only to be told: "It's a funny thing, Joe. We never had that guy's phone number." This was the same DePaula who had worked his way to a light heavyweight shot in the Garden by looking over the titanic likes of "Irish" Jimmy McDermott, a one-handed clover. But then again, one must forgive promoters. Their fantasies always are unfulfilled. Imagine if they were able to get St. Patrick vs. Mother Cabrini for fifteen rounds.

Now Sonny was a dishonorable man, as I've said. He understood his trade admirably. Asked to say a kind word about his opponents before a fight, he usually responded: "I'd like to run him over with a truck." No dainty doggerel that to entice the Dylan left and the older lib-labs. In fact, Sonny went so far as to say he'd like to leave his wheel marks on the executive board of the NAACP. No charisma.

One must know how to jerk and jolt the Liberal Establishment at the same time. Night trains have no subtle shift in gears; shifty roadsters are more the liberal style. It takes an Ali to tune their senses. Who could convince them he was a legitimate critic of the Vietnam war but a cat so sly he was contented to flunk the selective service test for years until the qualifications were lowered and he became eligible? So, like the unseated Saul, he then became a minister. One has to reread sports columns twice these days to decipher if they are about Ali or William Sloane Coffin. Will no one say amen?

Was Sonny Satan? Not really, but he'd make a helluva understudy. I first met him a couple of years ago in the Main Street Gym in Los Angeles, where he was starting his comeback. He sat in a small cubicle, naked and sweating after a workout. He just stared at me, not speaking while I waited to be assigned a furnace in his kingdom. In a booming castrato voice I finally asked: "Is thirty-six really your age?" Slowly, he looked up, and I looked down, hoping the Divine Editor would cancel that question. He boomed: "My mammy says I'm thirty-six. Are you calling my mammy a fuckin' liar?" After some neat verbal footwork, I convinced him Mother Liston would make George Washington out to be an old forked-tonguer, and, by God, he smiled. A big, wide-open grin that was as honest as his snarl. He talked of how he was the son of a sharecropper who had had twenty-five children and "whupped me every day." Hold your faint hearts still, you socially aware, that was not Sonny's bag. In the next sentence

79

spiced with his salacious grin, he paid his papa his due: "Twenty-five kids. My daddy was a champion at what he did, too." As his wife, Geraldine, said: "That man has mother wit." Sure enough.

It was a wit matured and gnarled in gutters, in prisons. The lowdown logic of every hustler who knows the cosmic truth that a bullet from a gun on the end of a pimp's silk suit travels faster and deadlier than the best left hook ever honed in a gym. But mother wit he did have, and his repertoire wasn't limited.

He could deliver a classic geographical put-down to a judge in the City of Brotherly Love when confronted with a speeding rap: "I'd rather be a lamppost in Denver than mayor of Philadelphia." He outcrazied the Crazies by announcing he was thinking of becoming a Catholic priest. Now that would have been a test of Pope John's liberalism.

He had a built-in shit detector second only to Papa's. When he'd beaten Chuck Wepner bloody for eight rounds in Jersey City, someone asked him if Wepner wasn't one of the gamest men he'd ever seen, and Liston replied: "His manager is gamer." A better line about boxing has never been uttered.

I spent five days with Liston in Los Angeles, some of them spectacular, some sour. You always could sense his mood from the way he used the word "shit." On bad days he grunted "Shith"; on his good days he strung the word out on a clothesline till it stretched to "Shee-ee-it." He would not talk about his losses to Ali, except to mumble: "I was overtrained for the second bout." On Ali's impending imprisonment he became a savvy Satan: "He like to say how pretty he is. They like pretty people in prison." A low-bred mother wit.

The final day I spent with Liston, we met a hippie when we were leaving the gym. He presented Sonny with a "fight song" that he wanted him to give to Sammy Davis, Jr., to sing on television. The song was a simple-minded rhyme, extolling Sonny's ferocity, and he got a kick out of it. The hippie then told him he'd like to make Liston a pair of sandals like those he was wearing. Liston put his huge, flat foot up against the hippie's and went into a Bunyonesque fable to the effect that there wasn't enough leather in the West to cover the great man's foot. The hippie loved the instant legend. As we left, the kid gave him a tin triangle with the words "Jesus, Mary, Joseph" pin-scratched on each angle. The boy said it was "to keep the champ safe."

As we drove away from the gym in his Cadillac, Liston turned the triangle over and over between his thumb and forefinger, extolling the madness of hippies. "Those cats are right," he said. "They don't worry about a fuckin' thing in the world."

We passed a campaign headquarters for Robert Kennedy (then still alive), and Liston exploded: "Tell me, with six million dollars, why the fuck do these people want to be President? All that money, and they want worries. That hippie is smarter. Their old man made all that money smuggling scotch, and they want to become President to tell the people to keep sober. Shit, six million dollars." I asked him what he'd do if he had $6,000,000, and the storm subsided as the country boy leaned his head back and in philosophical reverie replied: "I'd buy me the finest pussy in the United States of America." And, concluding his American Dream, Charles "Sonny" Liston with a flip of his thumb sent Jesus, Mary, and Joseph in flight formation into the middle of Wilshire Boulevard.

Was he the bastard everyone says he was? To many, yes. To others, such as Claude Brown, he was the only man alive who could have quelled the Watts riots. I'm not pleading for his life-style—a bastard, maybe, or, perhaps more fair, he did bastardly deeds. But he should be judged in context. He was better than the sport he practiced and the men who rule it. In fact, he was one of boxing's most legitimate sons. When greed, hypocrisy, and corruption complete their *ménage à trois,* a Sonny Liston will always be plucked from the breach.

And he was a lot better than the hucksters for sport who now so cavalierly dismiss his life. One could go into a social tract on that life, but Sonny would only stretch a "Shee-ee-it" over the analysis. He was what he was. A villain perhaps, but also once the king of the heavyweights, and it is only fitting that one should find his epitaph in a play populated by an aging king and a bastard:

This is the excellent foppery of the world, that, when we are sick in fortune—often the surfeit of our own behaviour,—we make guilty of our disasters the sun, the moon, and the stars: as if we were villains by necessity; fools by heavenly compulsion; knaves, thieves, and treachers, by spherical predominance; drunkards, liars, and adulterers, by an enforced obedience of planetary influence; and all that we are evil in, by a divine thrusting on—an admirable evasion of whoremaster man, to lay his goatish disposition on the charge of a star! My father compounded with my mother under the dragon's tail; and my nativity was under Ursa major; so that it follows, I am rough and lecherous. Tut, I should have been that I am, had the maidenliest star in the firmament twinkled on my bastardizing. . . ."

Amen.

January 14, 1971

Miami and the Stupor Bowl—Spectacles
of Vulgarity

The intriguing part of any spectacle is not so much the event itself but the spectacular vulgarity that surrounds it. One must be slightly raunchy in the soul to appreciate the October Festival in Munich or a Super Bowl in Miami.

All such gatherings would make worthy material for Brueghel—humanity on a bender with mouths either stuffed or raucously open, and everyone's fly unzipped halfway. The lout in me eminently qualifies as a citizen for such circuses.

And what better place is there in America for a nationalistic orgy than Miami, a city so steeped in the overdone it can mute the vulgarities it hosts? Even the Republicans felt at home here. But one shouldn't indict Miami for what drops into it, since geographically it is the cuspidor on America's barroom floor.

On the flight down (on something called a Yellowbird) one could sense the tone being set. Among my flight companions were two dogs (one a loquacious chihuahua) and a herd of minks of all colors. The pilot introduced himself over the intercom as Captain Peck, which submerged the fear of flying in my Roxy head, since I immediately recalled *Twelve O'Clock High*. And if one is to die, how better than with a cryptic captain and shrouded in mink? Besides, brethren, only the very young are entitled to mock the Miamis of the world. As one's blood and ideals become thinner, the sun, surf, sand, and some senility do offer solace.

It was pleasant, too, to escape the Eastern elitists and their endless ruminations about the evils of professional football and their assertions of its connection with war, racism, and sexism—arguments that seem rather superficial since neither Israel nor Biafra (nor about 200 other nations at war) has yet got an NFL franchise. And of course, there were the endless speculations about the two contestants: Dallas, where the unspeakable had happened, and Baltimore, where the unmentionable was hatched. Better the drone of a Yellowbird than the theories of shitbirds.

Miami is not without blessings. The old here seem to thrive. Indeed, instead of looking like gray park-bench rejects, they are quite handsome. The sun dapples their skin and bleaches their hair a downy white. And for the poor, heat seems the kindest of all human resources. Children's bodies are straight and strong, unlike those stretched globs of phlegm one too often sadly sees hanging around the street corners of Northern cities.

Only a cultural imperialist could fail to find humor in this city with its pink stucco hotels that evoke Zachary Scott, in white suit with gin and tonic, decaying on the veranda and its curbside phones which you dial from your car. The latter, naturally, are intended as another saved exertion on the heart—coronaries are conversationally big down here. A lovely old gent of a cabdriver, extolling the excitement of jai alai, told me: "Eight people had heart attacks and died during the matches last season." I decided to say nine to the jai alai games that evening.

Also, any city that can house Hialeah Racecourse must be granted a dash of soul. My own particular esthetic canon is that my final paradise must come equipped with a parimutuel machine. On a temporary basis, Hialeah was heavenly. It is a marvel of elegance: green, beautifully flowered and shrubbed, and heated to the right degree by civilized action and sunshine. Brightly polished chandeliers hang from the clubhouse ceiling, but standing beneath them was the real glitter. Every conceivable cloth ever woven by man was on display. There is none of that Yankee business about afternoon or evening attire—anything goes, from slacks to pant suits to leather De Sade minis and white go-go dresses fringed in fur to polo shirts done in banlon baroque. The flamingos on the infield lake looked like panhandlers in comparison to the crowd. But excess always has been my weakness, since I believe that in many instances the outlandish bespeaks life.

The mood of Miami seemed to signify a Dallas Cowboy victory. The hotels, restaurants, and bars were dominated by noisy Cowboy rooters: ladies who had ordered their faces from Neiman-Marcus' leather shop with their *machismo* mates who called the waitresses "honey" and ordered their dinner wine two bottles at a time to be followed by "some brandy, sugar. VSOP, if you have it." Steaks and stone crabs were being consumed like hors d'oeuvres, and bourbon and bullshit were the predinner appetizers at the bar while they waited for their tables: "Goddamn, I've been married to my old lady twenty-three years, and I've been in trouble for all of them"; "Christ, bartender, can you rustle up a round of bourbons? Shit, five-hundred thirsty people and only one bartender."

Shouts and salutations shot across restaurants as if they were convention halls, and at the two-bottle tables grab-assing took place during the courses, kisses mingling with steak fat, butter sauce, and some good old down-home spit. The yellow roses from Texas were howling under the moon over Miami, and the Colts were to be the final course—a Sunday dinner with all the fixin's. A healthy Cowboy burp was drowning out Baltimore, the cradle of the Silent Majority.

One watched the pregame activities featuring floats and frills, feeling as if he were meandering around in Zsa Zsa Gabor's brain. The weather at kickoff was perfect—sunny, but with a slight breeze to cool the combatants. My seat high up in the sun was excellent.

The predicted drama of the game was to be the confrontation between a great Dallas Doomsday Defense (some fodder for the Biblical Cassandras) and the golden, aged head and battered arm of Colt quarterback

Johnny Unitas. There was much talk as well of the Colts revenging their Super Bowl defeat two years ago by the New York Jets. This argument escaped me because I could not figure out how one can get revenge from a different opponent. What did Dallas have to do with Joe Namath's humiliation (both verbal and physical) of a Colt team that had been deemed invincible? Such logic is a little like screwing the sister of your unfaithful true love to get even.

The drama never materialized, but the game was exciting in spite of itself. It was a stage for frustration, immobility, and ennui. In place of the aging warrior trying to slay a hydra-headed defense, we were rendered Waiting for Godot with Vladimir and Estragon both seeming to want to spring into action, "Yes, let's go," only to be damned by the author's stage directions: "They do not move." But this mood wasn't set immediately, only hinted at during the first half. For a while, the Cowboys seemed capable of action.

Early in the first quarter the Cowboys recovered a fumbled punt inside the Colts' 10 but failed to get the touchdown when Craig Morton outrageously overthrew his wide receiver, Reggie Rucker, in the end zone. A hint. But some movement, because they scored three points on a field goal. In the meantime, the Dallas defense succeeded in making Unitas look ancient—not wily and ancient, just weary and old. Dallas once again showed sparks offensively on a long pass to Bob Hayes that, along with a roughing penalty, brought the Cowboys inside the 5. This time, Morton had his halfback, Duane Thomas, wide open on the sidelines but didn't spot him, so once again they settled for a field goal and a 6–0 score. Could it be possible that such a thing as a meek Texan could inherit the earth?

The tenor of the game finally was set when Unitas lofted a long pass downfield to Ed Hinton, who tipped it to Mel Renfro, the Dallas defender, who tipped it over his head to Colt tight end John Mackey, who ran it in for a 75-yard touchdown. Miami smiles on the old and volleyball. But Baltimore, not to be underdone, missed the point after, tying the score at 6–6. Estragon: "I can't go on like this." Vladimir: "That's what you think."

It was now Unitas' turn to atone for his brashness. Scrambling out of the pocket, he was hit hard and fumbled on his own 29. Dallas, disregarding design, drove to the Colt 7 and scored from there on a pass to Thomas, 13–7. At this point, Earl Morrall, the ghost of Super Bowl past, took over at quarterback for Unitas, who had injured his ribs.

Morrall brought his team down to the Dallas 2 in one of the few semblances of an offensive drive all day, then tried three running plays which gained a total of $\frac{1}{2}$ yard. One waited for the field goal unit, but it didn't show. Instead, Morrall threw an incomplete pass into the end zone, which gave the Cowboys the ball with seconds left in the half. One wondered what the hell was wrong with Colt coach Don McCafferty's brain. Was it so sunbaked that he didn't go for the field goal which would have left his club trailing only 13–9 with thirty minutes of football remaining?

As the second half opened, it was obvious that the pathetic pattern was irrevocable. Baltimore fumbled the kickoff, only to have the Cowboys drive to the 1-yard line, where they fumbled the ball back. It was like watching two sleazy stand-up comics trying to outdo each other. First, a slightly off-color joke, then a blue joke, a swish joke, a bathroom joke, and, finally, one dropping his pants for the final points on the applause meter.

Both teams threw away multiple scoring opportunities via 6 interceptions, 5 fumbles, and a combined total of 164 yards in penalties. In the end, Baltimore was more persevering. A late interception with eight minutes to go set up the tying Colt touchdown from the 2-yard line. With less than two minutes left, Morton was intercepted again.

It has become fashionable to blame Dallas' woes entirely on Morton's weak arm, but I won't buy that cant in these two instances. True, both passes were high, but his receivers (Walt Garrison and Dan Reeves) each got both hands on the passes and tipped them into defenders' hands. Professional receivers are paid good money to make difficult catches. If the criterion for receivers were to catch balls thrown into their stomachs, Brooklyn bars would become a prime scouting region.

With five seconds left, Baltimore's waiting ended. A 32-yard field goal brought them victory in the Stupor Bowl. It was an Irishman named O'Brien who kicked it and saved the game from going into interminable death. Odd thing that, eh, Sam, a Celtic savior?

And Dallas? As the ball went toward the uprights, they did not move.

January 21, 1971

In the Company of Two Madmen—
Frazier-Ali Fight

About two thirty in the afternoon on Monday the sun was shining brightly while snowflakes were falling like confetti from the Lord's balcony. Now that should have told a man something. If there was fiddling around in the firmament, what would be going on in Ali's head? Indeed, had he, like Prospero, called up these spirits?

The temptation is for the observer to call upon his mother lode of marvelous conceit and render the rendition of what *really* happened. Who but one who was battered for years by the good nuns is more qualified to discourse on the antics of religious maniacs? Mysticism and mayhem have long been the bread and butter of my philosophy. But an attempted journey through Ali's head requires a St. Augustine, not a reporter, so what follows is the humble account of a mortal who is not privy to the inner workings of saviors. In short, this is a confession of ignorance.

If it were cleaved open, the head of Ali would produce a Rousseau canvas populated with popeyed lions, eerie moons, and dozing black men. How else could one explain his estimate of the fight? According to the soothsayer, only his own journey around the moon in a spaceship or the discovery of a baby dinosaur alive in California (mark California) could be more significant than the fight. The Peaceable Kingdom on a dark bender.

It would be a futile gesture to paint the tableau of those who attended the Fight; better to know who didn't have the clout to be present, those poor souls forever damned to New York social limbo.

The horny sheet sharers of sex and ego promenaded around ringside before it began, demanding their due of recognition, which is not meant as a put-down since I did the flirtation walk route five times myself: my credentials winking at the cocoa flesh of the black ladies and the ivory tusks protruding from the hot pants of the lacquered ladies. It was delicious.

But the setting was best summed up on the way to the fight by a disgruntled nonticket holder who said: "The only people who can afford this fight are spade slumlords and white liberals."

The crowd was not Ali's by a long shot. Atlanta had been his night, a return from the political wars, a party in his honor given by intimate friends. Tonight the corporate heads in the prize seats would provide Frazier with a claque. Who else had uproariously cheered George Foreman for his Olympic Games flag-waving and his introduction by ring announcer Johnny Addie as "a man who is proud to be an American"? And they had had throat for Billy Conn—the donkeys letting out a huge Galway bray for him. Joe Louis, too, was smothered in a sea of sympathy by those who understand a man who is a credit to his race. In boxing everyone has a designated price seat in history.

But the crowd didn't matter simply because we were not only ignorant, but terrified. We are all slaves to sane design, but as early as the introduction we knew we were in the company of two lunatics—one (Ali) madder than the other, to be sure, but who can quibble about degrees of madness?

As they were introduced, both fighters do-si-doed around the ring, bumping each other and snarling psychic oneupmanships. In the first round

Ali did what he should—jabbed and moved, landing the right hand rather easily. Frazier, too, was predictable—a crab with a souped-up governor trying to envelop an elusive prey. Round two followed the same pattern with Ali successfully keeping Frazier off stride with combinations and jabs, but the lunacy was beginning to show its quirky head. Both fighters were giving running verbal critiques of each other's performance, each waving disgustedly at the end of every round. In the great show biz tradition they were ignoring the critics in the front seats and playing it broadly for the balcony, more so for the unseen balcony of the world on closed-circuit television. After all, who gave a shit for the opinion of a referee and a couple of honky judges when what really was at stake was the love from Lebanon and the bravos from Beirut?

In the fifth Frazier became Pirandello—that is, he became Ali and allowed Muhammad to punch him in the head for . . . laughs? At this juncture the crowd took solace in themselves, reassuring themselves that they weren't seeing what they were seeing and inwardly begging for some Eisenhower security and the sanity of a Marciano or a Louis. Or succinctly begging to have someone say it isn't so, Joe.

Enter Ali as Jack Johnson, the fantasy this fighter loves to live. For three rounds he laid on the ropes, letting Frazier pound him while he grinned, faked dizziness, swooned, and hinted at Victorian vapors. One was sure he was going to lie down with his $2,500,000 safely in the bank and his mitted hand on his pecker, dealing the Establishment the highest-paid fucking in history.

But no. In the ninth he decided to fight. Really fight, not laying on the ropes playing with Frazier's head as if it were the light bag in the gym. Such seriousness was contagious, and Frazier in the eleventh staggered Ali around the ring with left hooks. In the twelfth Ali fluctuated between pissing it, simply passing, then decided once again on punching. By this time his trainer, Angelo Dundee, looked as if he were being directed by Peter Brook—a lobotomized cheerleader. Brutal punishment was being exchanged willingly and accepted gleefully. It was a fight that could only be understood by the haunters of Forty-second Street skin flick houses. The world was being jerked off under a derby.

In the fifteenth Ali was floored by a tremendous left hook. He not only got up but ended the fight jabbing on his toes, a tactic that was forty-four minutes too late. I thought the fifteenth was crucial to Ali and scored the fight 8–7 for Frazier. This was a gross attempt to put numbers, logistics, latitudes, longitudes on an uncharted country—Ali's brain. One needs an anchor at sea.

Ali simply gave away his championship. Why? Jack Johnson, maybe. As one wag disgustedly said: "I could have seen *The Great White Hope* for two dollars and fifty cents." But then, one suspects Ali is not Eastern in orientation at all. Not even Yankee Eastern. He is, when it comes down to it, All-American. The return bout is scheduled for Los Angeles, and if miracles and resurrections are to take place, Southern California is perfect—a geographical gypsy tearoom. The sons of the surf and sun will in the future by divine scientology, tarot cards, astrology charts, Baptist rantings, and sidewalk scrawls unravel the mystery.

I always knew that Ali was the greatest faker (fakir) in history, but little did I suspect that, in vespers, when he was bowing to the east he was really pointed to the West.

Muhammad Greeley, I salute you.

March 11, 1971

When Happiness Used to Be a 12-Foot Set Shot

The great appeal of certain sports or combative contests such as boxing, bullfighting, basketball, or boudoiring is that they can be broken down to their simplest unit—one on one. Boxer against boxer, man against bull, man against man, or man against woman (though in this latter case one has to be terribly old hat to believe it). In short, there is a democracy of action, a one man, one vote concept, so to speak.

There is an economic democracy in some of these endeavors as well. One who is poor can always find someone to fight, someone to challenge him to a head-on-head half court basketball game, and, I hope, someone to woo. On the economic level, bullfighting must be dismissed; but little matter, since bull slinging was more renowned in my boyhood Brooklyn than bullfighting. Verbal veronicas drew the olés on the streets in that corner of the world.

But finally, it was basketball that fascinated us, simply because one needed only a ball, a hoop, and another kid. Fighting was reserved for monumental occasions, slurs on our girls or invasions of our turf.

And, as far as I can observe, the marriage of the kid and the hoop remains a solid hunk of Americana. The blacks in Harlem and Bed-Stuy still create schoolyard magic; the Irish in Rockaway still play their particular brand of aggressive, snub-nosed ball (Mike Reardon of the New York Knicks epitomizes this style); it still is the premier game of the Jewish kids on the East Coast; and across the breadth of the land, a hoop nailed to a garage door is as familiar as an "Honor America" bumper sticker. In its way, the game is one cohesive string, a full court pass from

New York to California that we have in common in the most uncommon of times.

But if one is to be honest, he must admit the rub, the technical foul between generations. He must blow the whistle on himself. Our own fantasies form the diet of sports—that on a God-given day, when our constellations are in order for a moment, we could compete with the best. Occasionally, I still Mitty about the mighty: Am I not capable of hitting a Texas League single off a major-league pitcher? With the aid of the 49er's offensive line, might I not uncork a dazzling 6-foot screen pass? Couldn't I, in a lucky moment, land a left hook on one of those beer-bellied heavyweights before he smothered me? Probably not. But a gossamer wing in the brain occasionally becomes airborne, and the marrow of the ego murmurs "maybe."

But when I get to thinking of challenging a professional basketball player to a nose-to-nose confrontation, the ego gives a reading as sensible as a Sears, Roebuck catalogue, saying: "No way you could afford it, sonny." To explain such a sensible response, one has to turn back the timekeeper's clock about fifteen years to remember how the game was played in his youth.

Let's get it straight. I was no dilettante in this game. I spent or misspent the better part of my youth playing basketball. During the summer months, I wore out sneakers by the pair, and in winter I shoveled a path in the snow from the foul line to the basket so that I could practice my lay-up and that classic Cousy maneuver, dribbling behind my back. When it rained, a friend and I practiced in his cellar (which had a seven-foot ceiling), shooting baskets into a homemade hoop adorned with a net made from his aunt's bloomers. What a parlor Freudian could do with that tidbit!

When I played school league ball, I was known for my devastating two-hand set shot (from 12 feet out), a shot that today is as useless in the game as a blacksmith in a Mustang factory. But what a shot it was! It took me about fourteen seconds to set up for it with my feet flat apart and my butt sticking out like Groucho Marx's, while my defensive opposite stood six feet away, waving his hands and grunting: Ah-h-h, Ah-h-h! If one threw a shot from more than 18 feet out, he was immediately sat down and suffered the scorn of his teammates for being a "heaver." Today a shot from 18 feet is like a conceded putt in golf.

Our professional hero in those days was Bud Palmer, the sportscaster who was then with the Knicks, who was the innovator of the jump shot. He usually threw this shot from inside the foul line, and it now would be considered a leaping lay-up. High school kids today cannonade with deadly accuracy from 25 feet.

But it is the pros who are beyond mere mortal comprehension. Earl "the Pearl" Monroe with back to basket spins in the air, lets go from 35 feet out, and starts to break to the opposite end of the court because he knows the damn thing is going in! Cruel, bloody revisionist without a sup of sympathy for history past.

And imagine trying to clear the boards against Reed or Alcindor! Or the humiliation of trying to dribble the ball across midcourt within ten seconds with Walt Frazier defensing you? Better to try to empty the sea into a sand hole by the cupful.

But rigor mortis finally set in on my fantasy in one of last season's play-off games when Jerry West threw in a 63-foot, one-hand push shot against the Knicks. When West was asked about his audacious luck, he flatly said: "It [the shot] felt good going off my fingers," the equivalent of saying, "I did it in six days and rested on the seventh."

Now this is not meant to be a crotchety carp. I still love the game and find it the most democratic we have. But these days, like most wise men of my age, I participate in the democracy on the sidelines, sitting on my duff in the paid seats—voyeuristically.

April 9, 1971

Guys and Dolls at the Spa

Whenever I find myself growing grim about the mouth; whenever it is a damp, drizzly November in my soul; whenever I find myself involuntarily pausing before coffin warehouses, and bringing up the rear of every funeral I meet; and especially whenever my hypos get such an upper hand of me, that it requires a strong moral principle to prevent me from deliberately stepping into the street, and methodically knocking people's hats off—then, I account it high time to get to sea as soon as I can.

—ISHMAEL in *Moby Dick*

Unlike Ishmael, whenever I'm spouting the blues, I don't look for an Ahab or a Pequod to offer me a whale of a time. Instead, I call Sam Kanchuger or Shirley Day, who graciously handle press relations for the NYRA, to book me passage into a racetrack. And there is no better time to brighten the November of the soul than in August. That's when Saratoga is in action.

Saratoga is the perfect setting for what race-going is all about. In its turn-of-the-century milieu a scruff from Brooklyn can, with the aid of good company, a straw lid, and a pair of binoculars, fantasize about his likeness to Diamond Jim Brady. Make no mistake about it: The odds-on appeal of racing is snobbery. No other action offers you the smug satisfaction of precisely charting your money's destiny, if you are right.

Good fortune at craps can be determined by a crack in the floor that can turn the cubes into Lady Luck or a disaster in drag. I gave up poker years ago, after holding what I thought was a winning hand, only to have had some good Samaritan keep anteing up for Lion's Head stickman Archie Mulligan, who had fallen asleep at the table from the effects of Puck's potion. Naturally, the conclusion was that the resurrected Mulligan beat my aces up with a paltry three of a kind and, on being roused, declared with brilliant coherence: "Huh? I wasn't asleep. Who turned off the movie on TV?" So much for poker.

The trotters should be left to those afflicted with bingo of the brain, and dog racing is for devotees of premature ejaculation. Though, I must admit, I did spend one intriguing evening at a dog track in Dublin. When the boxes opened, releasing the hounds, all the ignorant mutts, save one, bounded after the mechanical rabbit. My charge reversed his field and ran behind the boxes to head off the rabbit coming the other way. It was no simple solace that night to get drunk and reason that I had bet on the most intellectual hound in Ireland.

But flat horse racing offers you more. After a day of being cashiered at the windows, you can always walk out of the track thinking your failings have been shared by the handicap company of Degas, Lautrec, Dufy, and Hemingway. Men have made a life of lesser notions.

It is Saratoga that intrigues the most. Its atmosphere of a bygone time is infectious. The clientele dress to the nines, unlike Aqueduct where *de rigueur* seems to be a T-shirt with a pack of Luckies rolled up in one sleeve. The bartenders discover Delmonico manners, and even Harry M. Stevens Caterers (Home of the Limp Hot Dog) are struck with culinary inspiration. Perfect strangers talk to you, and *not* to ask you for spare change. All this is carried out under a canopy of stately elms.

What I'm promising you here is not the dream of financial reward but balm for an impoverished mind. Fiscally, I have had my bleak days at the Spa. For instance, one year I bet a horse that tried to mount another horse when the gate freed them. Not one to take passion lightly, I was impressed, till I realized the race was restricted to colts, but then the message of the sixties has been to look for prophets anywhere. The grace of Saratoga is that it is never boring, and there is always a story to be culled from the experience. This year was no exception.

I, my entrymate, the redoubtable "Tommy Sugar," and my lady took to the road and, as in "Adelaide's Lament," got off at Saratoga for the fourteenth time. As we sat at our table on the terrace, the day was going predictably: I was losing with more excuses than Martin Luther had theses, my love (an ungrateful upstart to whom I taught this game) was winning, and "Sugar" had been lurking near the $50 window, hoping to be adopted by a dowager who could give him the life he has never been accustomed to.

Into this familiar tableau walked a stranger who asked me if he could bum a cigarette and a look at my racing form. This intruder in the dust (it was a fast track that day) started making sounds as if he were a high roller. He then asked for my choice in the race, and being an escapee from the priests, I couldn't resist rendering spiritual advice. He proclaimed my choice was worth "a grand" and left our table for the betting windows.

"Sugar," a tout of human livestock, muttered: "A plunger, my ass. He can't even afford to spring for a pack of butts and a form."

It was a bit later when, much to my wondering eye, should appear our chap returned with a stack of $50 tickets that, well, could choke a horse. When we ran fourth, Gaylord Ravenal didn't even bat an eye, much less throw my body from our third-tier level onto the track.

Four races passed, and our friend had another nicotine fit. This time he was sold on a horse and merely asked our opinion. Like the Blessed Trinity, we nixed his choice and gave him ours (to be honest, we had good information). At this interlude (I had already cost the cat a grand) we swapped introductions on a first-name basis. He looked at us with the parable of the rich man and the camel passing through the eye of our table in mind and returned to his own. Thank God, went the collective sigh, who needs this kind of responsibility?

But our reprieve was short-lived. Waving ten $100 bills, he called to our distaff member (mispronouncing her name) and asked her to place the thou on our choice! After years of looking at my financial worth, my lady fell into shock, and I took the bet.

Now I had to carry this wad down two levels to bet in a crowd of 20,000 people for a guy who knew me as "Joe." If ever there was a candidate for the Will Rogers Award for never meeting a man you didn't like, this dude was it. The Saroyanesque ending was that our horse, Stop the Music, got up by a neck, and our man cashed for $3,200. His reaction? "Get me two more like that," he said, "and I might break even."

So the tout here is to get up to Saratoga for its closing weekend, away from malaise and misery, and take a fling at aristocracy. But if such elitism bothers your populist mentality, think about this: Where else would you find a man who was *really* behind you 1,000 percent?

August 24, 1972

Love Song to Willie Mays

When Willie Mays returned to New York, many saw it—may God forgive them—as a trade to be debated on the merits of statistics. Could the forty-one-year-old center fielder with ascending temperament and waning batting average help the Mets?

To those of us who spent our boyhood, our teens, and our beer-swilling days debating who was the first person of the Holy Trinity—Mantle, Snider, or Mays?—it was a lover's reprieve from limbo. No matter how Amazin' the Mets were, a part of our hearts was in San Francisco.

Mays was special to me as a teen-ager because I was a Giant fan in that vociferous borough of Brooklyn. This affliction was cast on me by a Galway father who reasoned that any team good enough for John McGraw was good enough for him and his offspring. So as boys, rather than take a twenty-minute saunter through Prospect Park to Ebbets Field, the Flahertys took their odyssey to 155th Street, the Polo Grounds.

In that sprawling boardinghouse of a park I had to content myself with the likes of Billy Jurges, Buddy Kerr, and a near retirement Mel Ott whose kicking right leg at the plate was then a memory, no longer an azimuth which his home run followed. The enemy was as star-laden as MGM: Reese, Robinson, Furillo, Cox, Hodges, Campanella, *et al.* So when Willie arrived in 1950, the Davids in Flatbush who had been hoping for a slingshot instead were bequeathed the jawbone of an ass.

Of course, we did have Sal Maglie, that living insult to Gillette, who thought the shortest distance between two points was a curve. But it was Willie who did it. It was he who gave the aliens in that Toonerville Trolleyland respectability. Even the enemy fan was in awe of him. He was no Plimptonesque hero about whom the beer drinkers in the stands fantasized. He was beyond that. His body was forged on another planet, and intelligent grown men know they have no truck with the citizens of Krypton. It has always amazed me to hear someone taking verbal vapors over the physical exploits of a ballet dancer while demeaning the skills of a baseball player. After all, is it not true that such as a Nureyev is practiced and choreographically moribund within a precise orbit? *I* should swoon at such limited geography, when I have seen Mays ad-lib across a prairie to haul down Vic Wertz's 1954 World Series drive? No. Willie, like Scott Fitzgerald's rich, is very different from you and me.

Yet, looking back on him (call it mysticism, if you like), I have the feeling his comet could have sputtered. This fall from grace, I feel, could have happened if he had come to bat in the final play-off game against the Dodgers in 1951. I was in the stands with a bevy of other hooky players, and I can't help thinking Mays would have failed dismally if he had had to come to the plate. He was just too young, a kid constantly trying to please his surrogate father, Durocher. Something dire surely would have happened: The bat would have fallen from his hands, or he would have lunged at the ball the way a drunk mounts stairs. Of course, this is all conjecture, since Bobby Thomson's home run was his reprieve.

Still, let the mind's eye conjure up the jubilant scene at home plate as the Giants formed a horseshoe to greet Thomson. Willie, who was on deck, should have been one of the inner circle, but he was on its outer fringes—at first too paralyzed to move, then a chocolate pogo stick trying to leap over the mob, leaping higher than all, which is an appropriate reaction from a man who has just received the midnight call from the governor.

But that's rumination in the record book. Now, the day is Sunday, May 14, 1972, the opponent those lamisters from Coogan's Bluff, Willie's recent alma mater, the San Francisco Giants. The day was neither airy spring nor balmy summer but overcast and rain-threatening. I liked that— the gods were being accurate. This was no sun-drenched debut of a rookie; the sky bespoke forty-one years.

The park was as displeasing as usual. Shea Stadium is built like a bowl, and when one sits high up, he feels like a fly who can't get down to the fudge at the bottom. An ideal baseball park is one that forces its fans to bend over in concentration, like a communion of upside-down L's. Ebbets Field was such a park.

The fans at Shea have always been too anemic for me. Even the kids with their heralded signs seem like groupies for the Rotarians or the Junior Chamber of Commerce: "Hicksville Loves the Mets," "Huntington Loves the Mets"; alas, Babylon can't be far behind. And today the crowd was behaving badly, like an affectionate sheepdog that drools all over you. Imagine, they were cheering Willie Mays for warming up on the sidelines with Jim Fregosi! A Little League of the mind.

But there were dots of magic sprinkled throughout the meringue. The long-ago-remembered black men and women from the subway wars also were in attendance: the men in their straw hats, alternating a cigar and a beer under the awnings of their mustaches; the women, grown slightly wide with age, bouquet bottoms (greens, reds, yellows, purples) sashaying full bloom. These couples wouldn't yell "Charge" when the organ demanded it (a dismal, insulting gift from the Los Angeles Dodgers), nor would they cheer a sideline game of catch. They were sophisticates; they had seen the gods cavort in too many Series to pay tribute to curtain-raising antics.

Mays was in the lead-off spot, and one watched him closely for decay. Many aging ballplayers go all at once, and the pundits were playing taps for Willie. This (and a .163 batting average) roused speculation about

Mays' demise. Nothing much was learned from his first at bat. He backed away from "Sudden Sam" McDowell's inside fast ball, a trait that is much more noticeable in him lately against pitchers who throw inside smoke. But he wasn't feverishly bailing out, just apprehensively stepping back. Not a deplorable physical indignity but a small one, like an elegant man in a homburg nodding off in a hot subway. He walked, as did Harrelson and Agee after him. Then Staub, as if disturbed by the clutter, cleaned the bases with a grand slam. Mets 4–0.

His second time at bat I noticed he shops more for his pitches these days. There is a slight begging quality, where once there was unbridled aggressiveness. This time patience paid a price, and he was caught looking at a third strike. This was more disturbing. The head of the man in the homburg had just fallen on the shoulder of the woman next to him.

In the top of the fifth the Giants roughed up Met pitcher Ray Sadecki for four runs. Also in the course of their rally they pinch-hit for their lefty McDowell, which meant that Mays would have to hit against the Giants' tall, hard-throwing right-hander Don Carrithers in the Mets' bottom half. Bad omens abounded. If a left-hander could brush Willie back, what would a right-hander do? And now the game was tied, and he would have to abandon caution. Worse, the crowd was demanding a miracle, the same damn crowd which had cheered even his previous strike-out. The unintelligent love was sickening. He was an old man; let him bring back the skeleton of a fish, a single, this aging fan's mind reasoned.

But one should not try to transmute the limitations that time has dealt him on the blessed. Even the former residents of Mount Olympus now and then remember their original address. Mays hit a 3-2 pitch toward the power alley in left center—a double, to be sure. I found myself standing, body bent backward like a saxophone player humping a melody, till the ball cleared the fence for a home run. The rest was the simple tension of watching Jim McAndrew in relief hold the Giants for four innings, which he did, and the Mets won, 5–4.

The trip home was romance tainted with reality. I knew well that Mays would have his handful of days like this. He still had enough skill to be a "good ballplayer," though such a fair, adequate adjective was never meant to be applied to him. But life can't be lived in a trunk, so I closed the lid on the memory of his lightning, and for a day, like an aging roué who has to shore up the present, I boldly claimed: "Love Is Better the Second Time Around."

August 26, 1972

Ali-Patterson Fight: Looking for a Daddy

Whenever Floyd Patterson enters a ring, he totes not only his aging bones but also the baggage of another time through the ropes with him. Like the doodads in the trunks in Scott and Zelda's attic, he gives illusion of a happier time.

Innocence in the American experience has always been the receding light on the dock, not the glaring, beckoning beacon of the future. In a time when nostalgia seems to be the opiate of the land—old movies, campy productions of old plays (indeed, even the children talk about the salad days of Woodstock), he has become something of a pugilistic Pabst Blue Ribbon commercial.

But on examination one finds there was always some stroke of voodoo emanating from his soft Chinese lantern interior. We took to him because he was vulnerable, beatable. The sad whistle in his soul was a call to the dog in all of us: that lovely glide back to the womb or the final security blanket of six feet of earth.

Other men in public life have had the same effect on us. Bob Wagner as a politician at times seemed so fragile that our most muted censure would crumble him. The runner Jim Ryun fascinates us in the same swooning fashion. Does anyone *really* believe his fall in Munich was not unlike the demise of the *Pequod,* a central drama rehearsed before the oceans began to roll over the earth?

It is for no small reason that those who had the audacity and the bad taste to win constantly (the old Yankees, the old Celtics, Jack Nicklaus) are disdainfully dubbed "machines." Even the politicians have perceived this sentimental swath in us. On the right Nixon talks about a mythical, maligned Silent Majority, and on the other side of the teeter McGovern cries, "Come home, America." Our classic literary theme now permeates all facets of our life: Little Boy Lost.

So, in the midst of this aura, it seemed fitting that my press ticket was lifted by the Garden, and I was forced to view the fight onscreen at the Academy of Music. No mini-tragedy follows, only an appropriate comic interlude.

Garden publicist John Francis Xavier (sometimes I feel like Little Eva on the ice floes—I'll never escape them) Condon told me I couldn't have a ticket, because the *Voice* ran no prepublicity on the fight. This reasoning seemed flimsy since this paper has always covered just the event, and indeed, it proved so. It seems Francis Xavier (I'm rusty on my saints and can't recall Francis Xavier's schtick; Francis of Assisi, if I remember right, talked to the birds—much more symbolic for one who has to deal with pugs) spotted a cartoon run in the *Voice* three weeks ago. It was a map of the United States with Florida shaped as a penis and Texas as testicles, with Nixon firmly gripping the latter. According to a reporter who was present, Condon declared my banishment on "unpatriotic" and "degenerate" grounds. If the *Voice* was allowed to violate ringside, he apparently mused, could *Screw* be far behind?

I could understand Condon's saintly consternation if the cartoon was a piece of spurious pornography, but since it dealt with a man who has finagled with ITT, rigged milk prices, and tipped the wheat deal with Russia to fat cats, who is adroitly juggling China and Russia, and who is 34 percent ahead in the polls, surely, it was editorially perceptive to illustrate that he has America by the—ahem—balls.

But in a fit of patriotic fervor Condon, who was not in a position to bug the Watergate for our Commander in Chief, decided instead to bug me. This tale is told not from personal pique but in the hope that Francis Xavier might receive one of those fabled locker-room phone calls: "F.X., this is R.N. We have the prescription to save America."

So it was with humility I climbed heavenward toward my seat in the upper balcony of the Academy of Music. The legions in attendance were, as usual, mostly Ali's, though occasional cheers for Floyd came from aging zoot suiters. It was great fun for a while. When Joe Frazier was introduced in the ring, Ali took a bogus temper tantrum and made forays to attack him. Frazier responded with mock aplomb, and one could hear the jingling cash registers of the future.

But when the bell sounded for the first, it turned rancid, as so many of Ali's latest appearances have. He has been pampered with adulation and martyrdom and seems to feel the sheer vision of him these days is enough. Of late he comes into the ring with that same passion play purity with which Dan Berrigan and Charlie Goodell enter a room. If Ali wants to give ethereal exhibitions, he should do it in the gym, not in the ring where his fans have to pay out big money they can ill afford.

He disdainfully toyed with Patterson, indulging in gaucheries that cost him the first few rounds on my card. Patterson, mustering old dignity, tried to make a fight of it, but he was pathetically miscast. Thirty pounds lighter, he pranced in his peek-a-boo style. Oh, he did some nice things intermittently, but one never lost sight that he was watching a charade. When Ali decided to stoop to conquer, he would do just that.

A right hand closed Floyd's left eye, and the farce was halted at the end of seven. For the first time in memory Ali's loyalists in the audience soured on him, and at the end of the fight Patterson received the cheers. When Ali, in a postfight interview, wanted to say "Hello to my fans watching on closed-circuit TV," he got more hisses than huzzahs. Patterson got his share of the emotional meringue by "putting up a valiant fight." Since he finished on his feet, the sentimentalists can always hope for . . . ?

97

One wonders if Ali's habits of jiving have not become his built-in excuse, his Patterson's disguise beard, for future disasters. He has claimed he shouldn't have played around in the first fight with Frazier, yet he compulsively did. There is reason to believe that perhaps the melancholy martyrdom of the sixties might finally have affected him, and he is dealing in feeling sorry for himself (the biggest indoor sport in America, as the George C. Scott character, Bert, cryptically noted in *The Hustler*). Are Ali's shenanigans paving the way for another defeat by Frazier?

Bob Dylan's remark about the need for cult heroes in the sixties tolls in the ear like a ten count: "These are bad times, everybody is looking for a daddy."

And somewhere down there on his plantation is that no-nonsense, laboring Daddy Joe Frazier, who just might possess the sublime knowledge that not only does all God's chillun got wings but that he is the cat to fold them. Ever so neatly.

September 28, 1972

Sunday, Super Sunday

It is with much distress I write this column. Instructional pieces have never been my forte, but I think the time has come for someone to write the compleat guide on how to view a Super Bowl—in short, to become the Dr. Reuben of the Pigskin.

The first prerequisite I offer is that all viewers should forget the word "super." It is not within the realm of man, unless you really believe there is a tabloid named the *Daily Planet*.

Speaking for myself, I have never been able to handle momentous occasions. This knowledge came early, when as a child I used to throw up before attending the Saturday matinee serials of Zorro and Fu Manchu (the pressure was unbearable). Subsequent major events were no better. At my first holy communion I was unable to swallow the host (now that's what you call "choking"). Serving my first midnight mass, I fainted dead away on the altar (I'm sure Shula wished Yepremian would have done the same).

Maturity didn't alleviate the condition. At wedding receptions I continually run into someone's pristine aunt who has a bun on and wants to have a fling before her sciatica renders her immobile. And at New Year's Eve parties I always feel as if I am trapped inside a George Grosz painting, where behatted clowns are trying to stick their tongues down the throats of their neighbors' wives at the stroke of midnight. No, the evidence is clear: Men are not made to handle heightened situations.

The civilized among us realize that life is really one long, innocuous Wednesday in mid-February. Days should not be greeted with vim and vigor but with the ritual of gagging the remnants of the night before whiskey vapors and cigarette phlegm into the bowl (commode, not Super), while you read passages in *Waiting for Godot*. Such a beginning assures you the day has nowhere to go but up.

Thus, Super Bowls should be approached in a Wednesday of the mind. I confess that in past years I have succumbed to flights of fancy about this event. When I attended the Minnesota–Kansas City contest in New Orleans, I arrived at my motel sporting half blood and half Remy Martin. To be "fresh" for the game, I decided to take a dip in the pool. The temperature was a gray 48 degrees as I looked down from the diving board at what I legitimately expected was a heated pool. For the life of me I couldn't figure out why other patrons began to leave the motel bar and room doors opened, their occupants eagerly awaiting my belly flop from a four-foot board. Even the Remy couldn't convince me the locals thought they had found a new Stanley Kowalski. But when I hit the 20-degree water, their curiosity was amply explained. Bordering on cardiac arrest, I barely made it to the side of the pool, and when I returned to my room and dropped my trunks, I had the horrible feeling I must have encountered a Danish surgeon in a scuba diving outfit underwater.

For the first half of the game I shouted for the Vikings to "hold that line," till a matron sitting in front of me asked if I was Bobby Breen who used to sing "Ave Maria." Later in the evening, when I toured the French Quarter in hopes of finding a figment of Blanche Dubois (flimsily frocked in Della Robbia blue), a sidewalk shill shouted at me, "Hey, buddy, come on inside. We got a broad here with forty-four-D silicones." Sadder but wiser, I flew home on National's "Lack of Desire."

My next foray (in person) was to Miami, where I observed the Colts-Cowboys supereffort. All that could be said for this event is that I have witnessed better pickup games between the White Rose and the Blarney Castle.

So I have learned. Now on Super Sunday Jeanine and I journey to the home of Bill and Miriam Sheed to watch the event. The only house rule was set down in print by Sheed awhile back in his majestic William Powell manner: "At my house we watch football with atrophy."

The cast usually is the same—the hosts, the abovementioned duo, Vic Ziegel, Larry Merchant (absent this year since he attended the game), and Martha Duffy, who confounds the cliché, since her husband, Jim (who hates football), is a football widower.

Political boobery, whether right or left, is disallowed—unless the line merits a laugh. The only significance to be found is in the merits of running, passing, catching, and blocking. At the Sheeds' we put on our philosophies one leg at a time. During the playing of "The Star-Spangled Banner" and the pregame prayer we run elegant post patterns to the bathroom or breathtaking Z-outs to the bar. If an interloper arrives and pronounces that pro football is why we are in Vietnam, we patiently explain that there are no known NFL franchises labeled the Tel Aviv Torahs, or the Belfast Boyos, or the Biafran Blood Brothers. As unfashionable as it may sound, we simply view football as a game.

Those who use sport as a metaphor for life never fail to bore me. The beauty of sport is that it is so unlike life. Sport is a universe unto itself with set boundaries, specific rules, a prescribed time span, whereas life is an unruly, quixotic brute. Sport is attractive, because it is undeniable order set down in the center of chaos. One could imagine Beckett would love the dimensions of a baseball diamond.

Another absurdity I will not truck with is that if someone evil adopts something you love, it then becomes tainted. After all, Hitler liked German beer and children, it is said Ian Paisley drinks Irish whiskey, Attila the Hun liked to fornicate, and Nixon adores football. I have no intention of relinquishing the above pleasures to the Philistines. End of cathechism.

The room had a Congressional flavor. On the right side of the aisle Ziegel, Miriam, Jeanine, and I were championing the Dolphin cause, while Sheed and Duffy filed a minority report for the Redskins. Sheed was the most "up" for the game, since a bet of a bottle of fine wine hung in the balance. No small matter this—Count Dracula wouldn't wager a jug of plasma offhandedly.

I had picked the Dolphins at the beginning of the season but had begun to waver after their play-off performances. My faith returned when Tex Maule picked the Redskins by 10 to 21 points in *Sports Illustrated*. One wishes Tex would make a definite statement on the existence of God. I would then know which style to choose—carnal or celibate.

Miriam entered the living room minutes before kickoff with a jug of vodka and a pitcher of Bloody Mary mix and slung some funk in her Southern Belle style: "Here's the vodka, and the gluck is in the pitcher." All agreed she would be tough to contain this day.

The Roman numeral VII was imposed on the screen, and Sheed and I, with our haunted Catholic consciences, tried to figure out which commandment this Roman version of a natural represented. We settled on the one dealing with coveting (one-on-one, no zone, mind you) your neighbor's wife.

Jeanine was stoic, but this was understandable. She reached her peak years back, when she had a wad on Baltimore to beat the Jets. She had prepared a shrimp quiche for the game. But as she envisioned her American eagles flying from her wallet with the grace of Namath's passes, the quiche was flung at the guests rather than served. Only those with "good hands" ate that day.

Martha sat erect, pulling for Kilmer. By the third quarter she had slid down into her chair like an embarrassed child in a movie house watching a gooey love scene. And since all the wooing was going the other way, a strange kyrie of "Shit, shit, shit" emanated from the recesses of the chair.

Ziegel is a constant. He starts the game with a manner as charming as Ronald Colman's in *Lost Horizon,* but after three quarters, five scotches, and two plates of food, he shifts into the High Lama. It took us several such games to realize that it was Ziegel's snoring, not a defect in the sound transmission, we were hearing.

At half time we realized that not an Executive Order, indeed, not even the executives' Executive could save the Skins. Sheed alternately ruminated over how many times Al DeRogatis said that Howard Twilley was "small, slow, but has great hands and can run a great pattern" and wondering if he could pour Thunderbird into an expensive bottle to cover his bet.

After hearing the phrases "would-be tackler" and "would-be blocker" scores of times, Ziegel mused that it would be brilliant to open a school called "Would-Be University" and achieve monstrous monetary benefits overnight from enrollments.

Miriam saved us once again by serving a spectacular French soup. The delicious smells that emanate from her kitchen alone can render a hearty man the gout. It was a damned shame the half had to end.

The tedium of the second half was alleviated by Yepremian's confusion over the worth of his extremities—his arm for his leg. Since this created pressure, we all had a chance to drink more-most-mostest. Ziegel also visited us for a brief moment from his transcendental meditation (really heavenly heartburn) to deliver a Bronx Jewish rendition of a Pedernales piety. "I won't," he intoned, "be the first President to preside over a Super Bowl defeat."

So it was over. The score you all know, so why bother? What was important was that it was not life or death, peace or war, patriotism or treason—just a game. The things that were super were the company and the booze and the super soup Miriam served in her bowls. Upon leaving many hours later, we renewed our yearly ritual. We awarded Miriam the game ball.

January 25, 1973

An Out-and-Out Mugging

When an object of invincibility falls, there is a very human need for theory. It seems that if we can concoct enough ifs, we can still hold onto the illusion of immortality. *If* the *Titanic* was moving only a few knots slower, *if* the *Hindenberg* hadn't received a strange spark from the heavens, *if* Ted Williams hadn't had to waste those war years, *if* that night Marilyn Monroe had called any of us who con ourselves that we're God's gift to women. Like Ahab, we can't seem to let the unfathomable alone.

The latest pondering of man's fate has to do with Joe Frazier. The cauliflower cognoscenti are expounding philosophies as delicate as Noel Coward's pajamas. Indeed, was it not Foreman but rather Ali's beating of two years ago that undid Frazier? This theology is the liberal equivalent of resurrection (the pain we suffer will be justified in the end). Or was it the weight, that ominous 8½ pounds Frazier was carrying (he was 206 when he met Ali and 214½ for Foreman—which doesn't exactly qualify him to play Falstaff)? Then there was the possibility that he "lacked desire," that he was "a fat cat ready to be knocked off." Ah, what would we sports nuts do without our "lacking desire" explanations? And on it goes.

I am not denigrating these sagacious observations, since when I'm Hyde-Parking it on some barstool, I have used much of the same dialogue. My particular pet is the "his legs are gone" theory. A god from the waist up can still punch in a garage door, but the legs are shot. I guess after years of betting on horses and cavorting with drunks, the legs have become too symbolic for me. But after trying to apply the above-mentioned host of humanities to Frazier, I just can't bring myself to believe any of it.

Before the fight I thought Foreman's style was made to order for Frazier. In past fights Foreman has never been a straight puncher. He threw right crosses so wide he seemed to be dancing a polka with an incredibly fat invisible woman. So it stood to reason that Frazier, who fights within the confining parentheses of his arms, would knock his head off.

Indeed, the opposite proved true. Foreman punched straighter than in any previous bout I had witnessed, and Frazier threw left hooks as indiscriminately as a Pontiff dispenses blessings on Easter Sunday. Also, there was a fantastic disparity in size, when one saw the two men meet in mid-ring for their instructions.

Only Tom Quinn (a local legendary left hooker to a select group which hasn't been traced yet) made a case for Foreman's awesome size to me before the fight. Quinn contended that Foreman's frame could easily carry another 40 pounds without a trace of fat. As he prophetically put it: "That guy shouldn't be fighting fighters, he should be fighting

Minnesota Vikings." And since Quinn refers to his tenure in military service as "when I was in the Corps," he is not a man to be taken gingerly on such matters.

Foreman, with brute strength, just bullied Frazier around the ring at whim. Of course, Frazier's style didn't stand him in good stead either. He fights with his face, catching four to land two. So the slow-striding Foreman didn't have to go looking for him, as he would have to do against Ali. And when Frazier crouched, Foreman had two foolproof remedies: With his awesome power he clubbed him on the top of the head (knocking Frazier down twice with such shots) or employed sweeping uppercuts to dismantle the crouch.

One caught a telling sign in the first round, when Frazier landed his vaunted left hook, and Foreman was unmoved by it. At such junctures wise men usually throw a dime to a friend to dial 911 for the Tactical Patrol Force. There is just no way to finesse the course of the bout: It was an out-and-out mugging. If anyone has ever had the experience of being beaten up by his older brother when the latter staggered through the door at three in the morning after striking out with his girlfriend, he could empathize with Frazier.

The final knockdown, the sixth, in round two was strictly out of the Joe Palooka-Humphrey Pennyworth genre. After setting up Frazier with two left hooks, Foreman threw a right uppercut that lifted Frazier cleanly a foot off the floor! Jazz like that just doesn't happen in real life, but it did. Foreman's performance was so overwhelming it's hard to conceive what Frazier could alter for a rematch.

So the conjecture now is where does Foreman go from here? Ali the boxer and Foreman the puncher would be a dream match. Not only are their fighting styles contradictory, but so are their life-styles—Ali bowing toward Mecca and Foreman waving a mini American flag. (One can almost hear the *Daily News'* Gene Ward chiseling his columns on ten tablets of stone.)

But it's doubtful this match will ever come off. There are too many lucrative, easy paydays out there immediately for Foreman, so at best an Ali bout will be a thing of the future, at a time when "The Greatest's" skills have been eroded by time.

As for Frazier, who has millions and a plantation down South, he ought to look closely at the fight films and meditate the merits of rocking on the veranda versus being rocked in the ring.

But it would be wise not to project Foreman too far into the future. Heavyweight champions of late have the tenure and stability of a government in a banana republic. How many nights past have we sat in saloons and declared: "Floyd Patterson has the fastest hands of any heavyweight in history," "God, Liston is indestructible," "Ali is the greatest heavyweight who ever lived," "Frazier is a machine, no one will ever beat him." But our history has shown us that our gods have an affinity to being stretched on canvas—though not in the memorial way they fantasized.

One last thought. If you disagree with all the prognoses I have set forth in this piece, don't blame me. My legs were weak when I wrote it.

February 1, 1973

Invitation to a Coronation— The War of the Roses

The scene was not simple to comprehend. A choice of A or B it wasn't; to like or not it was not. Like the race itself, there were too many divergent elements from which to choose. There was the crass and the class, the gauche and the gracious, debauchery and decorum, hokiness and high tone. Yet there was an undertone of innocence running beneath the whole affair. It was touching in that peculiarly American way.

Perhaps Secretariat had something to do with the mood. He was as beguiling a racehorse whose hoof has ever touched a track. But he was a three-year-old: a potential, a whiz kid in the wings. Our kind of stuff, that. As a two-year-old, he was nonpareil, so in our way we granted him a golden future. On freshman promise we automatically bequeathed him the Derby, the Preakness, and the Belmont, racing's Triple Crown. But in American life how many hotshots have turned into has-beens? Contrary to myth, we are not exemplary in tutoring our young.

Our literature has taught us that. Nick's Big Two-Hearted River twisted into an ugly red sea on a ceiling in Ketchum, Idaho; the cosmic Basil Duke Lee left his liver on the far side of paradise; and the garrulous Holden Caulfield hightailed it with his hat and hasn't spoken to us in years. But then again, maybe it isn't us at all, but the gods. Or is it the Christian God, the Christ Child who is jealous of early fire? The young Pete Reiser left his talent and part of his head on the left-field wall in Ebbets Field. The brilliant young pitcher Herb Score was struck in the eye with a batted ball as if it were a bolt from above. Ali's dancing feet were exiled for a philosophy, and when they returned, the million-dollar legs were reduced to 10 cents a dance. And there was James Dean, Janis Joplin, Monroe— shooting stars all. That was it: Comets always invite collision. It's a buried truth that we never fear for the mediocre. Was the message one of humility? Only He would be allowed to strut His stuff in the temple?

Thus, Secretariat was a colt that bred awe and dread, and his chore—

the Triple Crown—was not an easy one. It hadn't been done since 1948 (a more innocent and pleasing time to the Deity?) when the mighty Citation turned the trick. In recent times six horses have failed in the final leg, the Belmont Stakes: Tim Tam, Carry Back, Northern Dancer, Kauai King, Majestic Prince, and Canonero. Two of them came out of the race badly crippled and never raced again. So there was no doubt about it, it was an awesome stunt to pull off. When one thought about records in other sports, the significance of such an achievement magnified.

The two records in baseball that would *never* be broken, legend decreed, were Babe Ruth's 60 home runs in one season and his lifetime output of 714 homers. Roger Maris, with the help of an extended schedule and an asterisk, broke the former, and Henry Aaron, barring injury, should wipe out the latter by next season. In football the mythic Seven Blocks of Granite (each weighing about 180 pounds) would be the seven pebbles against today's 280-pound linemen. In track and swimming, records drop with the regularity of a hooker's drawers. So Secretariat was challenging a feat not accomplished in twenty-five years. He was odds-on to wipe out a quarter century of flops, and he had yet to win the first and most prestigious jewel, the ninety-ninth Kentucky Derby.

He started his three-year-old campaign in New York in March in the seven-furlong Bay Shore and eased the mental demons by winning easily. His next race was the one-mile Gotham in April, and he negotiated it in track record time. Strong hint that brilliant babe would in the Biblical sense one day become a man. But the important prep—the 1⅛-mile Wood Memorial, the first time he was to try his speed around two turns, was still to come on April 21. It was during the week leading up to that race that the Doubting Thomas in Flaherty began to surface, for two reasons. A strange blend of logic and mysticism started to whip about the psyche. The contradiction didn't bother me. It was a bit like enjoying an Irish coffee: the whiskey on the bottom, the cream on top. The Harry Truman show-me-I'm-from-Missouri side of me was disturbed by Secretariat's un- usually slow workout preceding the race. The guru vibes were created by a West Coast invader named Sham. Sham had just won the 1⅛-mile Santa Anita Derby in the quickest time at that distance recorded this year. But that was still logic. The magic—the caldron in my cranium was set bubbling by the horse's name, Sham. Earlier this year I published a novel titled *Fogarty & Co.* whose hero was a ne'er-do-well tippler named Shamus Fogarty, nicknamed Sham! If I had named him John, Bill, Harry— nothing; but Jesus, Sham! Next, I read in a column that Sham's trainer, Frank "Pancho" Martin, had been forced to give up the sauce because of a bum liver! Such is the stuff that makes a man spurn the true church. Flaherty was about to nail his theses on Secretariat's barn door.

Then there was Secretariat's trainer, Lucien Laurin. Last year when his

Derby winner, Riva Ridge, went sour, Laurin had copped more pleas than a three-time loser. Whiners have never been my lot. The big horse was owned by one Mrs. Penny Tweedy, a moniker to set off a Brooklyn scruff. She looked like those ladies who in my youth never would allow me into her house to play with her precious son. If it had to be, the street was okay, but heavens! never the house.

On the day of the Wood my reverse bigotry seemed justified. Both trainers had entered running mates with their big horses, rabbits to ensure an honest pace. But Laurin complained in print that he was worried Martin's three-part entry might "purloin" the race for Sham. What a genteel way, my anti-Establishment logic reasoned, to say the spic is going to try to pull a caper. Ernest, Scott was right: The bastards are very different from you and me.

Martin, in a fit of Latin *macho* at reading Laurin's remark, scratched his two other horses and went alone with Sham. Laurin, not given to fury, ran Secretariat and Angle Light as an entry. The outcome was inconclusive. Angle Light, on the rail, set a slow pace and hung on to win by a neck over the fast-closing Sham. Secretariat was a floundering third four lengths farther back. But since entries are coupled as a single betting interest, Laurin got his 10 percent trainer's end of the winning purse, and Angle Light's owner, Edwin Whittaker, got first money, while Penny Tweedy got a pittance for third. Hatcheck money, one presumed.

Laurin alibied again, Pancho was stoic ("next time"), and I fumed. So high in the air, Kentucky-bound with my luggage tucked away, I carried some voodoo mental baggage: a cherished nickname, Martin's (Luther's?) sacrilegiosity and liver, and a firm belief that if we weren't about to bring down the Establishment, we were about to show up a bum Penny.

No knowledge of Kentuck except Daniel Boone and a forced landing in a storm on an Army flight—not that much help, though, since the pilot thought we were in Kansas (yep, Yossarian). So one looked for a barometer among early encounters. The first of these was the cabdriver who picked me up at the airport. It's a native New Yorker malady to look for clairvoyance in cabbies. He was a kindly gray-haired gent—gents and senior citizens seem to be extensions of restful sunny climes, unlike the wizened old men that cruel urban centers produce. The cabby could have been a bygone colonel.

No such luck in my motel dining room for breakfast. The motel itself wasn't foreign but in that tedious tapeworm tradition of all the motels that stretch across America. The plastic glasses in the bathroom were wrapped in plastic; the room's decor was done by some decorator who couldn't distinguish hospitality from hospital. The room's windows were forever sealed, like Aida's crypt, and you inhaled the thermostatic air of thousands of your predecessors. A small monument to chloroseptic cuckoldry. But no surprises, one has been here before.

The motel manager greets you in the dining room. He is well encased in that "ole boy" lard. Greetings are delivered in deafening decibels, with the gush reserved for kissin' cousins. But it is breakfast time, for chris-sake, and the crow-of-the-cock conviviality has never been one of my strong suits. Since this carp is personal, it is set aside; sophistry will be kept in the stall. Not for long. He moves among the other diners, telling backslapping stories about "an old gal who had tits down to her knees" and another about "an ole nigger man walkin' down the road." Raucous eruption before eggs. A belle of a broad who is as hard as a three-horse parlay chimes in. Where is Scarlett with her fan, the wan Ashley Wilkes, and the debonair Rhett? *Could it be* that Margaret Mitchell *was* a great fiction writer?

Back in the room a perusal of the local papers offers little of what to expect from Louisville. It is all pre-Derby news. Every stray sneeze of an entrant is dutifully recorded, and the utterances of jockeys and trainers are treated with prophetic solemnity. ("I got the horse right here!") One learns that if New York inaugurated "radical chic" with composer-con-ductor Leonard Bernstein's party for the Black Panthers, Derby week produces kitchen couth. The society page notes the swells down among the bubbly, Sarmi dresses, yellow and white chrysanthemums, Italian garden lights, chicken breasts served with white grapes in a wine sauce, and the down-home humility of ham and grits. Thus it is recorded: All God's chillun got chitlins'.

A trip to the track, Churchill Downs, is needed to restore Americana, a flight from the chic to the coonskin. A Boone for the spirit. En route, one passed "Jones Church," and though you knew the white wooden building was christened otherwise, you smiled at the thought that it could have been for Ben and Jimmy Jones, the Calumet Farms father-and-son training team who led the devil red and blue silks into the Derby winner's circle eight times. A fitting true church for hard boots. A last glance at the newspaper gives off a sickening sort of twentieth-century decadence in an ad for a massage parlor. But it is not "Lola's" or "Corrine's" or "Marlene's" but "Sissy's." Sissy's, sisterly and sex a round robin do not make. Senti-mentality is once again secured. Sisters are to massage lumbago, not the libido.

The track is a glory. It is perfectly cast for the event. Harsh cement is at a minimum, as well it should be. (How could Dan'l track a bear on pavement?) Under the legendary twin spires of the Downs sits a friendly white boardinghouse that gives off the assurance management would never let you sleep through breakfast. The grounds and the infield were the green of an expansive gaming table, symbolically perfect, since bucolic betting is what the whole affair is about. So green saluted the eye and quivered the nostril. Pleasure and profit. God's green and greed's green deliciously in tandem.

The days leading up to the Derby swung wildly between calm and chaos. The early-morning rambling along shed row offered a preview of the contestants in preparation. Both the big horses, Secretariat and Sham, are coming up to the race perfectly. They are training well, eating well, and both sport coats that would tempt Sherman Adams. Trainer Laurin is taciturn, probably regretting his unfortunate remark about Martin, while Pancho is garrulous, outgoing, confident of victory, and the press identifies with him. Their affection could be based on Martin's more humble status in life, mirroring their own. Or did the name "Sham" also connote something to them? Perhaps being forced to file all that horrible copy or horseshit sidebars to be conjured had an effect. If bile could be booked, or spleen transformed into speed, it would be Sham in a cakewalk. The fourth estate would be first.

Sham himself was a beautiful rangy athletic-looking colt. A catlike creature who, if he were human, would have made a superb tennis or handball player. Maybe that was the problem. When one looks at Secretariat, it is impossible to transform him from animal to human. He was divined to be a racehorse. A gigantic glowing chestnut with three white-stockinged legs and an 1890 bustle-sized rump. One could set schooners of Pabst Blue Ribbon and bowls of pretzels on his magnificent ass. But there is a flaw. His ankles are too thick, unpleasantly recalling Irish Catholic virgins with whom one endlessly finished out of the money. The mind is as muddled as a hobo's stew: Sham, sociology, a slurred Spanish-speaking trainer, and alas, ancient horniness horning into handicapping.

The nights are not given to meditation but to rumor. At the Downs the press are regally treated (1,500 attended), and they revel in it. Like their under-the-skin brethren, the cops, they have reached their nirvana: free booze abounds. Parties and tall tales are everywhere. If you would lend them your ears, soused soothsayers would pepper them with predictions and calamities to come. "The track is so fast the speedster Shecky Greene will win it wire to wire." "Secretariat's running mate, Angle Light, has been sold to a mysterious source [Bebe Rebozo? Daddy Warbucks?] for a cool mil." "Secretariat's knees are shot, and he will be scratched." (This the gospel according to Vegas oddsmaker Jimmy the Greek.) "Martin is willing to wager a fortune on Sham's chances." The brain was more boggled by the bull than the booze.

And it isn't only the press. Every drunk in Louisville is a prophet, or is it every prophet a drunk? Drinking is attacked at a maniacal pace, and one gets that peculiar melancholy one always gets at heightened events in America. It is an inescapable conclusion: Americans are lousy at foreplay.

To let a good time happen or slowly be nurtured isn't enough. Enjoyment must be demanded. In the streets, in the hotel corridors, in passing cars everyone is carrying a glass of sauce. "Look, Ma, I'm drinking!" And if lavish tombstones are the topping of American death, stupid hats are our mausoleum to merriment. Every fool must sport a billboard on his head to attest to his joy. But the dumbness is democratic: The rich, the poor, the working stiff, and the dropout carry on alike. Aristocracy, middle Americans, and anarchists meld on the common ground of alcohol. The whole cacophony produces a dark Norman Rockwell canvas.

Yet when the day arrives, one mellows. A redemptive sun sits high above the track. It will be a day for savoring and salvation. In retrospect, one realizes that nothing intrinsically evil has taken place; indeed, it has only been frenetic, like those bygone Fourth of July picnics where neglected children squalled and nearly drowned, where the food was herbed with ants and sand, where beer cans grew into mountains that insulted nature, where middle-aged women mistook their sagging skin for sensuality and potbellied candidates for cardiac arrest chased footballs and frisbees and, foolishly, their youth. No, it wasn't decadence, but the sad curse of a people who couldn't comprehend leisure. A people whose motor was so tuned to automotive work it couldn't be governed down for a weekend of pleasure. Perhaps at this event they weren't out of kilter. The motif, after all, bowed to the motor: Speed *would* carry the day.

The seating smacked of social strata. The boxes belonged to the celebs, old oligarchies, young scions, and Southern belles who said "pardon me" so defenselessly you knew why half a nation went to war to protect their flowerhood. The grandstand and standing room went to those lacking clout, both black and white. The college kids and hippies were a hairy and half-naked foliage that sprouted out in the infield, and the press were given the imperial perch of the roof to monitor the manners of the species, both two-legged and four, below.

There were lessons to be culled from sights and sounds. A woman walked about with a gimmick-stiffened dog leash, as if it were tense from holding a real dog. Pathetically, she thought she was psyching the crowd; being hipper, they thought it was she who should have been curbed. Three couples pitched quarters in the parking lot, and one was touched by their improvised fun. David Brinkley in his box was reported to have said that he wished he was in the infield where the "real fun" was taking place. (Ah, aging Establishment liberals never cease to bark after the heels of trend.)

Mrs. Cornelius Vanderbilt Whitney touted tradition over trendiness. It seems that *National Geographic* wanted her to allow them to film her Derby eve party. In a remark so taciturn David would have been impressed she said she couldn't understand why *National Geographic* was interested. "I thought," Lady Bountiful said, "they did Ubangis and things like that." And a Bible Belt Cassandra, realizing that the hobby of horse racing ends in a dead heat in Hades, handed out the most definitive tout sheet of the day:

Want To Be A Winner?
Here's A Sure Thing!
"In a race, all compete, but only one wins the prize. It is only temporary."
—St. Paul in Corinthians 9:24,25
"I run the race of life with certainty that in Christ I will win eternal blessedness."
—St. Paul in Corinthians 9:26

The poor thing didn't realize she was touting a jock who has fallen out of the saddle. Surely now, Sham would win.

One waited high on the roof fluctuating between expectation and queasiness. A first Derby. The feelings were similar to those felt in boyhood awaiting a birthday party or a rare Saturday afternoon at the movies. Would the pageant prepared in the mind be reduced by reality? God forbid, as one's first Super Bowl? What is it that makes us temper our dreams with the built-in edge of disappointment? In short, the nervous stomach warbled, would it be love or only Asbury Park?

Then it happened. The call to post. The band struck up "My Old Kentucky Home," and the hair on the back of your neck quivered in combination from nerves and the soft high wind. All the rowdy raucousness of the past days melted. Boisterous drinkers suddenly became bittersweet as they sang, "Weep no more, my lady."

The colts, regally frocked and as mannered as beaus at a cotillion, pranced into view. Secretariat looked stunning, and one was ashamed for not backing him; not for the interior reason of Sham's name—that was magic—but because of the rebellious quarrel one held with his owner and trainer. Wasn't it Shaw who said that if he had one thing to change in his life, it would have been his parents? But a bed had been made, and I had chosen Sham as the sweetheart of my sheets.

There are always those who can't stand beauty once removed, and this day would be marred by them. As the horses warmed up, three bare-chested hippies ran out onto the track, waving their shirts. Poor, pathetic children cursed with the narcissism of the middle class. After all, hadn't

Mommy dragged them from their beds since birth to perform for guests in their Doctor Dentons? But what confounded was that they thought their presence had more significance and beauty than the collected thoroughbreds. Was it an extension of the same thinking that made them mar esthetically pleasing monuments with their inane scribbling? Indeed, perhaps the "love generation" with all its permissiveness carried with it its own peculiar curse. It was as if they had missed solitude or misunderstood it; thus, all their actions had to be done in consort. Maybe early cohabitation denied them the sad solo flight of masturbation, and now there was a deferred primal need to jerk off in public. What an irony if the kids of the fifties were blessed. Like Elvis, I swore at them to get off my bluegrass racetrack.

As expected, Shecky Greene broke first, and Sham, after much bumping, settled into third. (It was learned later that Sham had knocked out two teeth hitting the starting gate.) Going into the first turn, the mighty Secretariat was a distant last, and a screech went through the bankroll of the chalk players. By the time they had negotiated a mile Sham was in the lead by a length and a half, and the blue and white hood of Secretariat could be spotted moving up. It was then the shock came. Sham was merely running magnificently, while Secretariat seemed to have discovered a secret conveyor belt beneath the track. It was the most unbelievable sustained move I have ever witnessed on a racetrack—as if the inexorable hand of destiny were placed at the finish line reeling him home. He crossed the finish line two and a half lengths ahead of Sham, while the rest of the field was so far back they looked as if they were running for aldermen in neighboring Cincinnati.

Secretariat's grandeur stifled all regrets. He not only won going away but ran the fastest Derby in ninety-nine years. No remorse here; like Sham, only a couple of teeth were out of joint. Moreover, for a day Secretariat had beaten our peculiar curse. An innocent was still abroad.

So for all its sways between squalor and splendor the ninety-ninth Kentucky Derby was the most precious of possessions, a cherished memory. The hoopla makers took their leave in that tender tradition of Americans: Promises were made to acquaintances of one day to meet next year, or "We'll drop in and see you if we get up to your neck of the woods." The frailty of life: the inability to let go.

This Derby, this spectacle of varied human emotions, could be summed up as "That's horse racing," but that would be a cliché. Or "That's America at play," but that would be facile. Better to clock it as a few furlongs in the human experience. A tout delivered in modesty, I assure you, by a man known in some circles to have a penchant for sham.

June 1, 1973

111

Psyching a Jockey in a Nickel Town

The Man [Spiro Agnew] has the greatest command of the English language of anyone who has ever lived. Now, I want to make sure you get that right, the way I said that: not just any living person, but anyone who has ever lived.

—CHICK LANG, general manager of Pimlico Racetrack, quoted by Frank Deford in *Sports Illustrated*

Such sacrilege in the land of Mencken. Henry aside, one is perplexed by Lang's point of perspective. But then again, this is a town of crab cakes and curmudgeons or, as writer Mark Kram's grandfather said, "This is a nickel town, son." Perhaps such judgments are too harsh, or Yankee damnations. It would be fairer to characterize Baltimore as the Spleen of the South.

To explain: Henry and Spiro, though polemics and IQ's apart, both were rampant catechism teachers. Love seems too languid an exercise for the residents. Take the Baltimore Orioles, one of the finest teams in baseball in recent years. At World Series time the viewer would turn on the TV and stare incredulously at the thousands of empty seats in Memorial Stadium. My God, a World Series! This is the same town that rode Earl Monroe out on a rail, much to the delight of the champion Knicks— though it stands to reason that the state that produced Francis Scott Key couldn't appreciate rhythm. But the *pièce de résistance* of local perfidy came when Madalyn Murray had God 86ed in public school classrooms. My———, Henry would have dug that.

So it's for no small reason that they named their premier horse race the Preakness Stakes after a horse that was shot by his owner, the Duke of Hamilton. But that could be construed as love in some circles I travel in. In fact, the duke might be a candidate for canonization.

I said *their* premier race, but is it really? During the passage of the Preakness, the race has been run in Westchester, New York, and from 1894 to 1908 at the Brooklyn Jockey Club's Gravesend Course. Symbolism abounds.

The race is billed as the Middle Jewel of the Triple Crown, and maybe that's part of the problem. It is lost in the setting of the glorious Americana of the Kentucky Derby and the equine ennui of the Belmont Stakes. The distance of the race, $1\frac{3}{16}$ miles, smacks of netherland. The Derby distance of $1\frac{1}{4}$ miles is the classic American distance, and the Belmont at $1\frac{1}{2}$ miles the classic European. More confusion. In Kentucky they drape the winner in a blanket of roses, in Maryland in black-eyed Susans. But pause. It seems that in May Susans are out of season, so the horsey set uses daisies and colors the centers black with shoe polish. At Belmont one couldn't figure what the hell they drape the victor with, but the guess here is the plastic variety of floral, considering the quality of New York air.

Then there is the state song. When the band strikes up, you don't know whether to sing "Maryland, My Maryland," "O, Tannenbaum, O, Tannenbaum," or "O, Christmas Tree, O, Christmas Tree." This year some touches were added to try to give the Preakness an "identity." In an attempt to rival the Derby's mint julep, a black-eyed Susan was inaugurated, a mixture of rum and vodka (and you wondered why they wanted to lynch Rap Brown?). At the Belmont anything from a martini to a pint of muscatel goes.

Also, there was the "Preakness Song," with rhyming that would make Rod McKuen look like William Butler Yeats:

> IT'S SPRING! and it's time
> For THE PREAKNESS in beautiful Maryland;
>
> Win Place or Show!
> You really should go!
> To see the famous PREAKNESS;
>
> Join in the fun at Old Hilltop,
> Crab cakes and ice cold beer;
>
> I love it! You'll love it!
> At Pimlico (so)
>
> Come to THE PREAKNESS
> I said THE PREAKNESS
> At good old PIMLICO.

Such attempts will never solve the Preakness identity crisis. So it was fitting when six horses emerged from the paddock in a Pirandellian post parade.

A digression. In the democracy of geography, genius is found everywhere. We found ours in the presence of our cabdriver, one Andy "Humphrey" Bogart. The chap alleviated the aggravation of a traffic jam in the hot sun with one-liners that gave speculation he might be a bastard son of Henny Youngman. To wit: "Baltimore liberals always buy the New York *Times* but never read it. The idea is to get off the train waving it, so that everybody thinks you're informed." Besides, he was blessed with prophecy. He took one look at my rather square countenance (jacket, shirt, tie, short hair, a beard—but one that is very short and trimmed) and said, "What underground newspaper are you covering for?"

But his gem was the most original observation I have heard to date on

113

Watergate: "Nixon should have hired Japanese instead of Germans; they're a lot better with electronics. Hell, look at Sony. Besides, if the Japanese had been caught, they would have committed hara-kiri. The problem with Germans is they like to live too much." This perverse theory on the Watergate could be filed under crystal commentary or Japanese-don't-make-waves.

The track itself was a pleasant surprise. It has managed to maintain its quaint exterior and provide a modern, refurbished interior. Pimlico has none of the melancholy seediness of such bush tracks as the Fair Grounds in New Orleans, and the credit for this has to go to the above-mentioned Mr. Lang. The horses were something else again. Cheap nags were bounding in from left field, beating classier foes. And there was a hint of shenanigans, when one exacta that should have paid between $500 and $600 paid $322. Obviously, those in the know didn't bet the winner in the win hole (he paid $83.60) but threw it in with both hands on the exacta. New York *Post* reporter Vic Ziegel, the Keeper of Cosmopolite Corruption, commented: "If they tried that at a New York trotting track, they would have ripped the joint down." Indeed, all this could have been a plot. The place was loaded with "the New York liberal press," born suckers for class. Paranoia produced a memoirial metaphor: "Spiro Remembers."

To the calculating cognoscenti, the Preakness was a two-horse affair—Sham and Secretariat. The other four were garnish. Sham, though beaten in the Kentucky Derby by Secretariat by 2½ lengths, had his excuses. His head hit the starting gate in that race, costing him two teeth and forcing him in the course of the race to swallow his own blood. To boot, he had been bumped twice by another horse in the early going. But one was disturbed by Sham's jockey Laffit Pincay's comments in the press leading up to the Preakness. It seems he spent hours watching the film of the Derby and was in awe of Secretariat's stretch run in that race—as well he should have been, since it was the fastest final quarter in Derby history (23⅕ seconds). But his awe seemed reverential, a bit like Patterson watching the film of his first fight with Liston. One got the feeling Pincay was psyched. The Preakness proved it.

When the gate opened, a local speedster, Ecole Etage, took the lead, with Sham second and Secretariat last. The race wasn't a quarter old when Pincay was looking over his shoulder for Secretariat. He made the mistake of sitting behind a slow early pace instead of going for the lead, thus forcing Secretariat to catch him. Ron Turcotte, Secretariat's jockey, realized this, and when the horses came out of the first turn and into the backside, he shot Secretariat into the lead. This left Pincay in a shambles. Turcotte's brilliant improvisation dumbfounded him, and he just didn't know what

114

to do. Chase early? Chase late? For all intents and purposes the race was over after five furlongs.

Pincay committed the cardinal sin: He didn't play one on one. He should have used his horse's superior early speed to give him his best shot. It was like having Sandy Koufax throw a change-up on a 3-2 count in a crucial game with two out in the ninth inning. The result would have been the same (Secretariat won by 2½ lengths), but at least Sham would have been used wisely, and there would have been drama early.

Sham's dilemma is that he was born at the same time as a truly great horse, so he'll have to play Seymour Krim to Secretariat's Norman Mailer. And Secretariat? He is simply what Dickie III was hollering about in Bosworth Field. And the price would have been justified.

May 24, 1973

A Horse for All Seasons

A group of us, accompanied by the baggage of New York blasé, gathered early at Penn Station Saturday for an odyssey to Belmont Park.

The onus lay with the horse to convince us he *was* the Horse. His victories in the Kentucky Derby and Preakness, impressive as they were, were executed out of town, and well, out of town is out of town. Many a delectable bite has proved sour in the Big Apple. After all, this was the Belmont Stakes at a mile and a half, and as any professional punter will tell you, the get of Bold Ruler don't go a mile and a half. But maybe our skepticism had something to do with the heat or our mode of travel. The Long Island Railroad doesn't conjure pilgrimages to Lourdes.

There was the writer-critic puffing his cigar—nothing less than the stigmata would woo him. And there was the retired sea captain turned poet, who the night before had sailed the uncharted seas of martinis, now looking for a Bloody Mary to ring the rescuing buoy bell in his brain; his vision of life a catastrophic constant earning him the rating of the Beckett of the barnacles. And the authoress of cookbooks who thought Secretariat's probable odds of 1 to 5 was a fine ratio for a recipe but an obscene folly for a deuce. Add an artist—the novice of the group—the colors of the silks would probably dictate her choice. I had witnessed every kind of plunger, so why not a palette punter? A trio were left.

One true believer who had spotted the colt's greatness early in his career and had backed him with her cash and her heart every time he went to post. She had spent a sleepless night—not from dread but in anticipation, and perhaps this made her the toughest to take. Abominable optimism is a handicapping burden to those of sagging shoulders. As for me, I was cursed for the most monomaniacal reasons (the only ones that really matter) to root for Sham. Fittingly, the group was rounded out by a shrink. A native of Rumania, he had realized as a boy that his country had two exports: soccer and psychiatry. Existentially, he knew that as a circle the head is more fun to kick around than the ball and thus chose sorcery over soccer. Handicapping his companions, he pronounced: "We have the intellect, but I don't know about the heart."

But if truth had it, the heart was there, even though cautiously hidden. Like most who attended, we realized that if Secretariat was destiny's tot, we were to be handmaidens to history. No mean stunt in the sprint of life. If the horse was to be emblazoned in history, would not all in attendance be accompanying asterisks? We're a fragile weave who opt for immortality no matter how obscurely achieved. The Horse was going for the first Triple Crown in a quarter century. Indeed, had I not talked about Bobby Thomson's home run in 1951 as if I were one who had attended the multiplication of the loaves and fishes? One felt he heard the multitude at Belmont conjuring up the tale to tell to grandchildren not yet begat. And if the parentheses of my life were to be a home run and hoofbeats, it was more than I had bargained for at the beginning.

It was all there early. The preceding races on the card were bet with impatience. Damnable newsreels and selected shorts to be endured before the main attraction. His time came at five-thirty, when he took the track with Ron Turcotte up. As is his wont, he was alert, turning his head to check the crowd. Race caller Dave Johnson has a saying about such awareness in certain racehorses: "They know why they're out there, they know what it's all about." He had yet to begin his warm-up, and those mythical leather-souled New York horseplayers were giving him a standing ovation. The entire stands seemed to unfold like a coquette's fan. This was no rote accolade, such as the kids from Huntington and Babylon give the Mets regardless of performance, or the hip chant of Dee-Fense chanted to the Knicks at the Garden (hip in the sense that only the esoteric can spot defense, offense is a ball going through a net, the preserve of bumpkins). No, this was a tough crowd who normally clap for mutuel prices, not animals. Only once before in memory had this happened: when the ancient Kelso outgunned the younger Gun Bow through the stretch at a mile and a quarter.

It was now 5:38, and history entered the starting gate. For six furlongs it had the semblance of a horse race. The valiant Sham, who in the Derby and Preakness had given the chestnut a test of respectability (2½ lengths behind on both occasions), went in tandem with him. Sham's strategy

116

was like Floyd Patterson's in the second Liston fight: He had to embrace his destruction early from fear he would shy from it. Sham's fate was no kinder than Patterson's; his heart and spirit were broken early.

But unlike Liston, Secretariat's performance was without malevolence. It was much more deadly. He destroys competition by the sheer joy he takes in his work. By the mile he had seven, after one and a quarter 20, and when he turned for home, he had 28 lengths on his nearest rival. He was now doing the implausible, racing against himself and the clock or, as runner Jim Ryun once said, against eternity. At the wire he was a 31-length winner, breaking Gallant Man's record by an incredible 13 lengths. Great horses break records by 2 or 3 lengths, superhorses by perhaps 5 or 6 lengths, so what can be said of him? Only that if the Lord comes in a chariot, Secretariat will get the nod to handle the heavenly bit.

His magic was such that hardened horseplayers wept, and tip-hungry bartenders stopped serving sauce and watched the race on television. One bettor had wagered a $50 ticket on him in all three races of the Triple Crown and cashed none, saving them for posterity. An Englishman with a brigadier mustache cashing a large bet pledged 60 bucks to an Irish charity. It was a day when the form players didn't act according to form.

Horseracing history was ravaged, the memories of old times mutilated. Pick a horse from the past, use his clocking, and you find a barrier was broken. Triple Crown winner Count Fleet, who won this race by 25 lengths, would have been beaten by 21 lengths. The last Triple Crown winner, Citation, by the same distance. And if one could have got a stopwatch on Pegasus, the odds here are that it would be wise to have bet him in the place hole.

Such equine éclat has never been seen on an American racetrack. No horse in memory could carry his speed at such a constant pace over such a stretch of ground. His sire, Bold Ruler, charged out of the gate like a drummer hearing a dinner bell in a boardinghouse. Buckpasser came from behind like Dagwood Bumstead shagging a bus. But this one will pass this way only once. And there is a sadness here.

Since he was syndicated for more than $6,000,000, he is due to retire to stud at the end of the year by the shareholders' mandate. It is a tragedy for racing, so in need of a superstar, that this must be. But it would be a grand gesture, one classy last fling, if his owner, Mrs. Penny Tweedy, would send him to France to race in the Arc de Triomphe. To have a champion on both sides of the Atlantic would be a rhapsodic reverie to bequeath his fans. Our American in Paris.

We returned from our day contemplative. Talk was at a minimum. But it wasn't the heat endured or the gin consumed but those futuristic forays in the mind with young whippersnappers who someday will commit the sacrilege of comparison. The grandchildren were being mentally jiggled on the knee, and one felt the opening line for all would be the same: "I was out there the day Secretariat. . . ." The only question was whether we would ever get that damn mile and a half.

June 11, 1973

You Came a Long Way, Bobby

Not since the ghastly revelation that Bella Abzug employs a housekeeper has the Women's Movement suffered such a dark day as September 20, the date of the King-Riggs match. The contumely heaped on Riggs by women for his unprecedented contribution to their movement smacks of the ingratitude the Irish people leveled at Parnell for taking a sexual breather between battles. But then accolades are never the spiritual sustenance of saints and revolutionaries.

Pshaw! the sisters shout, Bobby was nothing but an old pork butt. The titular head of trichinosis! But I beg pause: Put away your doctrinaire defenses, your suet syntax, and you will realize this male was sugar-cured. Let us consider cases.

If male chauvinism were looking for a club (or, in this case, a racket) to humiliate women, would they choose a fifty-five-year-old, half-blind tennis player—who looks like a cross between Phil Silvers and a penguin —to champion their cause? Indeed! The man hits the ball with the ferocity of a sorority sister in a dorm pillow fight and walks as if he were a perpetual shill for Dr. Scholl's foot pads. If the much-maligned male were looking for a misogynist mismatch, would he not choose the number one of his gender—say, Stan Smith—to challenge the women's finest, Billie Jean King? Even lesser luminaries such as Arthur Ashe, young Jimmy Connors, or, conceding age, that marvel of a middle-age athlete, Pancho Gonzalez? These names were never considered. The ancient Riggs was chosen not for pigdom but to be a sacrificial lamb to the altar at which we all worship.

Yet the misguided sisters never saw this. One blushed during the past week at the sisters' lack of aspiration. Did they not ruminate what a victory over Riggs would really mean? In a prior match Bobby had defeated the other women's great (this year's winner at Forest Hills), thirty-one-year-old Margaret Smith Court. In turn, he was defeated by the twenty-nine-year-old Mrs. King. Thus, could not a malevolent macho justly claim that the male species could spot the inferior sex twenty-four to twenty-five years but not twenty-six? Did not the sisters see this insidious trap they laid for themselves? They set themselves up to suffer under the bullyboy yoke and joke that they were a quarter of a century behind their male counterparts. Could not one envision the articles in *Playboy* and the Teamsters' newsletter on "The Genital Gap"? If my words have become smudged and unclear, it is only because of the tears that fall like Riggs' lachrymose lobs upon my paper.

But at this jaunty juncture the sisters may demand just what it was that Bobby did for their movement. Well, I will set out to prove he took a sexual shambles and solidified it. To flush out this thesis, the sisters will not only have to exhibit patience but also suffer that most painful exercise, honest self-examination.

Over the last year the movement has been drooping like a pair of garterless nylons. In point of fact, it has been as flat as a pair of 1950 ballerina slippers from A. S. Beck. The Super Sisters have been savaging each other in print with Haley's M.O. regularity. The NOW conventions with their sexual juntas make Warren Harding's smoke-filled rooms look like an antechamber to Athens. Who should rule the roost (cock-a-doodle dandies never): Liberated straights? Switch-hitters? Ladylike lesbians? Radical lesbians? Or those who opted for the convent of the cunt, trickless teetotalers?

And in this most avant-garde of cities the stud side presented in the mayoral primaries a field so dismal that the self-respecting male contemplated a gesture of gelding himself in protest. He looked in vain for a fabulous filly to (if one may be pardoned) bring home the bacon. But, lo and behold, Gloria, Shirley, Bess, and Bella would not take the bit.

Then there was the campaign to have Congress pass an equal rights amendment. Was it defeated by a bevy of bourbon-swilling Senator Claghorns? Not so. The only red-necks involved where those mortified feminists whose bill was killed through the relentless campaign efforts of— gasp!—a woman. No, sisters, this has not been your season.

I suppose there was a smidgen of solace to be found. Gloria in her aviators and grimacing smile, looking like Smilin' Jack's Downwind Jaxon, was always good for another radical press conference at the Russian Tea Room. Or Ti-Grace might question the virginity of Mary, which was a shocker to the Buckley girls, but a yawner to dark ex-Catholics in Brooklyn and Queens. (In their midnight moments they are known to give you chapter and verse on how the deflowering occurred.) And there was the celebration of Susan B. Anthony's birthday in Washington that drew a crowd slightly smaller than is needed for an orgy in a Toyota. Of course, *Ms.* magazine, like methadone maintenance, could always be counted on to exhume that necrophiliac combo (their version of Evers-to-Tinker-to-Chance), Zelda to Marilyn to Sylvia. And Billie Jean this year, after nineteen years of campaigning, got Forest Hills to award the same prize money to women winners (a paltry $25,000) as to men. An achievement, to be sure, but not the millennium. (Speculation is that for cohabiting the court with Riggs this year she will earn a munificent half-mil.) To put the gorilla on a crew who think vociferous protest is a low, hidden, behind-the-hand whistle at a linesman who looks and acts like Alistair Sim is hardly Up Against the Wall, Fatherfucker!

Into this breach came Robert Larrimore Riggs. In a matter of a few months he coalesced a floundering, splintered movement into an Amazonian Armada. It bespoke the genius of sending the work crew on the Tower of Babel to Berlitz. Did Riggs deserve this bile? Well, not only the sisters thought so but male sportswriters as well. But the latter are to be forgiven, since for the most part they possess saccharine brains. Evidence is their infantile mania for nicknaming everybody and everything, the latest being "Triple Sec" for Secretariat. Ugh! How unsophisticated has the nation become that prattle about how women should be back in the kitchen, barefoot and pregnant, etc., is taken to heart!

No, sisters, the real porkers use thornier and hornier arguments, such as where are your Michelangelos, your Einsteins, your Freuds, your Napoleons, etc.? Riggs as a chauvinist is a sweat sock that won't wash. Perhaps, you say, but he did it for money, a ripoff of our ruptured romance. It is prudent here to remind that Riggs was once married to an heiress and could have lapped from luxury to his dying days. The time has come to spring the confession of the ages, a fact hitherto known only to the carnal cognoscenti—Bobby leaped the net volleys ago, he is a champion of the movement.

He devised his master plan because he was heartsick at the lethargy he witnessed in the struggle. Some say (though it can't be substantiated) that his mother was an early and formidable influence. The same sources claim (again no proof) that he attributes his fluky backhand to his mother's perverse penchant for nursing him with his head upside down, his wee bandy legs over her shoulder. Like Christ before him, he joyously took up his cross. The slight difference being that the Messiah, a traditionalist, preferred wood, and Bobby toted steel into the Astrodome. How happily he accepted the slur "hustler" (read here the mocking "King of the Jews"), thus liberating Xaviera Hollander and a score of suburban sluts from that appalling appellation.

It was learned by this corner that Bobby based his plans on two political precedents. The first, when Earl Long was approached by blacks demanding jobs in Louisiana hospitals, he told them he would secure the jobs but that they would not like how he went about it. Long then made a series of pseudo-racist speeches, pointing out that white women, "the flower of Southern womanhood," were being demeaned by the act of "handling and washing black bucks." Needless to say, jobs opened in abundance. The second was Jack Kennedy's response to a Southern Congressman who asked him to campaign for him. Kennedy said he would praise or damn him, whichever would help most. Riggs realized a standard match between a man and woman (it's been done before) minus vitriol would be no boon to the movement. So with these lessons in mind, the cunning codger accepted his crucible.

Moreover, it was his style of play that was most soul-cleansing for the sisters. By playing the baseline and allowing Billie Jean to be aggressive with booming serves and charges to the net (in and out), Riggs, like self-sacrificing romantics before him who allowed women to mount them while they passively lay back on the pillow, afforded women everywhere a practical exercise to dispel Freud's most despicable theory—penis envy.

So though it be true you came a long way, baby, you still have miles to go before you sleep unless you pay homage to Robert Larrimore Riggs' deliberate bow to love. Sisters, I plead, deep in your catgut don't let this prophet pass without praise. See him for what he truly is, the Samuel Gompers of future generations of cuddly little things in pink rompers.

September 23, 1973

Three: Mug Shots

Frankie Carlin, the Bookie

It was ten forty-five Saturday morning, and Frankie Carlin was finishing his soft-boiled eggs and his second cup of Irish home-brewed tea. His squat wife sat in a kitchen chair, dressed in drab wool slippers and a flowered smock, looking like a familiar house plant. He rose and slipped a light tan topcoat over his large frame and with fleshy hands molded his chocolate-brown hat into shape. It was time to go to work.

On the side molding of the front door hung a blue plastic holy-water font with a sculptured crucifix. With his right hand he took some water and made the sign of the cross, his protection against evil spirits. Carlin's devils dress in blue. He's a bookmaker.

Recently United States Attorney Robert M. Morgenthau, functioning as the Dow-Jones of the underworld, stated that the annual business of bookmakers in the metropolitan area was $100,000,000. Recently also, New York State announced that it would run a quarterly series of lotteries based on horse race results, the idea being to channel some of that money into the state coffers. So, contrary to the tenets of free enterprise, the state has set out to create unemployment in one of the oldest and most skilled trades in the history of man.

Of course this is all laughable to the people inside the trade. The trouble with reformers is that they equate their need for action with that of the general public and envision themselves as Nick the Greek every time they wager a quarter at a church bazaar. Mark Twain once said the world was made up of turtles and goats, and no matter how much you explained, the turtles would never understand the depravity of the goats. The turtles in the State Assembly passed their Mock Reformation on the theory that a gambler needs action only quarterly. It is the same as saying that if we put everyone in Yankee Stadium over the Fourth of July weekend for an orgy, the city would remain celibate for the rest of the year.

Carlin (a fictional name) runs his operation in the Prospect Park area of Brooklyn. He walks to work through quiet treelined streets. The houses are mostly brownstone and limestone, and the occupants fall in the lower-middle to middle-class income level.

Bookmaking, like everything else in our graduated society, adheres to economic class levels. The underprivileged bookie, like his clientele, usually hustles the street, taking action on a catch-as-catch-can basis: street corners, playgrounds, hallways. The middle-class bookie (Carlin's level) operates out of a permanent location. And those bookies who cater to the rich give all the advantages to the beautiful people: tell-a-phone credit-card action.

Carlin paused outside the window of a bar bearing an Irish name. He stood lighting a cigarette while he casually viewed the interior. The bartender waved a greeting. Carlin nodded. His office was safe; his workday was about to begin.

The bar was one of those classic Irish "male bars" that exist only in Brooklyn and Queens. It was strictly a no-nonsense joint, no frills, no extras, you came here to drink. A long mahogany bar dominated the room. Workmanlike whiskey bottles, without pouring spouts, formed a shape-up on the back bar. John Fitzgerald Kennedy's memory was encased on the wall between Irish and American flags. A shuffleboard stood against the side window like a low, sleek schooner in a bottle. The white marble floor gave a regimental click to every footstep. The only feminine-appearing thing in the place was a garishly made-up jukebox, but even that was denied; it was not plugged in.

Carlin draped his coat over a wooden booth. A guy in his twenties wearing a windbreaker, his slick hair sweeping back like jet streams, called down to the end of the bar. "Hey, Frankie, how about an eye-opener?"

"Sure, Richie, first today." Faking enthusiasm, Carlin turned to the bartender. "Make it a crème de menthe on the rocks, Lenny." Carlin turned and muttered, "I haven't even digested breakfast—Christ, this slop will kill me." Why take it then? I thought. "Look, if you don't booze with your players, they think you're playing it sober and trying to hustle them."

"Frank, mind if I join you?" The windbreaker was trying to feel out my presence.

"Sure, glad to have you—I want to introduce you to a friend of mine."

I shook hands with my new acquaintance. Still unsure of my presence, he played it cool. "Frankie, let me pay you the fifteen I owe you from the other night."

Carlin smiled, "It's all right, Richie, you can talk—he's all right."

Richie still seemed uncomfortable. "Here's the dog I owe you and give me twenty to win on Advocator." Richie moved back to the bar and started to mingle among the patrons. This was the last time anybody approached Carlin with trepidation all day; the word was out—I was all right.

All operations like Carlin's give their clients the benefit of the "dog" or the "marker," inside names for credit. Carlin explained: "The average working stiff is tapped out by Tuesday or Wednesday, so I let them place their action on the cuff. Come Saturday, he has his pay and he straightens out his tab. If they legalize bookmaking, is Rockefeller going to let the bettor hang a marker on the state till Saturday?" He frowned slightly, registering his displeasure at the governor's inhumanity.

It was twelve-thirty now, and the bar began to become more crowded. Saturday is a big day for Carlin, and this one in all probability would be bigger than most. At four-thirty every Saturday Channel 5 televises two horse races. This week the action was from Hialeah, and the feature was the Widener Handicap, a mile-and-a-quarter race with the value placed at $125,000 added. Hundred grand races always stimulate the bankrolls of the bettors; they have a mystique about them that is similar to a championship prizefight.

The projected star of the production, the incomparable Buckpasser, was sidelined with an injury on the West Coast. But this was lamentable only to the big-money boys who delight in picking up 20 cents on every $2 wagered—for the average bettor, Buckpasser's payoffs are as exciting as a dividend check on one share of AT&T. Carlin's clientele likes action, a quick turnover. So, with Buckpasser absent, the field was reduced to eight mediocrities, all going off at a decent price. In short, the Widener had become a "good betting race."

Carlin was now drinking highballs. He moved among the drinkers like a social butterfly at a cocktail party. But there was a lot more happening than chitchat. The action was being taken at all times, but even when you were looking for it, it was almost impossible to spot.

His performance was perfected by years of repetition. First he approaches the client and then bellows to the bartender, "Lenny, give this deadbeat a drink on me." The client feigns anger. "Lord, if you're buying, I'd better go to confession; the world must be coming to an end." A great curtain opener.

Scene two: the fabled Irish politician's "personal" touch. "How's Mary, Tim?" "Fine, Frankie, just grand." "The Pope will canonize that woman for living with a scoundrel like you." Some light jabbing and mock scuffling. The action is passed. Carlin gently slides the slip with the bet on it and the money into his pocket.

Find an exit line. "Tim, what are your Mets going to do this year?" "First division, absolutely." "My God, Carmine, did you hear what this crazy mick just said?" A young Italian kid seated two stools away smiles and answers, "All micks are crazy." Carlin booms, "Hell, Lenny, I'll buy a drink to that." What transition! Exit lines lead into new entrances. Right here in a Brooklyn gin mill, techniques Shakespeare couldn't master.

Ethnic joking is a big thing in bars like this. "That crazy clown thinks the Mets will wind up in the first division." Carlin places his highball glass on the bar. Tony slides a $10 bill with his bet slip folded inside toward the glass. "Mets, what Mets?" Theatrical outrage. Carlin takes the $10 and slips it into his pocket. Tony adds, "This is the year of the Yankees, with that beautiful Italian kid Joe Pepitone in center field. A new DiMag."

Carlin displays weary frustration. "Pepitone? Why do I bother with you when there's a good squarehead in the bar? Fred, drink up."

An old man drinking whiskey with an orange juice chaser delivers a stage imitation of a Swede. "Min-na-sota will win the pen-nant by seven games, by Yim-a-nee." The bar roars with laughter. It's all familiar; it's been in the repertory for years. The drinkers love the safeness of its familiarity. And Carlin moves along the length of the bar majestically. Not a line is missed; the interplay is beautiful. Alfred Lunt playing to revolving Lynn Fontannes.

Carlin now has many slips in his pocket. This is known as his "work," and a good bookie always protects his work. Checking everyone at the bar, he slowly moves to the back of the saloon. The back room is used only on special occasions like bachelor parties or an affair for some local kid going into the service. From it a large mahogany door leads to the cellar. Carlin opens it and disappears. The cellar is where his "bunk" or "stash" is located. His bunk is where he hides his work.

When Carlin disappeared through the door, not a head at the bar would take note of his movement. It was as if Lady Godiva were riding through Coventry; there was a religious dedication to blindness. The bunk is the most important factor in the bookie's business. And for a good bookie there are two unbreakable commandments about his work: (1) Don't let the police seize it; (2) never destroy it.

In actuality, it is preferable—and less expensive—to let the cops confiscate the work than destroy it. To be caught with wager slips is only a misdemeanor under Section 986 of the New York State Penal Law, but the destruction of one's work could mean grave financial losses. A bookmaker of Carlin's stature takes in up to $1,500 a week and as much as $500 on a given Saturday. If the word gets out that he has been raided and had to destroy his work, many of these bets miraculously become winning ones. The client, realizing that the bookmaker has no record of the transactions, claims he wagered on winning horses, winning teams, or what-have-you. The bookmaker, no matter how doubtful of the validity of the claims, must pay off the conjured wager to protect his reputation. When a bookmaker gets the reputation of a deadbeat or a welcher, his action dwindles till he finally has to close shop.

By three-fifty the action started to ebb. Carlin's work for the most part was done for the day. Late stragglers still approached him with bets on the televised races. Carlin kept moving from the bar to the cellar to deposit any new action. He seemed tired.

"Doesn't this get you down day after day?" I asked.

He smiled. "I don't get any wearier than a guy working a regular job, and I earn a hell of a lot more. Thirty years ago before I got into this I worked as a clerk in a small brokerage house earning three thousand a year. It seemed to me then that my laundry bill for white shirts was about two thousand. Where would I be today with them? Eight, nine thousand a year. Now I put in about five hours a day and I'm good for anywhere from 30 to 40 thousand a year. No, when I think of that, I don't tire of it."

"What about the pressure, the aggravation of the business?"

He patted his full head of hair. "It may be white, but it's still there, and I'm near sixty. Sure, you have to be on the lookout for the cops all the time; but guys with regular jobs come in here to booze, and you would swear to God they were the Fugitive the way their bosses hound them. Everybody's got aggravation."

He ordered another highball and raised it to me. "Do you know of anybody who has these working conditions? Besides the cops, what do I really have to worry about? Certainly not a lack of supply and demand. Some clown with a crazy long shot isn't going to break me. I've got enough collateral to cover me, and if any action is too big, I can always hedge off."

The term "hedge off" means that if a bookmaker is receiving too much money on a certain horse he can call another bookie (usually a wire-room setup) and place a good part of the bet with a fellow operative. This eliminates the chance of taking a severe financial beating on a particular bet. The hedge-off system also protects the bookmaker from being the sole target of a "sure thing."

Carlin deals only with flat horse races. He will take action on any flat horse on any track in the country. When a large bet materializes on a horse running at a bush track (a small out-of-town track), it is time to hedge off. Big money appearing on an obscure horse at an obscure track usually means the bettor has information, thus the danger of the "sure thing."

Carlin will handle only horses. "I'm no sportsman," he said. "That's where the big action is today, but I leave that to the big-money boys, the syndicate crowd. I operate alone. Besides, sports are too easy to rig. Who in their right mind would take action on college basketball? Those kids are so hungry they're easy pickings for any sharpie who waves a couple of hundred under their noses for a dump."

"What about the trotters?" I asked.

"If the college kids are looking for spending money," he said, "those old men driving the trots must be looking for retirement pensions. I wouldn't touch them. I stick strictly to the flats."

A man no bigger than five feet two, wearing a gray peaked cap, approached Carlin and handed him a slip with $2. Carlin read the slip and laughed. "Big Joe, are you still trying to break me with your crazy long-shot parlays?"

The little man grinned. "I'll get you yet, you big lug," he said.

As the small man retreated, Carlin motioned for the bartender. "Lenny, send Big Joe down a drink." Carlin turned back to me. "You see that little guy? He's a real sweetheart. He wouldn't bet a horse under twenty to one. I always like to see him catch a couple of long ones. He's been playing with me now for about twenty years."

Carlin excused himself and disappeared into the cellar again. No matter how small the ticket, he didn't want it on his person. When he returned, he laughed and said, "I'm going to have them build an escalator down to that place."

Looking at the clock on the wall, he said, "Four ten—that should be about it for the day." He looked at my near-empty glass. "Come on—drink up."

"How much does it cost you to buy drinks on a day like this?"

"I never count. These people are my friends. I've been operating out of this place nearly thirty years. I saw most of these kids you see here christened. Their fathers played with me, even some of their grandfathers. This very bar, I've been paying the rent in this place as long as I have been using it as a location. There are hundreds of setups like this around the boroughs.

"You know, John Q. Public thinks guys like me scoop in all the money and run home and bank it in the sugar bowl. Hell, I love to gamble as much as the next guy; that's how I got into this business in the first place. I always liked the horses. When I was with the brokerage house, over seventy percent of the employees liked to bet on one thing or another. We used to have this runner come around and pick up the action, but he was unreliable. Most days he was late, and others he never showed. So I got myself a small bankroll and started to handle the action myself. I was single then, and I lived in a small rooming house a couple of blocks from here, and in the evening and Saturdays I would come here to drink. The guys at the bar were always talking about betting and how hard it was to find a bookie, so I got together with the owner and I set up shop. After about a year things went so well I quit the brokerage house, and I've been here ever since."

"Do you still gamble?" I asked.

"Hell, I chase the ponies down to Florida a couple of weeks a year, and in August I chase them up to Saratoga. You know what the cops call us?

Degenerate gamblers." He snorted. "You know something? They're right. Very few bookies can stay away from the action themselves."

He was completely relaxed now, and he began to enjoy the whiskey. Sitting back in the booth, he talked of how television with its extensive coverage of sports has aided gambling. "The average guy sits down to watch a football game, and he likes to back his rooting interest with a five or a ten." When I asked him what events take the most money today, his answer sounded more like Daniel Moynihan than a bookmaker. "The Jews like baseball and basketball, but especially baseball. That's the biggest play today. The big-money boys like the one-on-one situation of the starting pitchers. Guys today follow Koufax and Marichal like guys years ago would follow Man o' War and Dan Patch. The Irish and the Italians like the horses and pro football. The Negroes and the Puerto Ricans, because they don't have the bread, play the numbers—sucker odds at five hundred to one; they get a pipe dream for two bits."

"Have you had much trouble over the years?" I asked.

"In any business there is always trouble. I had guys give me bets and welch. About eight years ago a couple of kids I knew since they were babies fleeced me for about seventeen hundred dollars. One of them would drive to Bowie in Maryland and watch the races and wait for a big payoff. When the payoff was official, he would run out of the track and call his buddy here in Brooklyn with the name of the horse. Then the kid would charge over here and dump thirty to forty dollars on the sure thing. It's called past posting. Normally, I wouldn't touch a ticket like that, but hell, like I said, I knew the kids all their lives. I wasn't going to refuse a bet with a neighborhood kid because he was about four minutes late. They stung me about four times; then I got wise."

"What did you do when you caught on?"

"What was I going to do? Beat them? Kill them? They took me, and that was that. I let everyone here know what they pulled; they never showed their faces here again. I have a lot of friends here, but I wouldn't let anyone lay a hand on them. I don't run that kind of operation, my friend—I'm no mobster."

"The kind of trouble I was really talking about was the cops," I said.

Carlin started to laugh. He told of how six years ago the cops began to lean on him. Every day there was a plainclothesman or two dressed as mail carriers or longshoremen standing at the bar. Carlin couldn't move. Then a brilliant idea struck him.

Since he couldn't circulate among the patrons and most certainly the patrons couldn't walk down to the basement to place their slips in his bunk, he decided to have the men's room redecorated. The bathroom is one of those museum pieces with gigantic marble urinals that Toulouse-Lautrec could have used for a shower stall. Carlin decided to replace the old plaster ceiling with a Cello-Tex one. The idea was that he would leave one Cello-Tex square loose and his clients, by mounting the urinal, could stash their action and their cash in the false ceiling. Carlin would remove his work late at night when the bar was no longer under surveillance.

The operation worked great for about three days till the plainclothesmen began to wonder if the bar patrons were plagued by kidney disease. Finally, his curiosity aroused, one plainclothesman decided to follow a patron to the men's room. Giving the guy a few minutes' head start, the cop pushed in the door and saw his suspect standing on the urinal with his arms stretched upward. Unable to explain his peculiar form of toilet training, the bettor wound up in cuffs while the cop mounted the urinal and flushed out the evidence. Carlin had tears of laughter running from his eyes at the completion of the story.

"What happened?" I asked.

"Let's just say it cost me plenty to get out of that one." Pointing to the end of the bar at a lanky guy in a sports jacket, Carlin said, "That's him. Since then we baptized him Johnny Highchair." His laughter was rich, and the best kind—self-directed.

"You seem like a contented man," I said.

"I am."

"No regrets?"

"I'll lay you seven to five no one can say that."

I laughed. "No bet."

The television set was now turned on. The voice of Fred Capossela nasally intoned, "It is now post time." George Widener's Ring Twice was an easy winner under a front-running ride by Billy Boland. Carlin was pleased by the result. Most of the big money he had taken in on this race was on Advocator, the favorite, who finished up the track. But he wouldn't know how his day came out till he heard all the results from around the country that evening at six-thirty on FM radio. Then he would balance his books. Sunday afternoon at one-thirty, after the twelve-fifteen mass at the parish church, he would wait for the winning bettors inside the bar. Their winnings would be in white sealed envelopes with their names on them inside his topcoat pocket. Every bet paid precisely, rounded off to the nearest dollar.

Saturday's results were now turf history. But come Sunday the papers would list the entries for Monday. And come Monday the bettors would be back again. Why? You looked up at the electronic picture, and television truly became educational.

There they were in the winner's circle. Ring Twice worth $24.40 to his believers. Seventy-seven-year-old George Widener winning his ancestor's race. Seventy-eight-year-old Wilbert "Bert" Mulholland training the winner. Dynasty! Continuity! Ring Twice, whose sire was Gallant Man, the Belmont Stakes winner, his stock reaching back to mysterious Arabia. Widener, Mulholland, Arabia—permanence, history. Carlin talking of generations of bettors. Man's passage through life. His history, his need to test overwhelming odds. His need for action.

This historic need. Why? One of their own, Nick the Greek, said it as neat as an inside straight: "The next best thing to winning is—losing."

April 4, 1967

Up the Up Staircase: Educating the Plebes

A group of about thirty sat thawing out in a stark classroom at Manhattan's New School. A rather buxom blonde turned to another female classmate and said, "I worked for Lindsay, but I couldn't resist taking this course." Her companion nodded in passionate agreement. When one weighed the sexual balance of the class (about 90 percent female), one surmised that, indeed, there was a "right" way to titillate women.

Then one heard the voice from the back of the room—as smooth and as warm as buttered rum. "Hi there, how are you this evening?" Muted sopranos chirped back to the majestic American Eagle. Then, to illuminate our dull horizons, he flashed his crescent moon of a smile. His eyebrows, like startled geese, flew from his forehead—William F. Buckley, Jr., had arrived.

Reeking of capitalism, he wore a mustard suede parka lined in sheepskin—a garment so magnificent that even the most strident Maoist would be tempted to turn in his quilted pajamas. With elegant fingers, he charmed into place the basket of snakes that was his hair. His exquisite sports jacket gave speculation that good tailors are still the weavers of our social conscience. His blue shirt complimented his blue eyes, and his red tie accentuated the ruddy handsomeness of his face. Only an infidel or a liberal would deny he was privileged to view a resident of Olympus.

He sat behind his desk and studiously put on his horn-rimmed glasses. His eyes scanned his lesson plan while his fingers played a silent sonata on the unyielding desk top. If this was Paul Goodman, one could surmise his silent music was Bach. But as Buckley's fingers strutted with a more militant tempo, you knew damn well it was John Philip Sousa.

Tonight's class, under the title "Issues and Problems in the City—a Conservative View," was to deal with education. Buckley opened his class by lecturing on the educational views of Albert J. Nock, author of

Memoirs of a Superfluous Man (a title the left might find appropriate for Buckley's autobiography). Nock, Buckley informed us, was a man who adhered to the classical concept of education. Learning should be composed of Greek and Roman tragedies—not classes in how to disassemble a car motor. Though he admitted the merits of the tune-up, Buckley felt such courses shouldn't be filed under education. To assure us Nock wasn't just another crank case, Buckley informed us "he was an ordained minister who left the ministry and his wife" and was expelled from college, because he was in "an advanced state of decomposition."

Buckley stressed the need for flexibility in education. "After all," he said, "part of my pedagogical training was building ships in bottles when I was seven years old."

Like shipbuilding, Buckley is an ancient art. He is the only male American I know who could enter a drawing room in jodhpurs and slap a riding crop across his boots and get away with it. He is that dream of English gentry Yankee farmers will never relinquish. His humor is as old as America itself.

W. C. Fields was the first to swat dogs and babies. With less cholesterol George Sanders sophisticated the technique. In the subterranean level of our soul William Buckley is of that class of men who smell like aged leather, who kick dogs and debauch the upstairs maid. He is indeed our last rake.

His pronouncements about the poor are outrageous. When asked what his initial statement to the Negro would be, Buckley said he would ask them to stop airmailing their garbage from their tenement windows. His disrespect for linear knowledge is audacious: "My fifteen-year-old son is an illiterate, he has read five books in his life, and four of them have been pertaining to sex." His view of national illiteracy: "In the nineteenth century forty percent of America was illiterate; the current rate of illiteracy is about two percent. In the nineteenth century the country was subjected to the Lincoln-Douglas debates; in 1960 we had Richard Nixon and John Kennedy. To me this doesn't offer a valid argument for literacy."

When a young female teacher asked irritably about "black power" moves to take over neighborhood schools, Buckley silenced her with the argument that *all* communities should rule their curriculum unless they were teaching anarchy or revolution. When the aggrieved young lady questioned the merits of courses in Swahili, Buckley said: "One would think that all the words in Swahili could be mastered in a week and a half."

Buckley is not a conventional teacher. He has the habit of ignoring his class. Like an elegant crane, he struts across the room oblivious to his audience. His heel touches first, then the toe, and to dramatize a point he stops in mid-gait and stands poised on one leg. Other actions are pure Stanislavsky. He pulls down a projection screen for no apparent reason.

134

Then he indulges in his own exercise program: He hitches up his pants, stretches his body, leans forward, and balances on his toes. His audience is isolated like whalers in their small boats as this awesome white Establishment figure hovers above them.

As only the rich can do, he explained how his father hired two tutors to teach sixteen children, including the Buckley siblings, instead of sending them to the public school system—and the process wasn't only superior but less expensive!

When queried if the private school system wasn't a citadel for race discrimination, Buckley scoffed. He felt the federal government should subsidize all parents who want to send their children to private schools. Everything is motivation: "Take the case of that young man who wrote *Manchild*—who only patronized reformatories, pushers, and whores." Patronized! Magnificent!

This is the man who with princely disdain said he couldn't give a damn about the Italian vote, the man who during the Civilian Review Board fight compared the cops to martyred saints. When his voice mentions liberalism, it takes on the ennui of Monica Vitti racing along a timeless landscape. In righteous indignation he deputized himself as sheriff of Fun City in prosecuting those who aid draft resisters.

When I introduced myself as a reporter for the *Village Voice*, the smile generated a flash of heat. "How is everyone at that hotbed of subversives?" Recalling an article I had penned in which Jim Reilly, the archrightist, accused the Conservative Party of being run "by gay bachelors," he said: "It was very effective—Kieran O'Doherty ran out and got married two weeks later." The charm of a Buckley administration would be that wit would reign supreme.

When one thinks of the prospect of the 1969 mayoral campaign, Buckley will be missed. Mario Procaccino will audit our budget with the vigilance of a local butcher. Frank O'Connor will campaign for everyone's Aunt Maud's virginity by claiming he will hire 5,000 more cops. In our city's great art of reverse alchemy, John Lindsay is such a case. Lindsay's problem is that he tried to become part of his city, while the hacks who preceded him were overwhelmed by it. The secret of this penthouse town is to reign above it. The Empire State is not to be ruled by peasants and reformers. Our future might not be desirable, but it is inevitable. Bill Buckley is the only monarch we have.

January 18, 1968

135

Wonder Woman Throws Her Bonnet
into the Ring

Mary McCarthy once commented that any woman who has ever had her arm twisted by a man realizes men are superior. Mary McCarthy has never met Bella Abzug, who is challenging incumbent Congressman Leonard Farbstein in Manhattan's Nineteenth Congressional District.

Challenging Farbstein is an old pastime among Greenwich Village reformers, and the end always has been the same—he devours contenders with the same ease Rockefeller digests blintzes.

And he is not going to be easy pickings this time around either. His ADA report card is in good shape; he has voted against military appropriations; domestically, he is on the "right" side of most issues; and in a district with a heavy Jewish voting bloc he led the group of Congressmen who walked out on Premier Pompidou's speech in the House, failing only to give the French goy a Bronx cheer on his exit.

So one wonders why the woman tries. Her backers claim they have a Wonder Woman.

Possibly the fault with past contenders was that they tried to finesse Farbstein out of his seat, but that's not Bella's style. The subtlety of the sweet science escapes her—she doesn't float like a butterfly or sting like a bee. She is strictly out of the Rocky Marciano school of politics: nothing fancy, just a straight ahead, two-fisted assault on the senses. Or as that cagey old philosopher Archie Moore once commented on encountering Rocky: "Man, did you ever get your head caught in a helicopter propeller?" And in the old Hemingway canon of getting in shape when you're trying to land the big one, Bella has slimmed down to her best fighting weight and added a new French haircut and a Bermuda tan to boot.

Abzug has a history of "cause" brawling that dates back over twenty years. After receiving her law degree from Columbia Law School in 1947, she spent time as a Hebrew schoolteacher, and in 1950 she traveled to Mississippi to argue the appeal of Willie McGee, a black man convicted of raping a white woman, a case she saw as a racist frame-up. McGee had been sentenced to be executed, but Abzug won him two stays in a two-year appeal fight, though she finally lost the case, and McGee was executed. She proudly tells of editorials calling for the lynching of McGee and his "white lady lawyer," as if to imply that there wasn't a rope in the South tough enough to do the job. But then, if memory serves me right, Wonder Woman was the sole possessor of the unbreakable lasso.

More recently, Bella was one of the founders of the "Dump Johnson" movement. She also is involved in the welfare rights movement and has been the national legislative representative of Women Strike for Peace since its inception in 1962. She serves as a member of the Lindsay Mayor's Advisory Committee, is the chairman of the Taxpayers' Campaign for Urban Priorities, was a founder of the New Democratic Coalition and serves on its state and national executive committees, and is an activist in the Women's Liberation Movement. ("I never served coffee to the boys in SDS," she poisonously purrs.)

She has been married for twenty-five years, has two grown daughters, maintains an elegant home in the Village, and probably cooks like Julia Child and shoots golf in the low seventies, but my male ego stopped me from asking.

Her furious activity over the years has gained her a host of enemies as well as admirers. Her critics claim that any defection from the Abzug Doctrine has been countered with Mafioso-like threats that she would use her political muscle to break them. Others claim now that she is mellowing, that is, becoming political to win across-the-board support in her primary fight.

One feels the first school of thought might have some substance since during her ardent moments it seems she might pacifistically beat you to death for peace. But the lady demurs. She says she never has been politically ambitious and her aggressiveness always has been on the issues and never personal. "I always was against internecine warfare on the left. It's the issues that count. My aggressiveness is not a personality thing."

When she threw her hat into the ring (a stunt she actually did for the TV cameras) at the Overseas Press Club last Friday, it looked like Ladies' Day at Yankee Stadium. The males present were all from the press with the exception of her husband and Michael C. D. MacDonald, one of the male Queenmakers behind the throne. Another closet Queenmaker fostering the Abzug candidacy is Doug Ireland, who has the distinction of being the youngest Old Leftist in America. He is the only twenty-five-year-old in captivity who knows more about Eugene Debs than Eldridge Cleaver and whose idea of alienation is not to be involved in a political campaign, or as one wag immortalized him in bathroom graffiti: "Doug Ireland is a Marxist Carmine de Sapio."

MacDonald is a natural for the Abzug camp, since he carries so many causes around on his back he might be regarded as the liberal Quasimodo. His loving burden is to get Herman Badillo elected to *anything*, which might have led to his favorable coverage of Arthur Goldberg in this paper last week (the reported deal is Goldberg for governor, Badillo for lieutenant governor), a Valentine that is not ringing many chimes on the New Left or among very many NDC reformers.

The morning began on a paranoid note when a large explosion was heard outside the building that sent the gathering scurrying to the windows. The crash proved only to be part of the demolition of a building across the street (traditional style), not the work of the current political Fourth of Julyers.

And the male press seemed ill at ease with the dominant distaff audience. Flanking Abzug on the podium were all females or "the real Silent Majority in the country," as Bella called them. There was Ellie Guggenheimer, suffering under the cloak of oppression in a full-length fur coat and a diamond as big as the Ritz. She was joined by Gloria Steinem and Lucy Komisar, who were suppressed sisters right down to mod boots. Seamstresses and domestics were nowhere to be found, and one had the suspicion he was witnessing another junta at the top.

But Bella brought the session down to earth, delivering a rousing speech in which she promised to be "no humble member of Congress who plays follow the leader and keeps quiet." She then went on to explain how she intended to lead the fight, both locally and nationally, to end the military domination of our tax dollars and turn the money back to the cities to cure their crying needs. As she enumerated these needs, she violently poked the air with her finger, like a cowhand on a toot shooting the shit out of the atmosphere. She went on to say she was leading her ladies on a march to Washington to tell Nixon: "No more men"—but here she paused too long, and the Sons of the Front Page gasped as if they were being slated for a program of genocide. But she continued the quote— "no more money, no more wars."

She said that voting properly is no longer enough, that what is needed is "an activist and a fighter," and that Farbstein is not that person because he has to be "pushed and shoved" into the right positions. She then read an endorsement telegram from Shirley Chisholm ending "Bella, Godspeed." One thought that advice was superfluous.

Then in a moment of political finesse, she introduced her handsome family and like a Southern belle tossed her bonnet across the podium, saying her hat was now in the ring, charming the gentlemen of the press and putting their worst suspicions to rest.

Bella doesn't associate herself with the Wild Bunch of the liberation movement. She doesn't go along with the notion of test-tube babies— sexually, she's from the old school. Nor does she look down on housework or "homemaking," as she calls it. She admits to having "help" in maintaining her apartment and simply notes that those who perform this chore should be justly compensated, complete with unemployment and health insurance. She feels women who go to business must be put on equal economic parity with men so they "can pay a living wage to those who make a career out of homemaking." If the guaranteed annual income comes about, Abzug insists all housewives should be included, since "homemaking is a profession." And, of course, the abortion laws must go.

But the thrust of her candidacy is that the role of a Congresswoman with her constituency is to "educate them, agitate them, and then mobilize them" (as she pounds her fist into an open hand). It is here Bella is on firm ground. One thinks that if other members of the House had had the courage early to try to explain to their constituencies that the war was robbing them of their children and their national treasure and causing urban decay, instead of panicking the first time they got flak from the American Legion, there might be some measure of decency and sanity in our national life. Bella doesn't seem the type to bend with the phony patriotic breeze.

Abzug is in for a formidable fight. Besides Farbstein's strength, her personal style is going to turn off a lot of voters. When she strides across a room, she is as formidable as James Arness in *Gunsmoke*. But in a political climate that seems to have been created by Antonioni (thank God for Spiro—he's the only thing that gets my adrenalin flowing these days), Abzug's hammer-and-tong approach to the issues might be a blessing to a weary America. One must consider noise is not always a nuisance. Good lovemaking, children, and life are also pretty raucous.

If the ladies would permit me a moment of condescending chauvinism, the thought of Bella hollering like hell in those hallowed halls of Congress just might prove a sexy scene.

March 19, 1970

The Cyclops Candidate:
Hemp High in the Saddle

Things are looking up in Kansas City or thereabouts. The current euphoria in the Sunflower State is due to the fact that Douglas County has a candidate running for sheriff who usually is as high as an elephant's eye. He is George Kimball, leader of the Lawrence Street People, pornographer extraordinaire, and the user and abuser of anything that defers reality.

The twenty-six-year-old Kimball recently left New York City at the request of the law and the bartenders' union to settle in Lawrence, Kansas. In this pure setting, Kimball began meditating about the sad state of man and benevolently decided to do something about it. With the aid of his street people, he began circulating petitions to place his name on the ballot to run for sheriff of Douglas County. This activity didn't cause much of a stir among the natives, since they figured Kimball would run on the Let-It-All-Hang-Out or the Vegetarian Grass line (George digs both spinach and pot); but an hour before filing deadline, Kimball filed his petitions as a Democratic candidate! And better yet, he is unopposed and will be on the official party line with Governor Robert Docking in November.

But the Establishment shouldn't despair, for Kimball is a man capable of snatching defeat from the jaws of victory. And though Jimmy "the Greek" Snyder, the Vegas oddsmaker, is not predicting a Kimball defeat in the primary, he currently is laying 8 to 5 that George will end up in a runoff with himself.

Who is this political phenomenon, this Midwest Mailer? He is the son of an Army colonel, a member of the Yippies, the White Panther Party (a minister of defense), the Lawrence Liberation Front, and the American Contract Bridge League (honest to God). He is hairy, unkempt, and has one glass eye which he will drop into your glass if you make the sorry mistake of asking him to keep an eye on your drink while you retire to the john. He is the author of a Girodias' opus titled *Only Skin Deep,* the only book I've ever read that had sticky pages. For Freudian reasons, Kimball refused to have the book issued in soft cover. His publishing party, held in a Village pub, looked like a Charles Addams review. Rumor had it that the ASPCA, acting in behalf of the pub's resident kitten, filed suit against a finger painter from Hoboken, charging the Mann Act.

But all this is not to suggest that George is not a man of real sensitivity. One morning, as I sat at the bar trying to recover from a sad night of the soul, Kimball was a comforting angel of mercy. I was having little success trying to stop the shakes with a morning drink, when Kimball, sympathetic to my plight, looked at me and said: "Don't worry, Joe, I've been both a junkie and an alcoholic, and, believe me, being an alcoholic is better." Now can a man such as that be all bad?

Kimball's best political moment in New York came the day of one of Jimmy Breslin's many "going away" parties. This one, I believe, was to honor an impending Breslin trip to Rockaway. Many of the local aspiring pols and chi-chi climbers had let it be known that Kimball's presence, because of his penchant for outrageous behavior, was not welcome. But the Kimball Crusaders banded together and insisted he attend. Kimball, a pariah of propriety, arrived at my house bedecked in his usual God-knows-what-stained dungarees (these were undoubtedly the same pair of pants that ran down the road alone in the Claude Rains' film *The Invisible Man*), his unmovable cowboy boots, his skin-grafted socks, and a tattered shirt. It would have taken a Weatherman's bomb to disrobe him. But with the aplomb of Fred Astaire, he looked at his magnificence in my mirror and said: "Joe, it's a formal affair, do you have a jacket that will match this?"

But it was at the party that he was truly splendid. The bar was popu-

140

lated with many of the city's top pols, and Kimball saw a great opportunity to put the fix in on a pot bust he was facing. He strode up to then U.S. District Attorney Robert Morgenthau, who was sitting with Mayor John Lindsay, and asked the law enforcer: "Do you have any fucking thing to do with the police?" The normally shy Morgenthau became even more reticent and mumbled, "Yes." George blandly countered: "Can you fix a dope rap for me?" Morgenthau looked shellshocked, and Lindsay seemed to be wishing for the hallowed halls of St. Paul's when suddenly Kimball offered to buy him a drink. The mayor, never wanting to appear unhip, accepted and ordered a ginger ale, causing Kimball to bellow: "I'm not buying you a fucking ginger ale. I said a drink." The mayor stuck by his pop, and Kimball proclaimed to all who would listen that the mayor was a tight-assed WASP. And since the day of the party happened to be Ash Wednesday, George surmised that if the mayor was anointed, he might loosen up. It was at this point that Kimball calmly placed the holy ashes from a bar ashtray on the mayor's forehead, and the bartenders decided to banish him to limbo. Lindsay and Morgenthau took a monastic retreat to the back room to "talk with Paul O'Dwyer," who, incidentally, had left the party an hour earlier. Now, be damned, Kimball had achieved the populist ideal—bringing government to the people.

George also is a genius of law and order. His pot bust occurred in a peculiar way. Walking the Village with a companion one night, he wanted to stop for a drink in a Mafioso bar. The bouncer at the door took one look at Kimball and refused him entrance. The funny thing about George is that even with a jaunty fedora and a raincoat flung over his shoulder he does not look like Frank Sinatra. Well, Kimball, always a vociferous civil libertarian, kicked in a pane of glass in the bar's door. Enter owner with gun. Kimball's associate, a man of renowned street smarts, quickly offered to pay $10 for damages, and the pistol-packing owner was amenable. But Kimball would have none of it. He stood in the middle of the street, Clarence Darrow fashion, proclaiming that his civil rights had been violated.

As he wailed, the sound of a siren was heard. The cops tried to settle the whole thing by imploring George to give the aggrieved party the $10 and move on. But by this time Kimball thought he was Joan of Arc in drag and demanded justice. After endless soliloquys, the cops took him to the station to be booked and ordered him to empty his pockets. And when Kimball put his hand in his right-hand pocket, he discovered three joints he had forgotten he was carrying. Immediately, he tried to cop a plea to relieve his kidneys or, indeed, pay the $10 or maybe even $20. No dice, said the cops, and when the pockets were emptied, Darrow was discarded, and George became the chief witness for the prosecution.

The upshot of the whole thing was that the $10 grew into a $100 fine which was paid by Lion's Head proprietor Wes Joice, who, if he ever cancels Kimball's bar tab, will become the largest political contributor this side of Dick Ottinger's mother.

Kimball's funky charisma has attracted unusual press coverage for a local race. The Kansas City *Star* has run a front-page feature with photo, Bill Moyers has interviewed him for a "What's Happening in America" series for *Harper's*, and local interest is being titillated by his green and white bumper sticker proclaiming "Kimball for Sheriff—Douglas County Needs a Two-Fisted Sheriff." (George's opponent has one withered hand.) When I asked him about the dubious taste involved here, Kimball replied: "Fuck, he can make political hay out of my one eye if he wants to." But if he tries, Kimball's staffers are ready to cut his opponent off at the pass with the slogan "Kimball Has *an Eye* on the Future." All's fair in love and gore.

Kimball's most visionary idea to date is the building of a subway in Douglas County, which some wag is sure to christen the Underground Railway. He also has made the wearing of guns *de rigueur* in Lawrence by toting a cap-and-ball Navy Colt. "Doc Holliday used to use one," he proudly proclaims. And though he favors gun control, he claims he won't hang them up until his opposition does. Obviously, neither will his saddle partner and one of his future deputies, Mary Ann Stewart, who wears a bandolier and carries a carbine. George also remarks that she's a mean woman in the kitchen and will cook for prisoners if he's elected.

Kimball has let it be known he will not be permissive with offenders if he catches his tin star: "I will preserve all natural resources and punish all those who fuck with them." Like all aspiring pols, Kimball's biggest problem is campaign funds. The main line of his support is from the Kaw Valley Hemp Pickers, but the war chest recently went bust when a group of the pickers were arrested for trying to sell fifty kilos to a federal agent. That's one thing about Kimball—like Caesar, he is as constant as the north star. No revisionist he.

Now, to me, Kimball sits tall in the saddle, but it is well known I'm no judge of political horseflesh, so I placed a phone call to Kansas' legendary half-breed lawman, the chronicler of Kansan cold bloodiness and the first wearer of a Mark Cross holster, True Man Coyote, to ask him if George had a shot. "You better believe it, bunny," he declared. "Any man who totes a gun and can sleep with one eye open has to be reckoned with."

August 6, 1970

Pug Taylor: Hard Hat

New York hardhats are organizing for action against bookshops featuring pornography.—July 10, 1970.
—Leonard Lyons in "The Lyons Den"

Only in America. The land of opportunity. Where else could construction workers—Nixon's Silent Majority—share the fabled inky bed of Jackie, Ari, Richard, and Liz? Surely a phenomenon.

But this is not all. Will it ever be possible again to walk by a building site with the curious innocence of a sidewalk superintendent? Without experiencing an ideological feeling? Gone are the days when the passerby can have burly fantasies of operating the steam shovel or climbing the high iron. Too, women no longer respond to the workers' whistles and shouts as sexual compliments or insults. Everything is deeper now.

Violence, the giant flags hanging from skeletal structures, the workers' mean stares at mods and beards have changed all that. Each building site has become a bastion of patriotism or a cage where apes scamper about, depending on your political persuasion. Salute or *Sieg Heil.* The hard hats are no longer voiceless or faceless, but the symbol of a political force to be reckoned with.

Nixon is the one who is responsible for giving birth to this new nation or this Frankenstein, and this is what is hard to fathom. Why have the hard hats rallied to Nixon? Certainly not out of identification with his life-style. Nor is it loyalty to a new embarkation. The war has been with us for years. Why couldn't Johnson muster popular support? The average hard hat would seem to be more at ease with LBJ, the prolific guzzler of scotch, the Texas hot rodder who was given to earthy dissertations on the mating habits of bulls.

But they let Johnson's Presidency die without a whimper. Here was a man they watched being mugged in state primaries by a theological politician who, for chrissake, wrote poetry as a hobby! Why Nixon?

A Wallace or a Joe McCarthy, to be sure, who projected themselves as feisty brawlers for the "regular guy" against the intellectual bureaucrats. And one wonders. These were men who had the barroom instinct to go not for the jugular, but for the groin. Both of them indicated that the legal democratic process was a large pain in the ass, a snake pit of *Red* tape constructed by those who want to thwart the desires of the real people. Thus, Wallace's solution of throwing all the bureaucrats and their briefcases into the Potomac. Nice and neat—a late-night gin-mill solution.

But Nixon? The darling of Republicans, Rotarians, 4-H Clubs, Billy Graham, Lester Lanin, and Midwesterners who belt the Bible more than the bottle. A man who dresses his Marine Honor Guard like a Prussian contingent of the Gay Liberation Front, the daddy of Julie, the father-in-law of David, the overseer of a romance so publicly icky it should have been packaged by Schrafft's.

This man now is the champion of a bunch of men who would drink anything that isn't nailed down, screw anything that would stand still long enough, and, like Sky Masterson, bet on the outcome of two raindrops racing down a windowpane. It seems unbelievable, but then there is that thing that sociologists term upward mobility. It's what the Irish call lace curtain, or what the immigrant parents of the working class refer to as losing the smell of the boat. To be anonymous, to walk among the better-educated white-collar workers as an equal, not a mick, a wop, or a polack laborer. The impossible dream that started so long ago on Ellis Island, the first step on the way to joining the All-American Club.

Thus Nixon. A man without accent, smell, or definable origin. Hatched in the only place truly devoid of European influence in America—Southern California. The class debater of Whittier College, the bench warmer for the football team (oh, the humility of it all), a man who thinks Knott's Berry Farm is really the harvest of the American Dream. (Indeed, he launched his 1960 Presidential campaign on that site.)

And I'm sure Nixon understands the hard hat who has fled to the suburbs, who cherishes his split-level or ranch house, who predominantly sends his kids to parochial school (most East Coast construction unions are Catholic, and Nixon's Irish descent and hard-line anti-Communism always have been attractive to them), and takes his action and suds at the Melody Lane, bowling a couple of frames on Friday night. This is easy to explain because this man would be Nixon without the majesty of his office.

But what about the others, the ones still living in the old ethnic neighborhoods in the cities, who make up such a large part of the work force? These are men who on Friday might heist only balls in ounce glasses and spend Saturday mornings over the *Morning Telegraph*. Yet they are for Nixon, even though their life-styles conflict like Andy Hardy and the Wild Bunch.

So for the President's edification, I would like to introduce him to Joseph Noonan Taylor, hard hat.

Joe Taylor is a thirty-nine-year-old steamfitter, a member of Local 638 of the Building Trades Council, whose president, Peter Brennan, presented President Nixon with an honorary hard hat at a recent White House ceremony. Taylor was born in the Red Hook section of Brooklyn and grew up during the heyday of Brooklyn's fabled gang wars. For years, he ran one of the toughest gangs in South Brooklyn, the Tigers, a feat that required not only toughness and daring, but a touch of tactical genius, since most of the rumbles took place in the green expanse of Prospect

Park. So if one were looking for a metaphor for working-class royalty, Taylor in the romantic mind perhaps could be looked on as a Henry V in pegged pants. Gang warring precluded the SDS, since a lot of terrorism and hit-and-run tactics were employed. But usually, these confrontations were of a territorial nature: an invasion of turf by the enemy or the usurping of one of the Tigers' broads. And since Taylor was a warlord, there were the fights of honor—one on one, their best against your best. Curbside chivalry.

Taylor attended Manual Training High School, an educational enclave that in those days was most noted for the manufacture of esthetic zip guns. He dropped out of school in his senior year, joined the Army, and was sent to Germany, where he completed his schooling and matriculated in what he did best—fighting. He boxed as a middleweight, working his way up in the ratings until he got a shot at the Army European championship, which he lost.

Today the middleweight body has aged into a heavyweight's, and Taylor's face is a record of a good offense and a dubious defense. The face, like ex-middleweight champion Joey Giardello's, is a masterpiece of a brawler's mug. The network of scars is as intricately woven as Spanish lace, and his nose reminds one of a perplexed traveler seeking directions. But like many such faces that have traveled the beaten path, it is a road map of humanity, blending gentleness and humor with the scars. He is affectionately known to his friends as Pug.

After his noncombat hitch in the Army, Taylor went to work loading grain in ships along the New York and New Jersey waterfronts. The grain handlers' local was an Irish father-and-son local (and "cock cousins from the other side"—greenhorns), and the characters who worked at this dangerous trade were mostly lusty and ribald. Taylor's father, Big Joe (so named for his peanut size in comparison to his son), worked the grain for a decade with my father, who had been the local's president years before the junior Taylor went to work there.

It was in 1956, after my own stint in the Army in Germany, that I met Pug Taylor. By this time Taylor was a Brooklyn street legend to rival Willie "the Actor" Sutton since both often received credit for brawls and capers they didn't know had taken place. Like most of us who came of age in the fifties, he showed no sign of even benign patriotism, except for our usual drinking in the American Legion post on Sunday mornings before the bars legally opened or for our admiration of the cult of the "regular guy." Mainly, we were active in the areas of hard work, beer guzzling, and gambling, plus occasionally indulging in that rarity of all rarities, that Halley's Comet of the fifties, a "loose woman."

In those days Taylor was the king of a bucket of blood called the Caton Inn where one was visually weighed in at the door to be placed in one's proper weight division. Georgia Gibbs heply sang "Dance with Me, Henry" on a sluttishly made-up jukebox, and there was an outside chance to grab a bouffanted comet by the tail. Sociologically, the blacks were not yet a threat, and bigotry was reserved for "kikes" and the most venomous Valentines for "the wops."

But for all the nasty trappings of the time, Taylor was neither a thug nor a bully. He was too busy contributing support to a household which had ten mouths to feed, and like all men who are truly tough, bullying was foreign to his nature. On the docks he good-naturedly endured the name Quasimodo, because of his scrambled features, and was the butt of many a mean joke, such as having a bucket of water dumped on his head down in the hatch from the height of thirty feet above on the main deck or the theft of his hidden cache of beer, the latter a sacrilege that insulted Irish heaven itself.

Indeed, I saw him fight only twice—once against his will when a drunken fellow worker taunted him mercilessly, and he tried unsuccessfully to beg off because he knew his protagonist had a plate in his head as the result of a war injury. It was only when he was struck that he hit back, using just enough force to get the job done, a strategy that seems to escape the man in the White House he now vociferously supports. Another time, someone saw this gentleness as a trace of punk in the aging warrior, and at a union meeting he accused the old-timers of dogging work, including Pug's father by name in the dog category. With a left hand so sweet and economical it could have fitted into a watch pocket, Taylor deposited "the Johnny-come-lately" unconscious across a desk where an official was intoning the Lord's Prayer for brotherhood among our union members.

Ten years ago the grain-handling business died in the Port of New York, and Pug and I parted company. He went to work in the construction trades, and I on to other dock jobs and finally to writing. Other differences occurred: His crew cut remained the same, while my hair grew longer. Time changed our early political stance: His views began to lean to starboard, mine to port. But we never lost touch. An accidental meeting in the old neighborhood or frequent run-ins on Saturday afternoons at Aqueduct Racetrack, where he would jokingly chide me for writing "for those fuckin' Communist newspapers," and I him for his latest beery affectation, drinking Miller High Life. But, mainly, like Sam Peckinpah's cowboys lamenting the coming of the horseless carriage, we reminisced about the old days when men were . . . : about the time on an Italian liner when Jackie "Scat" Whalen thought he had discovered some "great Italian white table wine" that turned out to be cruets of table vinegar, which we found out when we had drunk it all. It resulted in the worst dysentery disaster north of Mexico City. Or when Lulu Fleming, incensed at being fired for drunkenness on the job, tried to chop the breast line securing the mothball ship on which we were working with a fire ax, hoping to set a scurvy crew and its dead ship adrift in the Hudson. And there was little Mickey McLaughlin, a "ratter" whose timeless body scampered about the holds of ships, shovel in hand hurling-stick style, trying to swat bloated river rats to their eternal goal. Old-timers swore with gleeful piety that once they had attended his wake years before only to find him a week later in a shape-up.

And how many more: Salty Murphy, who was arrested for swimming with the seals in the Prospect Park Zoo at four o'clock in the morning, emitting what he claimed was a bull seal's mating call. Or Johnny "Woodenhead" Regan, who could filibuster a meeting hall better than Everett Dirksen. And of course, our gay stevedore, who is the only longshoreman on record to have his nose bobbed at Tough Tony Anastasia's ILA clinic on Court Street in Brooklyn.

It was a time when political and sexual bent shaped up behind the only thing that mattered in the working-class canon—could you put out the hatch? Now, all of us—older, more bitter, screwed from the left and the right—find the only safe harbor in reverie. Chronologically, we still are young, but politically battered and suspicious of each other's best intentions. So when we meet, all we can do is return to those thrilling days of yesteryear when, like nautical cowboys, we rode the waves together.

Today, when Taylor talks, he is conscious of his and his trade's newfound prominence. His words are no longer emotional but measured. He has a "public image." Reporters and TV crews are no more strangers who only seek the opinions of the exalted. He is aware that silent America is listening. A racial epithet will sneak into his speech only by accident, not by design. If what he is saying has repressive overtones, he tries to temper it with a judicial, fair, what's-good-for-America flavor. In short, he talks Nixonese.

And in this respect, he's no mean politician. Example: "There is nothing wrong with long hair," pausing to smile; "One of our greatest patriots, Nathan Hale, had long hair." Or the question of pot versus booze: "If dope is better for you than booze, how come they arrest pushers, not bartenders?" Agnew would get a standing ovation in every American Legion hall for such logic.

Taylor contends that he did not take any part in the beating of the high school kids during the Kent State Four Memorial service which took place on Wall Street and at City Hall. "I have kids in high school, and I wouldn't want a grown man hitting them. I don't beat up on fifteen-year-olds, but I'll tell you I wouldn't take shit from a college student. What's the difference between them and some twenty-one-year-old guy who walks into a bar and spits in your face? What would you do? I'd

147

knock 'im on his ass." Taylor insists, however, that he would not hit anyone merely for demonstrating: "That's their right, but spitting on our flag or burning it is something else. I did my time for that flag, and if someone spits on it, I'll break him up."

Taylor is separated from his wife, who has custody of their four children, another fact that doesn't fit the Nixon image of the *Saturday Evening Post* father in his blue work overalls with his aproned wife and his well-scrubbed brood. But most of the men with whom he works have remained married, not always out of passion, but in the parochial canon "for the good of the children." Others like Taylor, who live apart, lead the life of the proletarian playboy: boozing and wenching in hard-ass saloons with Saturday sojourns at the track, and they see no irony in their President's vision of them as the "real Americans."

In fairness to Taylor (and to most of the others in this situation), he takes an active interest in his children and proudly brags that they go to Catholic schools and attend church, though, in his words, "I haven't been inside a church for years except for the essentials—a wedding, a funeral, or a christening. I'm just good for special occasions." Occasions, I might add, that our mutual experience taught us had higher potential for sinning than saving. At these gatherings, "one's cup runneth over" but not in the sense Nixon's ball park belter, that Sultan of Salvation, the Reverend Billy Graham, preaches.

The point to be understood is that Pug Taylor and many workingmen are not some strange social phenomenon. They are baffling to mid-Americans who think all residents of big cities are the slick, urbane images they see at the drive-ins or, in their worst fantasies, pot-puffing miscegenationists. But they also are baffling to liberal, polished think-tankers, who can't believe them because none of their friends "thinks that way" or because they snobbishly view them as Neanderthals who go around buying war bonds and clubbing minority groups.

The fact is that inside every major American city are huge pockets of people still living in old ethnic neighborhoods whose life-styles might conflict, but whose ideologies coincide with the people of rural Kansas and Oklahoma. The pavement proletarians and the rural rotarians have in common a strong ethnic sense that takes in community, family, and blind patriotism. It is this ethnic coalition that Kevin Phillips explores in his book *The Emerging Republican Majority*.

Vice President Agnew garnered the same kind of admiration for attacking the New York *Times* and *Post* in many parts of Brooklyn and Queens (and virtually all of Staten Island) that he received in Houston.

The label "liberal" is spat out more venomously in these parts of the city than "Communist" (not really much in urban vogue anymore) or "nigger." The reasons are many. Working-class areas, not Manhattan's chic liberal fortress, are the first to be hit by integration and the violent problems it brings. When the economy falters, the building trades, the docks, and the factories feel it first and, sadly, hardest, since most working-class families' bucket got a hole in it for that rainy day.

And there is the war. Who goes? Surely the working class is at fault for failing to challenge an adventure that is robbing them both of their hard-earned dollars and their only true treasure, their children. But it's a tragic cycle—the neighborhood kids go away and don't return; and when blood is spilled in this culture, you revenge, not reassess. As one worker said: "Our kids are getting their asses shot off, and a bunch of fucking college punks with deferments are protesting." The stain of blood is thicker than not only water, but also well-meaning words.

How politically oriented is the hard hat (or worker) in terms of general activity in the electoral process? Well, luckily for Nixon, on the whole they are a hell of a lot more energetic than Taylor. "I've never voted in my life," he says. "They're not getting me on any fucking jury list."

But Pug admits his fellow workers have substantially higher marks in citizenship. "I would say about ninety percent of the guys on the job vote," he commented. However, his mathematics could be suspect, since his co-worker and buddy sitting next to him said he hadn't voted either.

Voting rolls would show that most of these men, if they voted at all, have been lukewarm Democrats following the old voting allegiance of their fathers. The real impetus for change at the polls was the emergence of Barry Goldwater nationally and William F. Buckley, Jr., in New York, though the latter has national stature as a spokesman for the conservative point of view. Once again, there seems to be a dichotomy. Goldwater for sure: tough, lean, shooting straight from the hip. But Buckley is another matter. It would seem he would be as popular with the working class in politics as George Sanders would be to them onscreen: goosy eyebrows, using a pencil as a sugar tit, speaking in tones so embalmed with ennui they could only enchant the Antonionis of America. In truth, Buckley would be the kind of kid who would have to circumvent the neighborhoods which now adore him to get home safely from school. But, perversely, this is his magic. The working class has found a verbal gun to shoot back at the intellectuals, the Jews, the Arthur Schlesinger, Jrs., the John Lindsays, and the Liberal Party, whose collected chants have fallen like a dirge on their ears.

There are strains of substance in their counterrevolution. Any lament from them about the decline of their neighborhoods or schools or the rise in welfare costs has been construed as racial invective. And, in the irony of all ironies, many liberal officials have set up task forces to find out "what they want." In Mississippi, they color their *they* darker. So a new force has been born, one which Joe Taylor relates to emotionally, but not electorally.

But this does not mean Joe Taylor hasn't opinions on all questions foreign and domestic. To him, all Presidents must be respected, and he finds no real distinction in the men who have held that office, not even an ould sod brother like John Kennedy. "You've just got to back the President of the United States," he declares. How far this backing goes depends on the issues. At home, Taylor comes across rather dovishly, though one suspects his new social standing has tamed "the Tiger" in him.

Taylor admits that his oldest daughter (age seventeen) has never attended a demonstration of any sort but insists he would not stop her "if she really believed it was morally right," though he adds that the protest would have to meet his criteria of civility and "not be a madhouse with rioting." Like most workingmen, he can't understand why college students challenge officialdom in any quarter. This, too, is gospel among his class—regardless of conflict with parents, church, elected officials, college administrators, they are the people who wear the hats, and respect must be rendered: "You can't tell me these kids are not being taught by people smarter than them. Who are they to take over a building by mob rule?" Who are they, indeed?

Haven't the Pug Taylors of the world been working at tough, dirty jobs for decades just to obtain a foothold in these institutions for their children, so they won't have to follow in the dreary footsteps of their fathers? And upward mobility doesn't mean having your child matriculate on the roof of a college building.

Though he is adamantly against the use of drugs, Taylor's background has taught him it is not a college or hippie phenomenon: "Twenty years ago, some of the kids I grew up with took drugs. What's the difference who gets hooked on junk—poor kids, black kids, rich kids? It's just bad."

He also claims he was not among the hard hats carrying signs lettered "Lindsay is a faggot" or "Peaceniks are fags." "I only carried a flag," he explained. "I wouldn't say that about anyone." Yet while we were talking in a Greenwich Village pub with many longhairs and beards populating the bar, he asked in a relaxed moment: "This is a big fairy hangout, isn't it?" The unpublic Pug Taylor.

Since he and his co-workers have become noticeable spokesmen, Taylor has given thought to many of our problems. Though he feels draft dodgers should be jailed, he would allow those draftees opposing the war to enter the Army and be stationed in noncombat zones. But on further questioning, one found this "humane" position had been reached through a process known as street smarts: "I wouldn't want one of them fighting alongside me anyway. They'd punk out, and that's the quickest way to get yourself killed."

150

And what about the protesters' claim that any compliance with the draft even in a peaceful capacity is "abetting the war"? Here the aging Pug flashed some nimble footwork: "If these kids buy cigarettes, should they be charged with abetting lung cancer?" A devout Spirologician.

Indeed, Taylor has mastered many homilies that would do the Vice President proud, but on reflection this is not so strange. Hasn't Agnew muckishly mimicked his more mannered mentor, Buckley? "Effete snobs," "Charlatans of peace and freedom," "Tomentose exhibitionists?" A strange ideological war is taking place here: The revolutionists rely on the quotations of Chairman Mao, and the counterrevolutionists on a thesaurus.

When Taylor is challenged about racial bias in his union (the building trades is primarily a father-and-son union), his response is that the ring around everything is rosy as the ins are so wont to say. "To be a lawyer, you have to pass a bar exam, right? To be a doctor, you have to pass a test, right? Everything takes time. These people can't expect everything overnight. It took me eight years to get my book while I worked under a permit."

Of course, what is missing is that many outsiders would be delighted to get a work permit since the pay received is union scale. And according to many builders, many more of these permits should be opened up, since New York City is going through one of the largest building booms in a decade. The stock answer to this is that the union doesn't want to overload its ranks (though with work permits they wouldn't), because they don't want to have massive layoffs when a slack occurs. Ring around it goes.

If at home there are hints at mercy, Taylor would export only mayhem abroad: "There is no good in withdrawing. We'll only lose face. We can't worry about China." The solution? "I think we should blow the balls off them all."

So stand or so straddle the Pug Taylors these days. The working class are the dangling men in our society: abused on the left and used on the right. One side spits on their flag; the other side shills them with it by draping it over the coffins of their children. How can men who have little more than their patriotism as entry fee in a power-stacked society say that their sons, their torchbearers who were going to carry their fathers' names to the Olympian heights of the American Dream, died for nothing? They can't. And why can't the other side try to communicate instead of caricature? It seems they don't want to.

The workingmen are now being patted by those they consider their betters, and they relish it regardless of the price. After years of limbo, the worker is having visions of the Establishment throne. Indeed, one worker carried a sign during the demonstrations, "God Bless the Establishment," praise for those who have picked their pockets for years.

More poignantly, another said as he was being showered by the capitalistic sperm of ticker tape: "This is the proudest day of my life." When you come from nowhere, it is a short trip to Nirvana.

So Richard Nixon, who has had to hustle all his life against big-money East Coast politicians who disdained him, has found a rapport with the workers who have spent their life beating the bill collectors. In a dark way, the President knows "What Makes the Silents Run."

But the sad thing the worker doesn't realize is though he finally has been allowed to play the game, he's getting no part of the action. He sacrifices his money, his chance for decent living conditions, and his children to the pot, but the same people do the dealing. The worker should remember the lesson of the gutter: The house always has the edge. Yet, that's the boobery of history—con men exist, because there always are willing marks.

Still, Joe Taylor wants in. But while his vision and aspirations are turned upward, he misses the cards being dealt from the bottom of the deck. And if the deck was passed to the liberal purists, one suspects Pug Taylor and his kind still would get a fast shuffle. Although they know they'll never hold the trump, they have the security with Nixon of knowing the buried card will be a spade.

Alas, everyone's answer seems to be retreat. The conservatives wax poetically about 1776; the Easy Riders pedal backward to the virgin land. It is that peculiar American schizophrenia—technically reaching for the stars while emotionally retrogressing to the unreachable outpost of social science fiction, our innocent past.

One can't blame Joe Taylor for wishing for "the good old days" of respect for flag and country, any more than one can indict Scott Fitzgerald for writing: "So we beat on, boats against the current, borne back ceaselessly into the past." Perhaps the reason this sentiment is so profound, why it attracts such disparate oarsmen, is that all of us pulling from our polarized port and starboard haven't the courage to look forward from the bow of our Ship of State.

Fall, 1970

Last Call to Cappy

A minor artist laid his larynx to rest this week. His work cannot be heard in a retrospective show unless one has an ear for the cosmos and can audit his nasal arias in the air that swirls around Aqueduct or Belmont

Park. His admirers have been legion for thirty-seven years, though his refrain has been the same. The man: Fred "Cappy" Capossela. His song: "It is NOW post time."

Of course, his artistry has appealed to a certain clientele—the punter, the plunger, the dreamer, the deadbeat, and the afflicted among those who follow the ponies. He has been the Tin Tonsil to the Jimmy Tomorrows of the world. And since I am a loyal legionnaire in that set, this is my last call to Cappy.

Small business, to be sure, in a world of corporate disasters; but then one shouldn't let pleasure pass without bidding adieu. These days the earth seems to be sitting shiva, so when one gets a chance to shake a leg and dance a jig, he should seize it. But why this man and why this sport?

I suppose I could intellectualize my love for horse racing by giving a leg up to Degas, Lautrec, Dufy; but that would be giving the reader a bum tip. When I was a fifteen-year-old Brooklyn kid and started to go to the track, I probably would have mistaken the names of that illustrious trio as the front line of the Montreal Canadiens hockey team.

It was the elegance in racing that attracted me, the sprint from the boredom of that particular hell called commonplace which was the enchantress. Years later, as an aspiring writer, I fell in love with another rube who flirted with blue lawns, green dock lights, and pastel shirts.

It was my oldest brother, Doc, who gave me my baptism by manure. The first horse I ever bet, Bottle of Ink, won and paid $19, which, in retrospect, has a rather nice, witchy touch. But Doc, like a gentleman golfer teaching a scruffy duffer, tutored me in equine etiquette: Any ass can win with grace. If you went racing with Doc, you learned how to lose a bet without a whine, how to spend like a sailor at the bar even though your bankroll had enlisted in the Salvation Army, and, most important, how to howl at disasters that the horseplayer's flesh is heir to. I still believe it was some murky metaphysician of a tout who started the singing of "Nearer My God to Thee," when the *Titanic* was taking its last gargle.

Fifteen years later, when my fortunes turned, I was assigned to write a piece for the New York *Times* on racing, and I took Doc to Belmont Park in the early-morning dawn. A beautiful, gentle world with "How Ya Do" manners, backstretch coffee laced with booze, and the best collection of legs outside a Busby Berkeley line. We sat sipping and talking to the late Eddie Neloy, whose talent as a trainer was exceeded only by his grace as a man.

Neloy took us over to one of the stalls to show us his great colt Buckpasser. Doc stared at the colt with the solemnity of a pastor viewing a full collection plate, and Neloy opened the stall door and said, "Go ahead in and pet him." Doc entered the stall with all the temerity of Humbert Humbert reconnoitering Lolita's sneaker and petted the great

153

colt's neck. He smiled a smile that beat the hell out of his years. A kid brother had finally paid for his lessons.

My racing partner now is one "Tommy Sugar" (his bookie's pet name for his prized punter), an Irishman who has the girth of one of the Budweiser Clydesdales. Sugar is a man of such singular sentiment he thinks Pegasus should have been given a urinalysis for his airborne performance.

This year he, my lady, and I traveled to Saratoga, the Lourdes of losers. Sugar, festooned in a white suit, looked like a cross between Diamond Jim and the Grand Kleagle. His stated intention was to bet a "yard" ($100) on the brilliant two-year-old filly Numbered Account. This struck me as being in character, but I was astounded when he commandeered our distaff member, with her camera, to the paddock before the race to take a photo of him with Numbered Account. As I looked on in amazement, the father of the bride patted his hair into place and, may Arnold Rothstein forgive him, straightened his tie! All that was missing was a tear and Guy Lombardo playing "Daddy's Little Girl."

Good times, indeed. But it's only accurate to call a fair chart. Many horseplayers are the most pathetic souls in Christendom. They moan, they lie ("I really gave the winner a shot, but I changed my mind at the last minute"), and they are some of the cheapest bastards I've ever encountered. I have had horseplayers ask me for 35 cents for a hot dog, so they would not have to break a dollar, because it was their betting money. But with the help of Lady Luck, I have managed for most of my betting career to avoid such deadbeats. As one studies "the Bible" (the *Morning Telegraph*), so he studies his racing companions—in search of class.

A chancy word that. Some have it; some don't. Class can be as elegant as an Astaire strut or as inelegant as Victor McLagen blowing his nose on the back of his hand. As Monsieur Baudelaire once instructed: "Harlots and Hunted have pleasures of their own to give. The Vulgar herd can never understand."

Through the years Cappy has been a continuance of class. So, when I heard he was to retire last week, I took a solo trip to the Big A to doff my lid for the last time. The portents weren't good. The Big A in December looks like the inside of Aida's tomb, and the players, bundled in winter coats, with watery eyes and noses, resemble a crew you would 86 from the White Rose. I made my way up to the announcer's perch atop the track to meet the man.

In a glass enclosure that looks like a flight deck from *Star Trek* (the universe being Queens) stood a short, natty man with a puffed-out parrot's stomach and breast. My first thought was that he looked like Walt Disney's Joe Carioca. On appraising the black suit, the white shirt and striped tie, and the black wing-tipped shoes, you realized he must be a

154

mean dancer at Italian weddings. Then the Voice spoke, and, by God, it was him, the chronicler of countless joys and miseries.

At sixty-nine he has that ambiguous quality of exhilarating and depressing the reporter. Exhilarating because of his ebullience, depressing because the reporter at his age seems older than his subject, and he still has thirty-five furlongs to catch up. Capossela's a stayer, Flaherty a sprinter.

But he is all I hoped that disembodied voice would be—generous, funny, and endlessly enthusiastic. Bloodlines: Brooklyn Italian; Training: Boy's High (a nice lack of formal schooling that warmed me); Track Record: a reporter for the old Brooklyn *Eagle,* turf editor for the New York *Evening Post,* a couple of seasons at bush tracks, and the Voice of New York Racing for thirty-one years.

Even recalling the Depression, when he was hustling $5 a day at Narragansett Park counting tickets, doesn't take the sparkle out of his voice. Only once all day does the voice falter, and that is when he mentions his departed wife. That, I suppose, is the price stayers have to pay. But that passes, the voice picks up again when we talk of the sport, the immortals: "Arcaro was the best jock I ever saw." "The two champions that impressed me most were Count Fleet and Kelso—they dominated their time." "In the eighty thousand races I've called, the greatest race ever was the Travers between Ridan and Jaipur. Two great horses going a mile and a quarter, noses apart, to the finish line. Unheard of." (Jaipur won.)

He lauded the men who spent millions unselfishly to build racing: "Joseph E. Widener, William C. DuPont." It is a voice capable of making immortals, a voice you would love to have eulogize you, because if any tonsils could sneak you under the Lord's wire, they are his.

But that wasn't what I had come for. I came to see him do it. Call a race. The bugle sounds, and the horses take the track. He signals for quiet and clears his throat, "Em-m, Mel, Em-m-Mel." He moves to the apex of his glass booth where the glass marries and juts out in a V. From the rear he looks like the conductor of a park band concert, no, more like a replica of one on a child's music box. He places a microphone around his neck and throws on the PA system. His pinkie, his baton, a dancer for sure: "The horses are *on* the track."

The PA system goes off, and it is time for Cappy to perform the occult. He doesn't memorize the horses by numbers, but by colors. Not too difficult if only primary colors were at stake, but cerises, turquoises, oranges, and hot pinks—a boutique that is going traveling on a forty-mile-per-hour merry-go-round.

"Purple, pink dots, pink dots, that's Social Spree, Social Spree is purple and pink. Turquoise, cerise, the cap is cerise, turquoise, cerise is Pagan Moon, Pagan Moon in the cerise cap." He has a ten-horse field down in four minutes flat, and he begins to chat and reminisce. The reporter worries. Won't this break his concentration for the calling of the race? "Not at all," the Voice replies. Such are the worries of mere mortals.

As the horses go to post, he runs down the field again. About a minute this time. He is at the podium now, the pinkie arched, the immortal lines —like "Come on up and see me sometime" and "Good night, Mrs. Calibash, wherever you are"—are about to be delivered. Up on tippy-toes, a pinkie downbeat the hopefuls' invocation: "It is *now* post time." He pulls off the whole caper without a hitch.

He confesses his mind goes blank after every race. "I couldn't tell you who won the last one. When my son was a child, he once said, 'My father is the best forgetter of anyone!' " Later he disproves this, when he recites about twenty lines of a poem he learned when he was nine years old. "I hated poetry, but in school they made me memorize that, and I've never forgotten it. People look at me and wonder, What the hell kind of mind does this guy have?"

So Cappy is off to write his memoirs, entitled what else? He will cut a record re-creating the greatest races of the century and tend his stamp collection. But he says he will be at Saratoga next August as a fan and a bettor. He says he's never bet a race that he called: "Dammit, I'd be looking for my silks, and probably no one else would get a call." Why the end? "God has been good to me. I've never missed a day's work because of illness and never suffered laryngitis. I don't want to push the Lord." Class turf people always sense when champions should be sent out to pasture.

From now on, his post will be handled by Dave Johnson, a thirty-year-old caller who worked the Midwest circuit and Hialeah. Mr. Johnson's method of calling? Well, he was an American history major, so he uses picture association. "It's a trick I learned when I had to memorize the points of the Yalta Conference and the NATO Treaty." Calling the fourth race of the day, he gave me this lesson: "My Turn To, I was on line at the bank this morning, and my turn was coming. Rumbottom in green silks reminds me of a green Bacardi bottle. Big Grin reminds me of a stripper I saw with a big grin. Simple Simon in a blue cap, that's what Simple Simon wore to the fair, a blue cap." Racing fans, the young man executed this perverse history lesson flawlessly. It was as if Houdini had a son.

And, since we are dealing in the occult, I have the suspicion that last Wednesday may not be Cappy's last call. I have kicked with cats who wouldn't stir at the sound of Gabriel's horn on Judgment Day, but if Cappy's voice came across the void announcing, "It is *now* post time," they would be jockeying for post position to run the race of their raunchy lives.

December 23, 1971

Running Against His Own Image

O, it offends me to the soul to hear a robustious periwig-pated fellow tear a passion to tatters, to very rags, to split the ears of the ground-lings, who for the most part are capable of nothing but inexplicable dumb-shows and noise.

—From Hamlet's speech to the players

What do they expect me to do? Come on like Al Jolson?

—EUGENE McCARTHY, 1972

Ay, there's the rub, it seems, between Eugene McCarthy and many of his critics on the left. Tatter-tearing has come to signify "soul," "heart," "gut," "empathy." One must understand the liberal mind: Demagoguery is as necessary to it as a pacifier to a colicky child. So how will Gene McCarthy fare this time around in his quest for the Presidency?

Already he has been passed over in some quarters as "a retread," accused of dealing in "the politics of necrophilia" (1968), and characterized as a man who appealed to the "intellectuals," a charge that seems to smack more of Joe Goebbels than Joe Hill.

So in a sense McCarthy is not running against the other Democratic primary contenders but against his own image or, to be more accurate, his image as conceived by his critics. He also is running against the Kennedy wing of his party, which seems to hate him more than Hubert Humphrey.

But this is understandable since 1968 was an affair of the heart wherein emotions eradicated logic. And old political passions, like old lovers, remain simmering on the back burner of the psyche.

The fact is that nobody wanted McCarthy in 1968 (myself included). We all had the central drama plotted out in our minds: Bobby Kennedy would challenge Lyndon Johnson. When that failed to happen, it was like going to a play you had been longing to see, but when you opened the playbill, a slip of white paper fell out, noting that the lead was to be replaced by the standby for this performance. The drama was the same, but could some Midwestern, straw-hat circuit understudy strut to it?

It was unlikely, the whole setting was wrong. The sixties was the decade in which the crotch conquered the cranium, and on first soundings McCarthy was as heady as Yorick's skull. But, in Shubert Alley tradition, the new kid turned out socko, and when the star decided to render a turn, some wanted the replacement to relinquish his role, others wanted to give McCarthy an exclusive run-of-the-campaign contract. So go affairs of the heart.

A counterfeit had stolen the dream, and bitterness on both sides grew. Kennedy and McCarthy advocates engaged in senseless savagery, only to be mortified by the TV debate in California which revealed both men taking practically identical positions on the issues. Then the bloody curtain fell in Los Angeles and was raised again in Chicago. And the left once again engaged in what it does best—devouring its own.

Since that emotional bender, I have read the most ludicrous charges leveled against McCarthy. Some examples: He was a quitter who didn't want the Presidency; he was directly responsible for Richard Nixon; he had no empathy for minorities (showing blatant disregard of his civil rights record). My favorite was when writers charged him with being "too egotistical" for having said that he appealed to the more educated, a remark he claims to have delivered in jest. Jest aside, the real joke here is a writer faulting anyone for possessing a large ego.

But did the Senator dog it, chuck it when he had a chance to be President? He stiffens in the back of the limousine en route to a campaign stop: "Some of the stuff written about my personality has been acceptable to me (parts of Jeremy Larner's book *Nobody Knows*), but this other business about me not trying is bullshit. When Bobby was killed in Los Angeles, it was the end for us. That summer was an exercise in self-abasement. With Bobby gone, we couldn't even pass the minority plank on Vietnam. Why the hell don't they attack the system that allows this to happen contrary to people's wishes?"

He went on to talk about how Pennsylvania gave Humphrey the votes necessary to guarantee the nomination—a state he had carried in a non-binding primary by over a half million votes. "The system is what needs to be attacked."

There is a subtle irony here—a candidate who is more cynical about the system than his supporters, even though they are always denouncing it. It was, after all, his critics who said he should have tried to forge ties with big labor, Mayor Daley, and state committeemen. And that's also understandable, because McCarthy was the surrogate of their dream. But could he have pulled it off?

Tom Wicker wrote in the New York *Times* that if Bobby had lived even he couldn't have gotten the nomination. It was a *fait accompli* for Humphrey. When one thinks of the energies expended by Kennedy and McCarthy across the land, then sees the image of Humphrey sitting in the countinghouse counting all the delegates, it's hard to belittle Wicker's prognosis. I, for one, never thought Lyndon Johnson had stepped down to allow either a McCarthy or a Kennedy to rewrite the history of his administration.

Sometimes what passes for cynicism are simply elementary lessons in life. But dreams die hard, and memory is an unrelenting shamus that dogs our days.

McCarthy's first stop of the evening was Charles Monaghan's house in the Park Slope area of Brooklyn. Monaghan is, in no particular order, the editor of *Book World,* president of the local political club (Central Brooklyn Independent Democrats), and a Jeffersonian maven of local democracy. The meeting room was filled with many who had marched for McCarthy in 1968.

McCarthy's entrance was typical of him. He doesn't seize a room but enters with the deference of a dinner guest who has been invited to fill out the table. He was given a vodka martini on request, then engaged a group in conversation about the Catholics (himself included) who had "adopted" Chinese babies by proxy through sending donations to missionaries. He concluded the discourse by wondering if the church knew how many Communists they had had a hand in adopting.

His banter warmed the crowd and the candidate, the martini working as a plenary indulgence. He seemed to circulate better than he had in 1968, and his advance man was eager to push the point by citing his busy schedule for that day: numerous radio interviews, meetings with various political groups, and a two-hour interview with the *Amsterdam News.* Handshaking and social amenities took about a half hour; then it was time for him to sing for his supper, in this case as at all political gatherings, a drink and a pig-in-a-blanket.

He briefly ran down his record: his early stand on civil rights, his call for a family assistance plan and a guaranteed income, his singular stand in 1968 on amnesty for draft resisters, and his challenge to Johnson and the war. He said he didn't like speaking formally and found it an ineffective format, so he threw the floor open to questions.

The gathering was largely Catholic, so his sins were the first order of business: "Why did you vote against Teddy for Senate whip?"

McCarthy answered that he didn't know what the flap was about the position of whip. "When the Democrats first put up Russell Long, I was against him, and everyone told me it was a meaningless issue. Look, the whip position has all the significance of the property room manager of a football team. Let's talk about something that matters. The Presidency of the United States." Once again, it was a question of who had more doubts about the system—audience or candidate?

The next questioner asked why he had given up his seat on the Foreign Relations Committee. "If I stayed, the committee would have added Gale McGee and two Republicans. With me dropping off, we got McGee and one Republican. You might say we won, since we lost a Republican." That lovely, perverse turn left the assembled bedazzled.

Then there was the nightmare question, delivered with the solemnity of a keynoter from Forest Lawn: "Senator, you talk of a fourth party. In fact, wouldn't that assure the election of Richard Nixon?"

"The question is not the defeat of Richard Nixon in 1972," McCarthy responded. "That is almost certain. The question is not who will be elected President, but rather the principles, the policies, and the programs to which the next President is committed before the election. Besides, in 1968, the polls showed that I was the only candidate who could defeat Richard Nixon. I was leading him by five points, and the party decided to nominate Humphrey. I ask you, *who* is irresponsible? If that's the grounds they want to argue on, I guess we can be irresponsible this time around." His audience, somewhat titillated by its collective irresponsibility, gave the Senator and themselves a rousing hand.

His exit was perfect. A Mr. Interlocutor fed Mr. Bones this line: "Why are you so late in announcing?"

"I'm not late announcing. In fact, I was the first to declare," McCarthy said. "I announced in Grant Park the night they nominated Humphrey. I told the people in the park I would never allow them to be taken in again by the politics of 1968. I said I would never lead a movement under the current system where the people were humiliated. I said then we would have to change the politics of 1972. And when I was in Grant Park, Hubert Humphrey was at the convention hall, standing on the stage with George McGovern on his left and Edmund Muskie on his right. Now, I don't know if there is any Scriptural significance in that." The audience knew it was out of its parish—nobody in politics pitches a meaner Bible than Gene McCarthy.

The last stop of the evening was in the Macedonian Church in Queens. The meeting was held in the church's gymnasium, no deterrent to a man who loves to use sports metaphors. A crowd of about 300 gave him a standing ovation when he came in.

He talked about how he had refused to sign a loyalty oath that he was not a Communist requested by the Illinois Secretary of State when he filed his petitions for the Illinois primary. "Now, as far as I know, the other candidates all agreed to sign the loyalty oath. This might not seem like a big thing to you, but this is the kind of thinking that has warped politics for twenty years in this country. How can we ask schoolteachers and those seeking public housing not to sign such a document, when their public officials bow to this kind of pressure? There is a principle here."

Mark him well. This is an issue that only a candidate of McCarthy's individuality would dare challenge. It's the same kind of courage that led him to debate Joe McCarthy in 1952, when he was a young Congressman (because better-known figures all refused), and moved him against Johnson in New Hampshire in 1968 (no other takers there either), and which led him to be the first major figure to campaign against Frank Rizzo in Philadelphia in 1971. There is a principle here.

There is a matter of style, too. McCarthy's quiet demeanor allows him to put forth radical thoughts in an acceptable manner. It's a neat political hat trick and not one to be demeaned.

When asked in Queens, a borough which thinks a Weatherman is Tex Antoine, whether he would free political prisoners, he replied that he would but added: "Half the people in jail in this country should be released, because they shouldn't be there in the first place, or they have been in too long."

When the applause became too emotional, he joked his way out of it: "Every year Lester Maddox releases one hundred people for Christmas. Nixon released only two—what grace!"

And within the shadow of Forest Hills he not only supported integrated housing but repeated what he had said in 1968: "We can't go on glorifying or perpetuating the ghettos. We not only have to have decent housing in the cities but also open up the suburbs."

McCarthy seems sterner this time around. He warns his audiences that in 1972 "we're going to have to deal in personalities." One suspects this is a threat aimed at Hubert Humphrey, since McCarthy said he could and would support a McGovern or a Lindsay; in fact, he would run joint delegate slates with them.

And he can get tough with a questioner who asks him if he has "empathy for minorities." "In an interview in *Playboy,*" he replied, pausing slightly to let the image of the nouveau riche skin magazine sink in, "George McGovern said he thought I was lacking empathy. I don't know how a man can talk about empathy. It's a matter of the spirit. And I doubt if McGovern can see my spirit unless it smokes. So I suggest you look at my record. In 1951 I was the one who brought up the plight of the migrant workers in Congress. I introduced a bill to include the mentally ill in Medicare. I wanted a resolution passed that the National Guard should not carry live ammunition unless the governor of the state concerned gets permission from the President. I don't think there are a lot of votes to be gathered from such proposals. Please—just study my record."

Nor, one can add, are there many votes to be gained from his urging to investigate the CIA and the military and to fire J. Edgar Hoover.

Finally, someone asked about the issue that had moved him into the national arena. How would he end the war?

With a quixotic candor you had to believe, he said: "I would ask the Pentagon to send me a general who knows how to disengage, an admiral who knows how to load ships in foreign countries, and an Air Force man who can take bombs off a plane—if the Pentagon could find one in two or three days." With a mixture of laughter and applause, he left to another standing ovation.

I, for one, would welcome a President with such wit. If we had the ability to laugh at our national follies, I doubt we would be in our current predicament. Also, I wouldn't mind a man whose aberration is poetry, since that art is a deliberate one and contemplation is not a flaw in a statesman.

But for those who prefer the "gut," it might be well to remember that what McCarthy did in 1968 took not only guts but a bit of the lower region of the anatomy as well. As far as his Celtic skepticism is concerned, well, the earth has always been closer to Samuel Beckett's "charnel house" then to Erich Segal's *Love Story*.

Thus, once again, he has put it to his party to reform itself, and one doubts if the result this time around will be any different. But it was he who said they always kill the messenger who brings bad news, and it was he who asked his party not to allow Adlai Stevenson to become a prophet without honor in his own party. So this is understandable, too.

With his quiet speech it is doubtful if he can catch the conscience of his own party, never mind the king. One waits.

But it would be shameful if his conscience was ignored, for in the end the sad song that would be piped would be worthy of a dark Irish poet: "The party's over. It's time to call it a day."

January 27, 1972

The Apocryphal Armenian

If you accept Holden Caulfield's critical canon that there are certain writers you would like to dial up for a chat, then over the years William Saroyan would have diminished my bankroll by dimes. Dostoevsky is more suited to a lengthy night letter and Samuel Beckett to a telegram—not exceeding the prescribed number of words.

But Saroyan, the hotshot drummer for life, the habitué of saloons and racetracks, the singer of love's old sweet song, is a man I have always felt was open to casual interruption. It is an assumption based on the fact that boozers have been known (at least onstage) to talk to six-foot white rabbits, and horseplayers will talk to anyone who would listen to them, if the riders on the racetrack special to Aqueduct are any indicator.

So awhile back, standing in a bar, I got my chance to talk to Saroyan on the phone. The conversation was arranged by his actor friend Val Avery who is also Armenian (they seem to be as rare as six-foot white rabbits). I said, "Hello, Mr. Saroyan," and he said, "Hello, Mr. Flaherty," and he asked me where I lived, and I said, "Greenwich Village," and Saroyan,

162

sounding like Joe in *The Time of Your Life,* said: "You live in a lovely part of the world."

In five minutes I tried to cover his literary career and told him I would like to meet him; but he was Paris-bound, so we both said we hoped to meet soon. Daring young men must be caught on the fly.

Then, a couple of weeks ago, I received a call from his publisher, Praeger, inviting me to attend a luncheon to honor his new book, *Places Where I've Done Time.* The day before the shindig I bet a two-year-old maiden to get into the swing of things, and the horse won and paid $17.60, so I knew we would have plenty to talk about.

Saroyan stood by a small bar set up in an upstairs room at the Brussels, looking like a grand old sea lion. He professed to be slowing down lately, having given up gambling for some unstated reason (probably he is just resting on his laurels) and also cigarettes and whiskey, because of an ulcer. He claimed that most of the stories spread about him were "apocryphal." One reasoned that this newfound moderation had to do with the title of one of his later collections of stories, *I Used to Believe I Had Forever, Now I'm Not So Sure.* But before becoming grim about his future, I remembered he had said, "Not *So* Sure."

The many stories, apocryphal or not, fit the writer and his work. Some I have read in an excellent reminiscence of Saroyan by Budd Schulberg, some I swear I read by Saroyan himself, and others I'm sure I've concocted myself. Little matter. Fancy is for the nocturnal of the world; fact is for those who think a worm is a just reward for rising early.

Saroyan's gambling has been the source of many of these legends. There was the time when he was working as a screenwriter for Budd's father, B. P. Schulberg, the producer, and felt guilty about the way he was earning his keep, so he took all the money he had earned in that period ($10,000) to the racetrack.

The story has it that Saroyan was about to drop the whole bundle on a horse when an old man (Saroyan's world has always seemed to be a planet without a middle; youth and old age are the only boundaries that matter) touted him onto another horse. Saroyan then was still a struggling writer, but with deference to one who had run more furlongs than he had himself he switched his 10 G's to the old man's choice. When the horses hit the stretch, the old man's was winning easily, but suddenly he faltered, then fell, and Saroyan's original choice went on to win the race. When the disconsolate old-timer approached Saroyan, the author simply put a hand on his shoulder and told him not to be sad because, after all, his horse had truly been the best horse in the race.

According to Schulberg, he never heard him mention that $10,000 again. Apocryphal or not, when I think of the Medea-like wails I have heard over a blown deuce, Saroyan deserves a big edge in class.

But my favorite story is the one about how Saroyan, losing $50,000 in a casino, drunkenly jumped on top of one of the tables and shouted: "I don't care what Freud says, *I want to win!*"

For anyone who has ever seen more in gambling than the multiplication of dollars and has had to endure the pronouncements of preachers and psychologists, that 1 & 1A entry of limitations on the spirit, his remark stands like a rock on which a plunger could build his church.

But besides the stories, I was fascinated with his work. It is now fashionable to dismiss Saroyan as a Johnny-one-note, a sentimentalist. But then again, Saroyan himself has said that to be a human being is to be sentimental. It has often baffled me as to why "dark" writing is received with so much reverence, while wit and fancy are cavalierly dismissed. After all, no dark writer is ever dark enough since none is able to tell you what being dead is like, yet a man of wit has no such boundary. If the critical essence of "seriousness" is the tomb, one should work once a year on Halloween in Harry Houdini's old house, waiting for a knock under the table, rather than review books.

But the sad part is that most people have misread Saroyan because he has always dealt with this subject. He admitted that such a critical approach confounds him. "It was always there," he said, "in all my work. Joy and death."

The evidence bears him out. The child in *The Human Comedy* indicts his brother for dying when he didn't have to. *Don't Go Away Mad* is set in a cancer ward; and in *My Heart Is in the Highlands* death is given one of the most humorous kicks in its dusty pants ever delivered on a stage.

An old man who claims to be "the greatest Shakespearean actor who ever lived" is the guest of an itinerant poet and his son. The old man, who is in ill health, finally decides near the end of the play to brook the Bard for the first time. He does Lear's death scene and, at its conclusion, dies. One shudders at such a bathetic scene, until the poet, looking matter-of-factly at the corpse, states that the old man really was the greatest Shakespearean actor in the world.

In a honey of a novel, *Rock Wagram* (one wishes it would be reissued), Saroyan depicts the death of his grandfather. The old man is dying, and he wishes for a melon, a perfect melon. However, there is only one melon in the cellar, and his wife dutifully trudges down to get it. But it is not the melon the old man had in mind, and he summons her to get another. The old woman repeatedly goes down to the cellar and each time fetches back the same melon for his approval, and each time he refuses it. After innumerable treks up and down the stairs, the crazy old man is satisfied—the miraculous melon has been found.

When the young Rock berates the old woman for indulging the man's madness, she chastises him and tells him of the duty of limitless love. It is one of the sweetest scenes ever written, as sweet as a dying man's quest for the sweetness of life.

But blah on death. He has done so much more. He wrote non sequiturs about 39-pound midgets before the absurdists knew they were absurdists; he was able to evoke the physicalness of place and food with the best of the naturalists. Moreover, he could sing of life and love, unlike many of the Turks, without pissing on anybody else's parade.

So, as the food and drink were served at the Brussels, the old man forgot about his ulcer and drank wine ("High tone," he pronounced it) and talked about places and writing. And one remembered that he still had that old trunk full of plays that sometime, somewhere he had claimed were better than Shakespeare's (he'll probably die to prove it).

He lapsed into the old tongue with Val Avery and told his special brand of jokes. When someone asked the secret to his success and longevity, he replied: "Not dying." And for this day you felt maybe he did have forever.

But that's sentimental. Like all of us, he will, but he's 8 to 5 not to go away mad. That's not sentimental. It's simply the lot of a Daring Young Man on the Flying Trapeze who has worked a lifetime without a net.

May 4, 1972

Requiem for the Last Radical

If I had to put up a religious symbol the way some people have crucifixes, or stars of David, my symbol would be the question mark. A question mark is a plowshare turned upside down. It plows your mind, so that thoughts and ideas grow.

—SAUL ALINSKY

When one thinks of "modern" American radicals, he is hard put to measure the masses of people they have helped. Reams of newsprint come to mind, bad-ass rhetoric, enough buttons to create a universe, chic fund raisers, graffiti, whining folk songs, and instant deification; but the scores of lives they have changed? Fair enough—the American underground is theater. But all this palls with the news of the death of Saul Alinsky.

Not that Saul hadn't a theatrical flair himself. A son of immigrant Russian-Jewish parents who grew up in a Chicago slum, Alinsky was cast out of the old Ben Hecht-Charlie MacArthur *Front Page* mold. A cigarette and a wisecrack made a constant couplet on his lips. Like most American men from a poor background, he hid his intellectualism as a street kid would hide a pair of argyle socks. One could almost picture his youth: Alinsky reading Tom Paine wrapped inside a Batman comic.

To my knowledge, Saul Alinsky was the last and only working full-time radical in America. He worked at it for nearly forty years, organizing his famous "Back of the Yards" movement (the slum described in Upton Sinclair's *The Jungle*), the Chicago blacks in the Woodlawn project, the Rochester blacks against Eastman Kodak, the Mexican-American grape pickers, and the middle-class whites in his Proxies for Peace action. He also has left behind him the Industrial Areas Foundation, which is a training ground for radical organizers. No buttons or slogans, though.

His ideas and plans of action can be found in three excellent books: *Reveille for Radicals, Rules for Radicals,* and *The Professional Radical,* his conversations with Marion K. Sanders, so I won't dwell on them here. Rather, I would like to evoke the spirit of this extraordinary man, with whom I had the pleasure of spending a few days. I believe a man should be eulogized in the way he lived, and Saul Alinsky claimed he loved the virtues of irreverence and good humor, so let's try to stick to that.

A couple of years back when NET was planning to do a segment on Alinsky teaching radical organizing at Antioch College, the producer, Bob Fresco, asked me if I would like to host the show. The deal, however, was that Alinsky would have to meet me first to check me out.

I brought along a young lady who admired his work, and we met at the St. Moritz bar for drinks. For the first ten minutes Alinsky talked to my date about the spectacular mini-skirt she was wearing. Then he and I, in the best street accents we could muster, swapped our lives and hard times. It was evident that I had two things going for me: the fact that I had worked as a longshoreman and the unsheathed gams seated beside me.

But as a raconteur Alinsky reduced me to a minor-leaguer. "When I was organizing the grape workers with Cesar Chavez, we had our first conflict when we sat down to dinner," he said. "They had all this belly-burning Mexican food laid out, and I said to Cesar, 'If you're going to get me to do any work, we'd better get some fucking steaks around here. You might think this stuff is soul food, but it's as bad as kosher cooking to me.'"

I want to get one thing very clear. I do not do what a lot of liberals and a lot of civil rights crusaders do. I do not in any way glorify the poor. I do not think that people are specially just or charitable or noble because they're unemployed and live in crummy housing and see their kids without any kind of future and feel the weight of every kind of indignity that society can throw at them, sophisticatedly or nakedly. Too often I've seen the have-nots turn into haves and become just as crummy as the haves they used to envy. Some of the fruit ranchers in California steam around in Cadillacs and treat the Mexican-American fieldhands

166

like vermin. Know who those bastards are? They're the characters who rode west in Steinbeck's trucks in "The Grapes of Wrath."

—The Professional Radical

Alinsky then went on to speak about FBI harassment. The FBI had taken pictures of him leaving a younger woman's cottage early in the morning and presented him with the photo evidence one day when he arrived at the Washington, D.C., airport. "The trouble is," he said, "that people bow to the FBI when they dig up this kind of evidence. I asked them to produce evidence that Hoover was sleeping with anybody! I told the bastards to go print the photos; it would do more for the sex lives of aging Jewish men than anything else in America."

Then he sashayed into youth. "You know," he commented through the ever-present cloud of cigarette smoke that hazed his face, "I debated William Kunstler once, and I said that in five years Rubin and Hoffman would be a vaudeville act." Then with a chuckle he added, "You know what Kunstler said to me? 'No, you're wrong, Saul. They'll be *producing* vaudeville acts.' He was right."

We went on for about two hours, but the Antioch trip was not yet settled. As we were leaving, he held my lady's hand (all this, I must admit, was carried out in baroque good fun) and said: "My dear, you should never have heroes. But if I'm to have an admirer, I'm glad she is as beautiful as you."

I decided to turn the tables and, grasping Alinsky's hand, said solemnly: "Saul, you're just what I've always wanted to grow up to be."

His face registered serious shock. "Really?" he asked.

"Yeah," I replied, "a dirty old man."

He roared laughing and shouted to Fresco: "When you come to Antioch, don't bring that Irish son of a bitch with you." It was settled. Antioch was on.

The problem with those kids is that they always want the third act, the resolution, the big drama. They want to skip the first act, the second act, the tediousness, the listening. Actually you do more organizing with your ears than with your tongue.

—*The Professional Radical*

Antioch. A sun-dappled April day, frisbees flying, students running barefoot in the grass, yapping dogs at their heels—all marred by the painted graffiti on the buildings. Alinsky stood there in a raincoat, puffing his cigarette and looking at the scrawls: "Revolution! It looks like the inside of a shithouse."

I wonder now if those middle-class kids with their "right ons," "pigs," "Establishment sell-outs," and precious Mao T-shirts ever knew what they had in their midst. A man so weary from his travels he had airplane tickets the thickness of a deck of cards in his pocket. Those womb children whom he tried to teach so patiently to win, to win something real, to teach that revolution—especially in a country structured as ours—is gained by inches. I hope now that their clichés gag them, and they know better. I hope they no longer talk of "moral victories."

He told them he knew all about moral victories: "When I was a kid at the University of Chicago, we had a football team that used to get their asses kicked eighty to nothing. The day after a game the coach, Alonzo Stagg, used to announce in the campus paper that we had won a moral victory. I learned moral victories were bullshit early in life."

To watch him try with good humor to bring practical organizational thoughts into their heads was a little sad. It reminded me of Yves Montand as the aging revolutionary confronting the Young Turks in *La Guerre Est Finie*. Alinsky's message was the war is *never* over. But perhaps they did learn. Maybe all those George McGovern organizers were sitting in the auditoriums of the hundreds of colleges at which he spoke. It would be a grand epitaph.

I also wonder if they ever noticed how many times he mentioned death in his speeches. It haunted him, yet he overcame it. I remarked on it to him at Antioch, and he ruefully smiled. "You're very perceptive," he said. "I've had a few personal tragedies. You know, kids ask you why you live life. What the hell can you say? Like the guy said about Mount Everest—it's there."

The last time I heard from the old warrior it was pure Alinsky. He made an early-morning phone call while he was in town for the publication of his last book; and he was leaving again in a few hours, so we couldn't meet.

"I was in the airport at Shanghai last week," he said. "I was talking to a Communist organizer, and I gave him a copy of your book (*Managing Mailer*). I told him you were one of the most brilliant revolutionary theoreticians in America. If they buy that," he cackled, "it ought to set back the party a fucking century." That's how we left it.

I promised I wouldn't be sentimental, but perhaps I can sneak one by him. If there's another turf out there, and some cats are cooling it in purgatory and looking for someone to bail them out—well, cheer up. Your main man is on the way.

June 29, 1972

Howard Cosell: Happiness Is Hyperbole

If Harold Pinter was to have a recurring nightmare, it probably would go something like this: He has written a new play full of his patented, precious pauses populating a wasteland of words, and he is casting a male lead. The earth, let's say, is a Kate Millett sugarplum dream—defoliated of men, except one. But, since the show must go on, Pinter must cast him. This one remaining actor who struts the stage is Howard Cosell.

Words, words, words. Talk is Howard Cosell's answer to Sophie Portnoy's chicken soup. To talk is to cure everything.

Just who is Howard Cosell? A sports announcer, to be sure; currently a television property, who has appeared in such nonsporting shows as *Nanny and the Professor* and *The Dean Martin Show;* a huckster in a commercial for, if not sporting, supporting Fruit of the Loom underwear. But more than these, Cosell is what college girls refer to as "a life experience."

Let's start at the beginning or "the top of the show," as Howard calls it. The *Times* called to ask if I would like to profile the Wizard of Words. Fine, I said, but cautioned that Cosell and I had once crossed swords in the past. (I had criticized Cosell in the *Village Voice* for what I thought was a mean-spirited eulogy he delivered on the occasion of ex-heavyweight boxing champion Sonny Liston's death. With the quickness of instant replay, Cosell took to the air the next day and, like an outraged Quasimodo, poured a caldron of hot, steamy words over my head.) But I promised I would try to make contact and made the initial phone call to Cosell.

Switch to one of those mornings-after the flesh is heir to, when the inside of my head resembles the floor of Madison Square Garden the day after the circus has left. The phone rang ever so early, the Voice on the other end of the line. It is a voice as recognizable as those of W. C. Fields, Mae West, and FDR.

The words emerged separately, spaced, it seemed by dashes, each goose-stepping behind the other. "Joe—this—is—Howard—Cosell. In—all—due—respect—to—your—creative—ability, do—you—believe, with—respect—to—things—past, you—could—render—a—fair, unbiased—profile—of—me—for—the—New—York—*Times?*"

I answered in a hyphenated stutter.

"This—is—what—I—want—to—know. On—the—grounds—of—journalistic—ethics—do—you—believe—you—should—disqualify—yourself—from—this—assignment?"

I began to realize how Cardinal Mindszenty must have felt. After some billing and cooing (after all, I'd criticized him on only one issue), Cosell decided to go one on one with me.

"All—right. The—hell—with—it. We'll—meet—at—my—office, and—we'll —have—lunch. As—I—said, I—respect—you—as—a—creative—writer. Your —work—is—beyond—rebuke, even—though—you—were—dead—wrong— about—Liston." Round 1: Cosell.

Cosell works out of a cubicle in the ABC building on Sixth Avenue. He sits behind a cluttered desk, a telephone receiver seems permanently grafted to his ear and an unfiltered cigarette to his lips (he is a two-pack-a-day man).

He is a nervous man; his nicotine-stained hand shakes quite visibly. Tall and lean, he dresses in mod clothes that do not seem to suit him. This is not meant to be a knock against his tailor, merely an observation that most men are trapped in some time period, and Cosell's style wasn't nurtured during the kicky sixties or seventies. It is not a flaw—who among us could picture Eisenhower in bell bottoms? (One reflects that even his younger partner on *ABC Monday Night Football*, Frank Gifford, suffers from the same malady. Gifford's coiffured, helmet haircut seems out of synch, too. "The Giff" will always be remembered with that Tony Curtis, fastback look of the fifties, when he was the darling of the football Giants.) But with Cosell, the threads are a bow to the updated necessity of the cameras, not a matter of conviction. He tells you he is a square, a family man, a sentimental man given to crying.

"My wife is everything. She is the star of the family. My God, without her, I'd be nothing. I don't know how she ever married a guy with such an ugly mug."

True, you wouldn't put such a face on horseback to ride into Atlanta to rescue Scarlett O'Hara, but Cosell's mug has something. It slopes downward like a ski slope for Lilliputians. It's the kind of face you'd be likely to see in an old *Batman* episode: there are curves of high camp in the profile. And perhaps that is one of the reasons Cosell is the hottest thing in sports broadcasting.

Most announcers' pans look like bowls of well-arranged Farina, and their delivery is equally bland. Cosell is too rich, too baroque for early-morning digestion. He is to be sampled after evening cocktails. Maybe some genius at ABC realized this, and that's why he was slotted into the late Monday night games. It is inconceivable he could be so popular if he were broadcasting on Sunday afternoons. Imagine returning from church and switching to Cosell. It would be like leaving a curate to go and be bombarded by a bishop.

Cosell is an odd mixture of the critic and the self-parodist. He hits his profession for hiring too many ex-jocks and "shills," instead of qualified reporters. His special dislikes are many major-league baseball announcers who have become adjuncts, or housemen, to the clubs they cover, thus eliminating any tough criticism of the game.

"Why should the FCC grant licenses to clubs who hire announcers as salesmen? Look at what happened to Red Barber. When he demanded that the cameras pan the empty stands at Yankee Stadium during a game, the club fired him."

Cosell has great respect for Barber, as well as Curt Gowdy and Vince Scully. With Agnewesque alliteration, he says: "They are the best under the strictures and structures of our industry."

Then, there is the other side. Cosell disclaims his importance (though his critics swear he is an egomaniac). "My God, I enjoy what I do, but we are still dealing in the realm of sports. Football is not a game played in a cathedral."

He is given to self-parody of his vaunted vocal style, both socially and professionally. Walking through the corridors of the ABC building, he stopped a secretary and with promethean earnestness announced: "Marie, I—must—have—you. My—dear, I—crave—you. I—must—have—that—body." Or, spotting an ABC executive: "Ed, I'm—sorry. But—that's—show—business. The—rumor—is—that—you're—out—on—your—ass. I—pity—your—poor —wife. She—could—have—married—a—talent. But—take—consolation. At— least—now--you'll—know—if—your—wife—really—loves—you. Eighteen— months—on—unemployment—will—be—the—bitter—test." The victims glee- fully received the bantering assaults as if they were blessings.

Professionally, he has laughed at himself through a number of com- mercials and guest shots on television shows. His most notable Cosell-on- Cosell was an appearance in Woody Allen's movie *Bananas,* in which he covered the assassination of a South American dictator (presumably for *Wide World of Sports*), then did a running commentary on the honey- moon high jinks of a couple in the film.

But a perfect example of not-the-real-turtle-soup—merely-the-mock oc- curred right before we left his office for lunch. A local sportswriter who felt Howard had snubbed him at an event in Houston called, wanting to know if the rumor that Cosell hated him was accurate. "My God, ————, all the world is not a one-hop grounder to Bud Harrelson. A man hates wars, a man hates ghettos, a man hates what is happening to the environ- ment—but a man does not hate sportswriters. Disregard those damn silly rumors, and, as usual, I look forward to seeing you soon." The absolution granted, he looks up and says, "Let's go to lunch."

We walk around the corner to the Hotel Dorset, where Cosell greets and is greeted, and we are led to a shiny black vinyl booth that resembles those patent leather pumps of—what else?—the fifties.

"The place is not that well publicized, but it is a marvelous little place for food and a drink. Make note of it," he demands. "Keep it in mind." Immediately, I rate it next to Lourdes as a watering hole. It is at such moments, as with jolly old St. Nick, that you laugh in spite of yourself. It is the Voice again, the tonsils which can bring drama to a routine luncheon. It is such an infectious weapon that not only pros such as David Fry and Bill Cosby imitate it, but also, on any given night in a sports' saloon, five guys can render a Cosell imitation.

There are the many apocryphal stories about it. One of my favorites: Cosell returns to his apartment one night and finds he has forgotten his keys. He rings the downstairs bell, and his wife, Emi, shouts out the window, "Who is it?" The Voice from the pavement rises heavenward, "Emi—Cosell, here—on—the—corner—of—Sixty-third—Street—and—Third Avenue—in—the—most—majestic—city—in—the—world—this—is—Howard— Cosell." One's mind goes back to Scripture and imagines he can hear Alexander Scourby playing God to Cosell's kvetching Job.

We order drinks (Cosell is a martini man) and begin to talk. The conversation gets around to marriage, children, love, work, and all the crucial third-and-one situations of being alive. After a while I began to wonder who was interviewing whom. But this, too, is part of the Cosell mystique: He has the knack of the father confessor.

On a subsequent evening we board a cab, and the burly driver tells Cosell that even though he disagrees with his views, he respects him as a man. Then the hackie laments to Cosell that he is in terrible pain, because he has been circumcised that very day! For about ten blocks Cosell sits shiva in deference to the driver's loss, and, as we debark, Cosell has added another lifetime fan.

Minutes later over drinks Cosell holds his groin in sympathy and exclaims with a shudder: "God, I can't think of the pain. At his age it must be excruciating." Much to the cabdriver's credit, he didn't blame the briss on Mayor Lindsay. Another Cosell first.

Switch back to the Dorset. More drinks. Since Cosell plainly is a man who can handle his cup, I ask the obvious question: "Were you drunk, Howard, as some reporters said, when you threw up in the broadcasting booth the night of the Giant-Eagles game and had to leave the air?"

Cosell, dry as Carry Nation, denies it. "The charge is absolutely absurd. I thought I was having a stroke on the air. I rented a car that evening and was driven back to New York. If I was going to die, I wanted to die with my wife." Cosell goes on to explain that he checked into a hospital the next morning, and the diagnosis was a flu bug in his inner ear. His detractors will tell you that is a helluva place to pour a drink, but he stands firm. "If I was drunk, I would have been fired four hours after I left the air, but what can you say once a phony story gets circulated? You managed Mailer and Breslin, and they had to take crap in their time [the scalawag in me bowed to that nice diplomatic touch]. As Harry Truman said," he continues, " 'If you can't stand the heat, stay out of the kitchen.' So now,

172

when the question comes up, I say, like W. C. Fields I always get drunk before a show in Philadelphia."

The passage is vintage Cosell. In one breath he had managed to incorporate a Pulitzer Prize-winning author, a columnist with the natural appeal of Damon Runyon, a former President of the United States, and a legendary comic. If you are going to torpedo Cosell's ship, you had damn well better aim for the grand salon.

It is approaching four-thirty in the afternoon, time for Cosell to tape his two network shows, *Speaking of Everything* (general topics) and *Speaking of Sports*. He informs me that I am to be his guest on *Speaking of Everything*. Once again I feel like Charlie to his Edgar. We have known each other for approximately four hours, but on the show he introduces me as "a throwback to the great ones—Brendan Behan, Scott Fitzgerald, James T. Farrell, and perhaps Sean O'Casey." In 240 minutes he has taken me from the Irish kitchen table of journalism to the Hibernian banquet setting of Arts & Letters. I think about firing my agent.

We finish up, and he does his sports show solo, stopwatch in hand. He launches into an attack on the monopoly of professional sports, keying on New York Giant president Wellington Mara and his impending switch of franchise to the Hackensack Meadows in New Jersey. He calls the move venal, greedy, and shoddy; he cites how Mara received $10,000,000 from the AFL to allow the Jets to move into New York and now is deserting the city; he lambasts Governor Cahill of New Jersey for spending $200,000,-000 on a sports complex while his cities, particularly Newark, are decaying. The Tonsils beckon Washington and the denizens of the Halls of Congress to investigate and indict the whole kit and caboodle under the antitrust laws, because it's about time the damn lie that professional sports are games is exposed. "They are business, big business." The stopwatch clicks, and he finishes like a horse with his nose on the wire.

It is this type of gutsy performance that makes Cosell the best in his field. There are journalists who are tough, but in the eunuch world of broadcasting there is no one who can carry Cosell's glove.

Cosell's hostility to the Giants' greedy machinations has made him unwelcome among the Giant management and court fops who gather at Mike Manuche's on West Fifty-second Street. Manuche's is where the Giant apologists meet, and, since he began his attacks on Mara, Cosell has shunned the place, though the owner is a personal friend. "Mara, like George Halas [the owner of the Chicago Bears], is living in the past. They think you can run a football team like a family, with the owners as father figures. That's passé. These kids today are too smart to buy that crap. They know it's a business, and they want top dollar, not pep talks, for their performance. And many of the New York sportswriters, not all, mind you, are just as bad. They have been shilling their readers all season about a Giant resurgence, a rebuilding process [Cosell is right about this], and, my God, they have about four or five real professionals on the whole team!"

As regards head coach Alex Webster, Cosell says simply: "He's a nice big bear of a man." Which is his kind way of saying Webster is cuddly, but not coaching material.

The issue that catapulted Cosell out of the ranks of broadcasting hacks in the hearts of some and into hell in the minds of many more was his defense of Muhammad Ali aka Cassius Clay, when he was stripped unconstitutionally of his heavyweight crown for refusing to accept military conscription on religious grounds. In numerous interviews and essays on the nationally telecast *Wide World of Sports* Cosell not only addressed the champion by his Muslim name, but defended him as the true champion until the point he was found guilty beyond all court appeals or rightfully lost his title where he won it, in the ring.

Aside from Cosell's moral stance, his interviews with Ali made for some of the best theater seen on the tube. A sometimes truculent Ali would badmouth Cosell (or were they both engaging in an elaborate put-on?) to the point of delivering veiled threats of physical harm, till Cosell, like David, equipped only with his syntactical slingshot, would woefully accept. "If it comes to that, I suppose that is the way it will have to be."

Cosell says that he received thousands of insulting letters and that threats were made on his life, because of his stand on Ali. "Many of them beginning," he relates, 'You dirty Jew bastard.' "

I had heard him use that phrase three times in the course of our meetings and asked if he had "rabbit ears" about his Jewishness. "You're damn right I have," he replied. "Growing up in the time of Hitler, I always knew I was Jewish." Then, in half indictment, half charade, he gives the Cosell stare, the "Just how do you beat your wife?" accusation. "It was Irish bastards like you, from St. Theresa's Parish, who used to chase me over the back fences when I was coming home from school every day on Eastern Parkway."

So, to find the essence of the man, let us return to those thrilling days of yesteryear, when Howard Cosell entered this planet earth, and a doctor spanked his upturned pink behind and instead of a cry heard, "This—is—Howard—Cosell."

He was born Howard William Cohen on March 25, 1920, in Winston-Salem, North Carolina, the son of a Jewish immigrant from Poland named Isidore Cassell (he changed his name when he landed in America). His father worked for a credit clothing chain, and his work caused him to move his family through various Southern towns until the early twenties, when the Cohens came to rest in Brooklyn.

Cosell attended Alexander Hamilton High School, where he was sports

174

editor of the high school newspaper and ran for the track team, an activity, one presumes, that was valuable in his pursuit of those little flowers of St. Theresa.

When he graduated, he enrolled at NYU and majored in English literature before going on to law school, a circumlocution that prepared him for his future role as both the Devil and Daniel Webster.

He went to work as a law clerk for $10 a week, but along came World War II, and in February, 1942, Cosell enlisted. He was stationed at the New York Port of Embarkation which was the jump-off point for troops bound for Europe. In the span of a year he reached the rank of technical sergeant, and it was at this juncture that the future denouncer of the Establishment did the unspeakable—he entered Officers' Candidate School.

Cosell rose to the rank of major and in 1943 met his bride-to-be, Mary Edith "Emi" Abrams, who was working as a secretary at the Fort Hamilton base. Emi, a girl of Welsh-Dutch extraction, married him a year later.

After the war Cosell opened his own law practice at 30 Broad Street, and he and his wife and their new baby lived with his parents. It was a bad time for Cosell, emotionally and financially. But then again, consider Cosell's character: How could anyone expect him to prepare anything with the word "brief" in it?

It was in the early fifties, Cosell's talisman decade, that things began to break for him. He was involved in incorporating the Little League in New York, and ABC approached him to put together a radio show on which the kids would ask the pros questions. The show was set up as a noncommercial public service program, and Cosell agreed to emcee it without pay. It was scheduled to run six weeks; it lasted six years.

He maintained his law practice until 1956, when ABC made him an offer to do ten weekend sports spots at $25 each. It was a marriage made in metaphorical heaven: The mike and the mouth had found each other.

The following year he was given a nightly TV network sports show. (The format was a first and has never been duplicated.) In 1961 he brought his sandpaper eloquence to what is now the nightly local *ABC Eyewitness News,* on which he held forth till June of this past year.

In 1962 Cosell entered the documentary field, forming his own company, Legend Productions. His first documentary was titled *A Look Behind the Legend,* a profile of the Sultan of Swat which brought Cosell together with network bigwig John Gilbert and Roger Kahn, who had written an article about Babe Ruth for *Esquire.* The film drew raves and was followed by eight other documentaries, two of which won awards for journalistic excellence from the Council on International Non-Theatrical Events.

But the making of H. C. Superstar was to come through Cosell's color coverage of heavyweight championship fights (his first was the Patterson-Johansson go at Yankee Stadium) and *ABC's Monday Night Game of the*

Week, which Cosell works in trinity with Frank Gifford and Don Meredith. Howard, for those Scripturally inclined, is the one who appears as the tongue of fire.

It is fitting that boxing should have caused his breakthrough since it is Cosell's favorite sport. "There is no event like a heavyweight championship fight," he intones, "and I'm not talking about a Quarry against an Ellis. A great one. Like Ali-Frazier. It has all the excitement and anticipation of what a great event is supposed to be. Man reduced to his essence, brutality, self-discipline, pain, and tragedy. I suppose it's what Hemingway saw. The essential qualities of man exist in boxing, and I won't apologize for my feelings about the sport."

Nor will the accountants at ABC, one gathers, apologize for the brickbats thrown at Cosell & Co. for their Monday night telecasts. The boys are money in the bank. They have garnered audiences up to 40,000,000 and have broken into the Top Ten (No. 7) in national ratings, which is unheard of for a sports show. Cosell claims most of the criticism directed against him has come from "certain" New York writers. The "quality" publications and sportswriters around the country have been unanimous in their praise, he declares, and runs down a list of names with the agility of Old Joe McCarthy.

But Cosell (the word "quality" aside) is on firm ground here. The Monday night show is generally lauded by the experts, and like Huey Long, Cosell also has "the little people" on his side. He has more offers for speaking engagements than he can fill, more commercial offers than he cares to handle, and enough love letters pour into ABC to satisfy the appetite of a Rubirosa.

Even the execs at ABC are loyalists. "When people watch a one-sided game on the other channels on Sunday, they don't even talk about it on Monday," one said. "If we have a turkey on Monday night, Tuesday at the bar they still talk about our broadcasting team, and Howard's the reason."

Then why does Cosell overreact to criticism? The tough guy, the badmouther, the Archie Bunker of sports? Well, underneath, Cosell is a bleeder. Like a borsht circuit comic with a tough shtick, he wants to be loved.

Too, the Cosells are a tight-knit family, and the father tries to shield the roost. "My daughters get terribly upset when something nasty is written about me," he says. "I don't like to afflict them with that kind of pressure and pain." His wife, Emi, a woman of easygoing grace and charm and a ready laugh, agrees. "It upsets the children, and some of it is so unfair."

His concern is not an act. Over dinner at P. J. Moriarty's with his youngest daughter, Hilary, Cosell tells her: "In tomorrow's paper you'll read that Buster Mathis called your father 'cruel and inhuman.' " He referred to the *Wide World of Sports* coverage of the Ali-Mathis fight. The network thought the fight was so dull they showed only a few rounds and accompanied the video portion with a sound track of waltz music.

The family motif also is played out as one watches the busy Cosell trying to rearrange his schedule so that he can be at his older daughter Jill's side when she gives birth to her second child.

It is evident that Cosell is in love with his newfound life and is sensitive to anyone or anything that threatens it. This is humanly understandable to anyone who has ever had to scuffle for a buck. But he is genuinely awed by his good fortune: "I can't believe this past year. It's beyond my imagination. Don't get me wrong. I love it, but I realize something like this can go on for only so long."

Cosell is also generous in that way the poor who have made it are: He picks up checks. Not ostentatiously, but as if it were his round. And like a gambler in the chips who buys an expensive watch that is hockable to remind him of past disasters, Cosell keeps part of his speech in the pawnshop of the past—his quite elegant apartment on the East Side is "the flat."

According to Paul Zimmerman, author of *A Thinking Man's Guide to Pro Football* and a critic of Cosell, Howard is generous in other ways. Zimmerman, a confessed football "purist," thinks Cosell & Co. interfere with the game on the Monday night telecast: "They don't pay attention to the game, and all that damn talk distracts me, so I end up missing plays. But ABC's technical coverage is so good even these guys can't mess it up." Yet in the next breath Zimmerman relates how generous Cosell was to him when his book came out. "He plugged it for me, and I have to say he has helped some out-of-work writers find work. I guess you would have to say he is a generous guy. I just wish he wouldn't let his ego get in the way of his performance."

Zimmerman went on to tell me that a friend of his in the Midwest just adores Cosell. "My friend told me, 'If you spent your life speaking to audiences of Rotarians, you'd know why I like that funny-looking bastard with the weird voice.' And, you know," Zimmerman concludes, "when I walk into my living room and hear those other dullards on the tube, I say to myself, my God, there are far worse than Cosell."

In a way Vic Ziegel, an urbane, witty sportswriter for the New York *Post*, echoes Zimmerman. Ziegel wrote what he thought was a mild criticism of Cosell's sportscasting, and he received flack, not from Cosell, but from an ABC executive. "He comes on too strong for my taste," says Ziegel, "and furthermore, I don't think he is that knowledgeable about boxing." But then he shrugs and grins: "But offer me twenty announcers, and I guess I'd take Howard."

The truth is that Cosell is overly defensive. No man is right all the time, but Cosell vigorously tries to defend his more apparent bloopers by citing people who agreed with him and pulling complimentary letters from his pocket, as Lyndon Johnson used to pull out his popularity polls.

The Johnson imagery, though, refers only to the polls. Cosell is an ardent dove. "I visited a veterans' paraplegic hospital the other night," he told me, "and it would break your heart. A black veteran put his arms around me and told me how his people were on my side for my defense of Ali, and he started to cry. I broke down and wept with him. I'm going back to that hospital once a month from here on, and I'd like to take some of my right-wing friends with me."

Cosell's closest tie with a right-wing mentality was Vince Lombardi. "I truly loved that man," he says, "a dedicated, lovely man, but we couldn't stand each other's politics." Cosell even has praise for Spiro Agnew—not for his politics, but for his one-liners. "Agnew said in a speech that Ralph Nader comes weekly to *Wide World of Sports* to take courtesy lessons from Howard Cosell. His politics are lousy, but you have to admit, it's a helluva line."

Maybe that's why Cosell creates enemies. His love for the one-liner, the put-down. His most constant critic is New York *Daily News'* sportswriter Dick Young, whom Cosell labels "for decades the best baseball writer in the business." Young commented: "Cosell can dramatize the day of the week. Moreover, he shouldn't call other people shills. In this business nobody gets interviews with superstars without being nice to them, they just won't come on your show otherwise." But even Young mellowed on Cosell: "In his early days he was the best interviewer of his time."

Only Jimmy Cannon, the syndicated columnist, sees no redeeming qualities in Cosell: "I just don't want to hear him. I wish he'd disappear. He makes a utility infielder missing a grounder sound like a verdict from the Nuremberg Trials. He's the Tiny Tim of the airwaves, and Meredith is nothing but a rube comic."

Cosell couldn't disagree more with the latter remark: "Dandy Don has more natural native intelligence and wit than any man I know. You would never know it when you look at that charming man, but he has had many sorrows in his life." And on Gifford: "I really love that kid. Faultless Frank had his problems in the early telecasts, but he worked like hell to conquer that job, and by the end of the season he was great. In fact, he was making even better cracks than Dandy and me."

Perhaps the one who came closer to the truth than all the rest is former *Look* assistant sports editor Jared Lebow. "I don't know why the hell they all rap Cosell," he said. "He's a sports reporter, not Richard Nixon. Besides, he's fun. Don't these guys realize he's great show business? Out there in mid-America they hang banners from the stands about Howard."

Show biz. The love of the shtick. That really is what is irresistible to

Cosell. The comic who longs to play Hamlet (Cosell would like to do politics), but who can't resist doing a turn. Some of those turns: He introduces Meredith by saying that since ABC is the third network, they decided, in their losing tradition, to conduct a talent search for the biggest loser they could find, and who else could it have been but Dandy Don Meredith?

Second chorus, the 21 Club: Walter Kennedy, commissioner of the NBA, comes in, and Cosell loudly announces: "Ladies and gentlemen, I would like you to meet the man who single-handedly destroyed the great game of basketball. Truly a magnificent detriment to the sport." (Of course, Kennedy joins the party for drinks and dinner.)

A late lament, Cosell's flat, night: A phone call to Don Klosterman, general manager of the Baltimore Colts. Subject: The Colts' surprising loss to the New England Patriots in the last game of the season which allowed the Colts to face the weak Cleveland Browns in the play-offs rather than the mighty Kansas City Chiefs. Ugly rumors have appeared in the newspapers about a possible Colt dump. "Klosterman, Cosell here. With me is a radical sportswriter who is going to smear you and your team for dumping the Patriot game. He knows you dumped it, I know you dumped it, and the nation knows you dumped it. Wait for the exposé." Cosell giggles maniacally and hangs up. Klosterman, his sleep murdered, puts in a night like Macbeth. Like Mailer, Cosell understands Advertisements for Myself.

A REPRISE: In—a—nation—populated—with—political—pygmies, where —monosyllabic—midgets—monopolize—the—microphone, where—charlatans —shill—sports, where—ex-jocks—devoid—of—jocularity—lull—legions—into —listlessness, there—is—one—Mensch—of—the—Microphone. His—star— rose—in—the—East, when—he—isolated—pass—receiver—Inky—Blumenthal —on—slow—defender—Siggy—Rothstein—and—had—Inky—cut—in—at—the —blue—Chevrolet—before—Hank—Stram—ever—thought—of—it. Remember, you—heard—it—here—first. So, don't—vacillate—in—your—vespers. Thank—the—Coach—of—the—Cosmos—for—that Nemesis—of—Network— Nada, Howard—Cosell. This—is—Joe—Flaherty—reporting—on—sports.
P.S. May all his sins be remembered.

Summer, 1972

Four: Fancy Flights

My Summer Vacation, or
Notes from an Underdog

In Robert Rossen's *The Hustler* George C. Scott, after observing Paul Newman's psychological makeup, turned to Jackie Gleason and cryptically pronounced sentence: "Stick with him, he's a loser." It is braggadocio to say let no man write my epitaph, but after the last three weeks Mr. Scott's words are forever chiseled in my heart.

Three weeks ago my wife and I planned to start our summer vacation. Our destination was Lake Mahopac in upstate New York. My plans—two tranquil weeks at my mother-in-law's house. Notice the loser tendency: Who spends his vacation at his mother-in-law's? The only problem was transportation. There are many modes of transportation to Lake Mahopac but not for dog owners. You see, I own a wire-haired terrier named Gatsby. You know, that sad Midwesterner who forlornly looked at the light on Daisy's dock. Beginning to get the picture, old sport?

The obvious move was to buy a car, a simple enough exercise in the American way of life. A car—the purchase that keeps the Great Society in gear. Simple! Innocent! Not for the Flahertys.

The American romance with the motorcar has always eluded me. By use of flashback (falling calendar pages and racing locomotives) I will describe my first automobile purchase in Los Angeles seven years ago.

The object of my affection was a 1953 Dodge. How proud I was of my first middle-class possession. I was an owner, a state-registered owner. For two months I drove this great whalelike vehicle in a sea of finny mechanized sharks. Then, like the old man of the freeway, I began to hear the sounds of death. Great groans rose from the hood. Simple trips home became agony. The Dodge moaned dumbly for a place to die. With a heavy heart, I brought the car to a mechanic (an abortionist, Detroit style). The diagnosis: the transmission was dead.

Like the wife who marries the image of her first drunken husband again and again, I was doomed for repetition. After a proper time in mourning (I'm Irish, you know), I decided to choose a new mate. This time, for

183

luck, I switched brands. The owner of the 1951 Chevrolet I was eyeing was the president of the savings and loan company. Savings and loan on the West Coast is not to be confused with the liberal decadent bankers of the East. Everything seemed in order, and I took the plunge.

The Chevy performed admirably fine for six weeks. Then the Chevy's behavior pattern turned to knocking, hissing, and spitting oil. My Chevy became a crime in the streets. Angrily, I called the salesman and complained about the racing disorder in my engine. With great superiority he stated that the treatment I gave his car was at best niggardly. So was established the tune-up of the sixties. Before we shift to the present, let me state the Chevy suffered death of the transmission.

"Those who do not learn from the mistakes of history are doomed to repeat them." (A mechanic wit.) I, like the Republican Party, pay no heed to past history. The year was now 1967, and I needed a car. A co-worker had a 1963 Rambler for sale. I had no grandiose dreams about a Rambler, but at least it wasn't an Edsel. After much self-examination, I decided to buy. Now everyone is ready for an O. Henry ending—transmission! Only in literature are neat endings possible. The Rambler was stolen.

Maybe! The possibilities are infinite. I had just come from having the car registered. To celebrate my courage, I stopped in the Village for a few drinks. I ordered Irish whiskey and milk, Freudianly described as fathers-and-mothers. (I'm Irish, you know.) Was it stolen? Did I move it? Did my over-thirty-year-old conscience donate the Rambler to the hippies? I'm afraid I'll never know.

It was a long hot August. My wife and I stared at each other. Johnson was blowing up North Vietnam, and H. Rap Brown was blowing up Detroit (not the automobile factories, much to my disappointment). I had to get away.

After five wasted days of my vacation, the phone rang. A friend called and asked: Why not use his car for my vacation? Tears of joy ran down my face. Who said humanity is dead? Friday night we joined our friends for a bon voyage highball.

To say the least, my friend is a talented fellow. He is an excellent psychotherapist (I say this because he has never suggested I give up drinking). But he suffers a common weakness with me. Such things as nuts, bolts, and screws not only confound him but seem to have an active animosity toward him. (Nuts, screws, joints, bushings, rods—what filthy minds those bastards in Detroit have!)

But back to my friend's trouble with mechanical objects. In an attempt to reproduce seltzer water for our highballs, he attached a Polaris-type missile to a flask of water. After much shaking, the missile exploded off the flask and nearly denutted him. The water remained water.

Ignoring this ominous sign, I borrowed the car anyway. Sunday morn-

184

ing, with wife and dog in tow, I started out for the country. It is useless to explain distance in terms of miles to New Yorkers—time works better. But first one pertinent fact: The car had a weak suspension system and a dangerously low tailpipe and muffler (there's that Krafft-Ebing terminology again). Well, after six blocks, or eleven minutes, I struck a loose cobblestone. The loose cobblestone struck the low muffler. The low muffler bent and smashed into the. . . . A familiar lament rose from underneath the car. My wife cried, my dog howled, or did my wife howl and my dog cry? I looked westward toward Detroit. We had cracked the transmission case.

Slowly, I worked the car back home. Hurriedly, I opened a bottle of whiskey. Speedily, I emptied it. I remained in a rather foggy state for four days. The car finally was fixed for the mere sum of $220.

Lately, George Romney has been complaining that he has been brainwashed. Now, not only do I think Mr. Romney should be brainwashed, I think he should be lobotomized. Anyone who has made his fortune producing these greasy deadeners of the soul would be a menace to this country in 1968.

Well, the end of the shaggy car story is drawing near. I presented the repaired car to my friend with the story of the disaster. Courageously, he offered me the loan of his vehicle again. Wisely, I refused. Why not, he suggested, all drive to the country for a weekend? Feeling the exhilarating release of responsibility, I agreed.

Showing a marked improvement, we reached Forty-second Street before the muffler fell off. Back in Brooklyn with more whiskey, I decided to give up.

But when another highly optimistic friend (he swears the riots are the start of urban renewal) heard of our plight, he packed us into his car. Without further incident, we reached the lake Saturday night.

Sunday morning I woke up and made my way to the water. My kidneys were sore, my bankbook naked, and my soul weary. With the little energy I had left, I dove into the water. Nick had finally made it to the Big Two-Hearted River.

September 14, 1967

Pub Shark Racks Up the Hustler from Chi

The Lion's Head bar in Greenwich Village is one of the few existing patches of Thurberesque terrain where one can escape the god-awful decency of one's wife and home. With its wood-paneled walls and mahogany-colored liquid, it combines the best dark security aspects of the womb and the coffin. The tenor of the conversation is baritone. In this troubled world the talk at the Lion's Head is usually about sports.

Poets in residence spend their most creative hours drinking boilermakers and trying to recall Slats Marion's 1947 fielding average. Local sportswriters gather here to souse and swap stories. Pugs who decide to break training and tipple can be spotted at the bar. The pub's fleet of bartenders with their sailing hang-ups are all frustrated Ahabs. It is not a place where a young lady comes looking for romance. In fact, the only broad in the pub's history ever to achieve the horizontal position was bowled over by a French horn player demonstrating how to run Green Bay's fabled sweep. In its own way, it is a swinging New York Athletic Club for marginal people.

But like all Village bars it has its touches of the exotic. Ex-IRA cadre harp about the queen's sexual habits and conspiratorially talk about "the rising of the moon." A band of folk singers, who use the pub as headquarters, occasionally (after thirty-seven Irish whiskeys) demonstrate their social consciences by staging a lay-in on the floor. In the best spirit of ecumenicism, Jews tipple as ardently as Irishmen. And in the ever-infringing world of lace curtains, the Lion's Head remains a man's saloon.

But lately a melancholy mood began to prevail at the pub. With the Super Bowl a thing of the past and the baseball season still too far away, the local jockos fell into a conversational lag. Then in a moment of isolated sobriety, day bartender Don Schlenker stumbled on a solution. The pub boasts of one of the best pool shooters in the Village—ex-collegiate champion finalist Normand Poirier. Poirier is a former New York *Post* reporter whose supremacy with a cue was never challenged till Mike McGovern, an editor for the New York *Daily News* and self-described "Chicago hustler," threw down the gauntlet. Bartender Schlenker, with outraged civic pride, arranged a match between Poirier and the usurper from the West. Or as one local devotee of Warner Brotherese stated: "Poirier is going to take on the hustler from Chi."

Since the pub is a Village bar, a simple sporting confrontation didn't seem enough. Ideological reasoning began to overshadow the match. Talk spread about the West against the East, the liberal *Post* versus the conservative *News,* a symbolic showdown between the hawks and the doves, and alas, the supremacy of left-hand English over right. Both contestants agreed to a Tuesday night match, and Poirier declared he was ready to defend the honor of the Village on the field of green.

On the night of the match a squadron of cabs transported about twenty Villagers to a classic midtown poolroom. As the group made its way down the concrete steps to the emporium, the Broadway set stared in amazement.

The one female spectator, Jeanine Johnson, a dazzling movie script researcher, hobbled down the stairs with one leg bandaged and supported by a cane. (Miss Johnson archly said she received her infirmity skiing on the slopes of Sixth Avenue, where she slipped in dog dung.) Being the first female presence to enter these hallowed portals since the statue of Mother Cabrini was placed above the cash register, she was treated with elaborate politeness. A Runyonesque character with a gray fedora as large as the roof of the Houston Astrodome held the door open for her.

As the bearded Schlenker passed through the door wearing a white carnation to indicate his role as promoter, someone grunted: "Tell that creep the florist shop is across the street." Poirier, a dedicated athlete of the old school who was reported to have quit drinking seventeen minutes before the match, was already practicing on the table with McGovern looking on. The spectators took their viewing places; not since the Last Supper have so many beards been gathered around one table.

Leon Seidel, the rotund Lion's Head owner, dressed in Irish fisherman knit sweater and looking like Gertrude Berg playing Victor McLagen, racked the balls. Amazed outsiders gathered around the table trying to decipher what the hell was going on.

The game was to be decided at 100 points, and Poirier promptly took the first rack 9–5. Both players were obviously nervous, but McGovern's shooting arm seemed to be doing a private shing-a-ling. Poirier, playing oneupmanship, asked the nonresponding McGovern if he was "nervous." Poirier, whose face, like a crumpled question mark, has a constant inquisitive look about it, sensed McGovern's inadequacy and began to run him off the table. After three racks, the game had all the drama of an arm-wrestling match between Sonny Liston and Shirley Temple.

After a while the real show was on the sidelines. One had entered a time machine where the world had stopped in the early fifties. Pants legs were still pegged, every blue jacket was bullet-ridden with silver splashes, and wavy black hair was so pomaded it glistened like ebony skating ponds. Everybody's Pygmalion seemed to be Leo Gorcey. Miraculous medals hung over form-fitting T-shirts, and pinky rings as ostentatious as the opera box lights at Lincoln Center bedazzled the onlooker. The timekeeper admonished a heckler over the loudspeaker: "Jack of Diamonds, leave the outsiders alone." The Village innocents had entered the world of the hustler—a dollar down and thirty-nine weeks to pay.

The only downtowner who could have passed for one of the sharks' own was Lion's Head bartender Al Koblin. Looking to add some dash to the occasion, Koblin had recruited a camp wardrobe worthy of Susan Sontag. With the slim elegance of Fred Astaire dancing a Mike Hammer skit in the fifties' *Bandwagon*, Koblin decked out in pegged pants, a dark blue shirt, and a porkpie lid.

Demonstrating the credibility gap between "the beautiful cultured people" and the subculture of our society, a local sharpie asked if Koblin wasn't "a hustler from the Coast." Archie Mulligan, the pub's maître d', cryptically replied to his inquisitor that Koblin was "Chalky from Staten Island." Since some kind of repartee was established, Mulligan was next quizzed about Village poet Joel Oppenheimer, who sat viewing the match with his beard and his hair teased into a wall-to-wall bouffant. Mulligan, forming his mouth side-pocket style, said Oppenheimer was "a physicist from the University of Heidelberg on a sabbatical and heard of the game through the vine." When the *Voice* photographer arrived on the scene, he was told he was allowed to shoot his own people but to "keep your camera down because a lot of guys around here don't like their picture taken."

Meanwhile, back on the table, Poirier was defeating McGovern by a score of 100–49. If McGovern is a Chicago hustler, he has a premier career as a New York welfare case. If the evening had any social significance, it was certainly dubious. Eugenia and Suzy didn't give it a line. Jackie and Lee were nowhere in attendance. But unlike those masked capers of the jet set, the Villagers' evening out had a distinct touch of balls.

February 15, 1968

For Whom the Bull Tolls: Making a Bust of Papa

After a short happy life or after a long sad one, when the soul makes its final journey across the river and into the trees, peace should come at last. But the memorable dead are such salable commodities that even death doesn't bring solace.

The common among us after our demise suffer such minor indignities as plastic flowered wreaths emblazoned with our role in life: father, husband, son. Occasionally the clergy will chant prayers over us we never used or grant us attributes we never possessed. For years of live heterosexuality, in the end we are powdered, lipsticked, coiffured, and laid to rest in the Lilac Room of some Mafioso funeral parlor. But these are minor indignities.

The exploitation of the famous dead has become a major industry. Martyred Presidents become material for key chains, syrupy poems, bumper stickers, and political career launching pads. The names of airports and avenues are renamed in their honor, only to have our supreme social critics —the cabdrivers—call them by their original names. The latest of our notable dead to suffer this demeaning process is the old shit detector him-self—Ernest Hemingway.

Last week at the home of sculptor Luis Antonio Sanguino on West End Avenue, the press was invited to attend an unveiling of Sanguino's bust of Papa, which is to be placed in the town square of Pamplona near the bull-ring. A Xeroxed press release informed us that Sanguino was one of the finalists for the FDR Memorial in Washington, D.C., and among other works he had created a seven-foot statue and three figures in rock salt for the International Salt Company of Scranton, Pennsylvania.

Sanguino, a native of Barcelona, was commissioned by the town of Pamplona to sculpt the bust. Dressed in a yellow sport jacket and a white turtleneck, with black lacquered hair and mustache, he looked like Marcello Mastroianni in *Divorce, Italian Style*. Precious ladies perched precariously on the end of a couch, their elegant fingers entwined around their napkin-mummified highball glasses. Instead of Nick's bread crust dipped in bacon fat, the guests were served hors d'oeuvres so elegantly slim they had all the corporal substance of communion wafers. Besides the various sculpture and paintings, the room was dominated by a contingent of Spaniards speaking the mano-a-mano tongue and making only occasional passes in English. A young, tightly tailored man in wraparound sunglasses caught the Heming-way mystique—he was a perfect veronica.

The big moment was about to arrive. The guest of honor, Mary Heming-way, rose to unveil the statue. Her tanned face and white hair blended to-gether like a sun-flecked beach. Seeming as if she was looking for the nearest exit, Mary Hemingway asked: "How do you unveil it?" After receiving her instructions, she removed the covering, and a huge head of Hemingway stared down on the proceedings. Applause filled the room, and Sanguino, patting his hair into place, posed with Mary Hemingway and the bust. Next, one Amador Marin, who described himself as a friend of the house, rose to speak. Marin said his speech would be like that of the master—"succinct and lucid in style." Very dryly Mary Hemingway said: "Either one or the other would do." Marin, ignoring her and his promise, went into an endless spiel of convoluted Castilian prose worthy of a gaucho Faulkner. After reams of purple about ringing bells in Pamplona on the day of the unveiling and allusions to *For Whom the Bell Tolls,* Marin went into Hemingway's value to Spain as a tourist attraction and gushed about Mary and Papa's many trips to Pamplona. Mary Hemingway, getting in high editorial gear, cracked: "Also with many other wives." Marin finally finished his novella and sat down.

The grateful guests started to look for refills, when the door to the next room exploded open and five musicians costumed circa MGM Ricardo Montalban burst into the room playing castanets, guitars, and accordions, and shouting "Olé, olé." A group of Spaniards grabbed Mary Hemingway's hands and did a peasant dance. Then, my God, it really got eerie. The bust, which wasn't cast yet, began to rock back and forth on its base from the dancing. Panicky guests, like all the king's men, moved forth to keep Papa intact. Expediency overrode passion, and the dancing ceased.

After a round of whiskey to fortify us, we were besieged again. Jim O'Brien, an aide from Mayor Lindsay's office, delivered the next dirge in the best Irish mortician manner. O'Brien, like all career politicians, began to shift the names of the famous around in the attic of his mind like old trunks. Then, eyeing Ernest eyeball to eyeball, he summed it all up: "I'm sure in that happy land he's in now, he remembers New York." With this, Mary Hemingway made for the door.

O'Brien and a young West Side reformer were both wearing PT-109 tie clips, and one got the feeling that this once exclusive crew has grown into a flotilla of delegates in this election year. The guests then began to approach the bust to deliver their critical opinions. A young woman in a slouch hat à la Lady Brett walked to the bust. In that classic New York museumgoer pose, she placed her right leg forward and bent her torso backward. Her buttocks evaporated, like soft clouds, into her inner universe. Her maidenhead arched forward toward the bust about to spout an esthetic announcement. "Breathtaking," she intoned. "He captured everything." Her mate added the finisher: "Yeah, even the beard." The bust with its Mount Rushmore grandeur vacantly surveyed the room.

As the guests were preparing to leave, a blonde and a brunette went to fetch their coats off the bed. The brunette's cloth coat was lying under the blonde's massive sable, a fur so formidable it would have ruptured King Kong. The blonde, with all the delightful bitchiness of Margot Macomber, turned to the brunette and cooed in that baby talk only big broads employ: "I hope I didn't crush your itty-bitty little coat."

At the end, one thought of what Hemingway himself would have thought of the evening. Maybe the latter-day Hemingway, who concerned himself with the squabbles (or *phffts*) of his friends Walter Winchell and Leonard Lyons, would have enjoyed it. But when the current of his prose ran as clean and as true as the Big Two-Hearted River, he would have found it unendurable. But he wasn't deserted. Mary Hemingway did all a wife, a lover, and protector could do in these exploiting times. In his absence she served as Papa's shit detector.

May 2, 1968

Realpolitik in the Parlor: Family Entertainment?

I am a symbolic man. I was lying on the couch in my living room clad only in my drawers, my legs slightly open as the delegates began to vote, waiting for the inevitable. I believe in dressing for the occasion.

I also am a vindictive man. The powers that be refused to grant press credentials for what would have been my first national convention. This was a slight I chose to ignore. Men of fertile imagination should never allow themselves to be defeated by mindless bureaucrats. Refused access to the real convention, I created my own Chicago.

Every night before the convention began on TV I would enter the living room (where the TV set is) through the kitchen. Here I would pop my credentials (a First National City loan book) in the toaster. My wife, unsympathetic to my symbolic ritual (after viewing the fifty-six remaining payments), would sarcastically say such things as: "You have enough credentials to seat the whole goddamn Associated Press."

On entering the convention floor (the living room), my wife and I engaged in a credentials fight. For two nights running I refused to seat her father, a Knights of Columbus right-winger. In this irreligious household it was necessary to import my mother to open each session with a prayer. The prayer usually summoned heaven for the return of Al Smith, pleaded with God that Negroes should act like the Irish, and, Jesus willing, I would go back to high school, get my diploma, get a normal job in the Telephone Company, stop drinking and disgracing her and the memory of my departed father in front of the neighbors, and shave that shit off my chin.

But something was missing. The living room was too congenial—there wasn't enough oppression. To rectify this I called up my brother, a Brooklyn cop, and invited him over for beers. When he arrived, I opened the door and delivered a soul-searing indictment. *"Sieg heil!"* I shouted.

Casually, he walked past me and said to my wife, "Christ, is he drunk already?"

For safety's sake, chairs were kept far apart in the living room to keep the hostile delegations from each other's throats. With the proceedings under way, we began to choose favorites. I sat alone on the couch rooting for Don Peterson of Wisconsin. When O'Dwyer condemned the Chicago cops and the war, my mother said, "He was probably English on his mother's side." My brother mused that "Mayor Daley must be a sweet guy to work for." And when Dan Rather of CBS got punched to the floor, my father-in-law was moved to comment that it was a shame "some other smart-ass journalists didn't get floor credentials."

By this time my wife was suffering her usual four-year paranoia. (In 1964 when the Republicans nominated Goldwater, she hid under the bed, like Millie Perkins waiting for the trucks with the hiccuping horns.) This year she swore that when they played "Happy Birthday," Lyndon was going to jump out of the cake naked and by joint acclamation receive the nomination.

Though the rhetoric on TV was endless, I soon discovered my liquor supply wasn't and ordered another quart from the local store by phone. Ten minutes later a twelve-year-old black boy delivered the merchandise. My father-in-law answered the door and in his usual boorish right-wing manner paid for the jug and tipped the boy excessively. My boozy liberal conscience offended, I invited the boy into the living room (over his protestation that he had to return to work) to have a glass of soda. With arms around my diminutive brother, I led him to the empty couch where I was sitting. Suddenly, he bolted toward the door and said to my wife, "It must be tough on you, lady, married to a honky chicken queer."

As my father-in-law and brother bellowed with laughter, my over-thirty violent psyche remained constant. As I moved toward confrontation with my brother, suddenly imperialistic tentacles encircled my neck and tried to garrote me. "Pig—police pig," I shouted, with the last gasps of my free breath. Out of the black void that was enveloping me, I heard my wife's voice: "Hold still, you drunken clown, before you choke to death in the baby's mobile from 1-2 Kangaroo." When I regained my dignity, like Washington bidding his troops farewell, I announced that I was going to the Village to the Lion's Head to drink with "my own kind." Hearing this, my wife seized the baby and stepped in front of the door, chanting, "Hell, no, you won't go."

When everyone was sure that I was too immobile to move, they bade my wife good night. My father-in-law was murmuring about the merits of lesbianism; my mother was mumbling something about may God and the Holy Father in Rome forgive her, but if the Irish have been reduced to producing the likes of McCarthy, O'Dwyer, and myself, maybe there was something to be said for that damned pill after all. My wife unilaterally withdrew to the bedroom.

Alone, I waited for Hubert Horatio Humphrey and the decision I have been pushing into the back of my mind for months. As Scott Fitzgerald once wrote, the dark night of the soul was upon me. It was Nixon-Humphrey. It was 1964 again, the same ball game, only the contestants were different. Jesus, my conscience screamed, anybody but Nixon. Maybe Hubert will put it all back together in his acceptance speech. Just maybe he'll applaud the minority plank and condemn Daley's cops. Maybe, maybe, never.

If the trouble with Gene McCarthy's speaking style was that (like Wagner) he never climaxed, the trouble with Humphrey's is that he is like Liszt—he has premature ejaculations every forty-seven seconds. And that

192

was not all—the band on the platform gave him a drum roll every time! When he was through, I felt like St. Paul after he got knocked off his horse—I never wanted to mount anything again.

It was that zombie hour between the dead night and the living morning when I said it. "Cleaver!" To my disappointment nothing happened in the heavens. My God—don't You even recognize a defection of an ex-altar boy to an animal cult named the Black Panthers? It just couldn't be as casual as this. There should at least be some pagan ritual. The drinking of blood? Impossible—my mother cooked the roast beef for five hours today to kill the trichinosis.

Unceremoniously, I went to bed (where was my soul? in the lower depths or up on the lofty rooftops?). In my newfound blackness only my wife's exposed buttocks gave forth illumination. I reached out to the familiar softness of that secure white cloud. "Good night," she said. Laconically, I replied, "Good night, David." And with the strains of "God Bless America," as sung by Anita Bryant, floating in my head, the light flickered, and I blacked out on Campaign '68.

September 5, 1968

When Maggie's Brood Gathers for Christmas

I suppose that those who regard Christmas as humbug have a point. Age turns that once candy cane stocking, the soul, into a withered sack of coal. And each year the coal becomes harder and blacker. God knows, it is for no small reason. Yet what other holiday is there? In times of cold and hot wars and domino theories, amid cries of racial genocide and visions of wooden boxes draped in pieties, it is impossible to have the pilgrim spirit and celebrate a national Thanksgiving. And Halloween vanishes with our firm legs, flat stomachs, and our flair for innocent vandalism.

In the old Irish neighborhood where I grew up, Easter Sunday was both mystic and material. As boys we knew someone was going to rise from the dead, One who, we felt, if He was as tough as rumored, shouldn't have been in that predicament in the first place. Since Lent was over and we were young gourmets, it was a time for celebration. It meant we would at least be spared my father's recipe for porgy (transported all the way from County Galway), a dish that called for such esoteric ingredients as water, salt, and a porgy, or my mother's Friday night fling at "real eye-talian spaghetti," which was concocted from a noodle with a German name and a can of Campbell's tomato soup. Of course, Easter also meant a hand-me-

193

down suit from a cousin who was "better off." A garment both my mother and my aunt judiciously would agree "needed a little growing into" but was fine for the day; so you wound up walking to the altar rail to receive communion looking like Toulouse-Lautrec in Wilt Chamberlain's threads.

But all this rambling has been a smoke screen to cover up the fact that I am, in fact, a sucker for Christmas. The magic has changed, but never diminished. One is tempted to recall a Christmas of his boyhood, but such memories are best left to the toy chest of the mind to be saved for one's own children. In these years of national sadness, perhaps one should paraphrase Fitzgerald and not chug our toy trains back into the safe past, but go forward to find hope in the present.

Christmas now is Maggie. She dominates it. She's my mother. A small Irish woman who alternately (or in combination) follows the teachings of Our Lord and Vince Lombardi. My own children, Liam and Siobhan, are not yet two years, so they have no awareness of the occasion. But every Christmas Day, my three brothers and their collective eight children, my widowed aunt, her two children and grandchildren participate in a gathering of the clan at Maggie's railroad flat in the old neighborhood. My father has been dead for twenty-five years, and one doubts he would have allowed so many micks in the same room, except for a union meeting.

Plans for the day usually start at the end of October, when Maggie calls to say she "can't do it again this year." Twenty-some-odd are too many to feed in the small flat. It is then that I ritualistically offer to help by organizing my own and my brothers' wives to do part of the cooking in our homes and transport the results to Maggie's to help ease the burden.

Always, it is a tactical mistake of the first order. Maggie has her yearly moment in the sun, and she'll be damned if she's going to share it. If Simon had offered my mother a hand to carry the cross, she would have kicked him for trying to horn in. So, after a period of breast-beating and lamentations, the old girl decides she'll go it alone, because she doesn't "have that many years left anyway." On this glorious note, we begin Christmas.

Now the guest list should be examined. My oldest brother, Doc, who manages a food store, and I make easy companions as long as we confine our conversations to Arts and Letters—the horse. Doc is not without spirituality—he has been known to be moved by such miracles as the nine-year-old Kelso taking the four-year-old Gun Bow in the home stretch. And he has to believe in the miraculous, since he married a girl from Northern Ireland, which in my family is integration.

The next brother in line is Billy, and that's another question altogether. Billy is a cop. Six feet three, hair of black, teeth of pearl, a vision in uniform that moves the old women at the wakes to look heavenward and mutter: "Jaysus, isn't he grand?" In brass-buttoned blue coat, he is the embodiment of why we came to these shores. It is enough said that our conversation is limited. Brothers feign civility because of blood. His wife and I have no such bond. She is a tall German-American girl with a spirited left hook, who for the life of her can't figure out why *Time* magazine didn't put Richard Daley on the cover as Man of the Year.

My younger brother, Eugene, is the classic youngest brother, who ecumenically breaks everyone's heart and bankbook. At twenty-five he has had more careers than George Plimpton. Every family has a ne'er-do-well, but, God, how do you tolerate him when he's a registered Conservative who preaches "self-motivation"?

My Aunt Nonie is, in the best sense of the phrase, a merry widow, whose mere presence is a gift to us all. Her youngest (and unmarried) son, John, presents no problems, since his hawkish tendencies are confined to the battlefield of the New York Giants and the Chicago Bears; and her married son, Billy, is a schoolteacher who always is placed next to me at the table so birds of a feather may. . . . So we gather with all the ideological unity that brought the Democrats together in Chicago.

Maggie wants a table-sized tree, or lately one of the plastic variety, but Billy annually insists that she can't do that to the kids and arrives a week before with a monstrosity that looks like the bastard son of the one they mount at Rockefeller Center. It is delivered with the promise that he will set it up, which he never does, so when we arrive on Christmas Day, Deirdre has another sorrow to lament.

Since the dining-room table seats only six, we eat ranch-house style, in four or five shifts. Maggie and Nonie run a food shuttle back and forth from the kitchen, reheating the food for every serving. String beans recooked four times are a delicacy not to be believed, nor should one have to attempt it. Too, there is a certain want of Christian charity: Someone steals all the skin from the turkey in the kitchen, or one of the kids eats all the marshmallows from the top of the sweet potatoes.

The living room is bedlam. The children are ripping the wrappings off the gifts, all of which are perfect except for the fact that they were given to the wrong kids. At this juncture, we have a setting for a Lilliputian brawl. Maggie, who believes godliness is next to cleanliness, scampers around picking up the discarded wrappings, managing to throw out some of the gifts in the process. By accident one year, she nearly discarded Eugene's infant.

Fully fed, we haul out the booze and begin to talk. Doc starts to cry about Eugene, lamenting that "he never knew his father." Billy's wife offers the opinion that a stretch in the jug is what Eugene really needs. Maggie accuses me of getting drunk and for the ninth year in a row says that I'm ruining her coffee table with whiskey stains. One year, Kevin, Eugene's oldest, accidentally decapitated one of the wise men in Maggie's manger under the tree, and the 230-pound Eugene carried the statue around in his pocket in sheer terror until we found glue to put the wise head back on the man. Billy's wife swore I put the kid up to it.

Finally, something magical happens. We play a collection of carols and Irish tunes on the phonograph, and we forget our differences and remember our likenesses. We talk of my father and Nonie's husband, Jack, and we laugh at the absurd odyssey of our lives. We touch and hug for the first time in a year, and to everyone's astonishment I dance with Billy's wife. Our boyhood friends arrive for drinks, and Salty Murphy, a burly Irish dockwalloper with a tenor's voice as light as Jim Corbett's jab, sings "When I Die, I Don't Want to Go to Heaven, Because I Found Heaven in My Mother's Arms," and Maggie and Nonie cry.

So there we sit—a family once a year. And I guess that's what brings us there. An unimpressive lot. No Madonnas and no Princes of Peace. Maggie and Nonie and their brood, whose collective grace is their staying power. And as long as we stay and still populate cradles, who knows? We may yet beat the humbuggers and people the earth with men of goodwill.

December 7, 1969

A Christmas Valentine to Maurice Sendak

If it is permissible at Christmas to mix one's Hallmarks, I would like to send a Valentine to Maurice Sendak for Christmas pleasures past and present. His books not only have given me great joy but have found me favor with my youngers and betters.

One young enchantress named Minja Steinman has loved me for over eight years, because I'm capable of endless rhyming to Sendak's *Chicken Soup with Rice*. A particular favorite of my son Liam is *Pierre,* the boy who said, "I don't care" to everything until he was swallowed by a lion. We both deliver the "I don't care" line in a mock basso profundo, trying to scare the hell out of each other, only to wind up giggling. Of course, in the end Pierre *does* care and triumphs over the lion, which probably is why sons are attracted to the tale; but I've always wondered about my fondness for it. Does Pierre finally represent to me a hip Christian who can outfox a lion, unlike those saints with names such as Desperation and Futility that the good sisters extolled to me in grammar school? They were mealy-mouthed losers. Even Victor Mature, in breast armor as large as a Brooklyn manhole cover shielding each nipple, was no match for the lordly atheistic lion. But Pierre is. Pope John would have seen cardinallike potential in the boy.

Then came Sendak's *Where the Wild Things Are,* a book that delighted every tyrannical tyke and terrorized his parents with their bush-league neuroses. Here was a boy commandeering an island populated with assorted monsters with the aplomb of a ringmaster, while we elders were emotionally incapable of an evening walk to purchase a newspaper. How could we possibly understand the boy's courage and spirit when we were locked behind chains and police locks, intricate bell-and-buzzer systems, and peepholes? Children today must possess the savvy of *The Dirty Dozen* to gain entrance to an apartment house to trick-or-treat on Halloween.

My own son, I'm proud to say, is a Sendak sibling. Recently, when his baby-sitter (of over a year) went to pick him up at nursery school, he refused to recognize her. He had expected his mother to call for him and had not been informed of the switch in plans. For twenty minutes he calmly sat while the best Montessori minds grilled him and with Le Carré cool claimed he had "never seen the girl in his whole life" (all of three years). Visions of baby-snatching plots were dancing in the progressive educators' heads. Such capers are to be cherished.

But it is this season that Sendak has blessed us with his masterpiece, *In the Night Kitchen,* which, I believe, will take its place in classic children's literature. I shouldn't really use the qualifier "children's" since the book has given me as much pleasure as anything I have read all year. I've read it about ten times now, and it still has the one ingredient that goes into making great books—magic. It has been fondly reviewed, but I think the reviewers have missed what the book is about. There has been comment about its "sexuality" and the display of the hero's genitals (I gather, a breakthrough for children's books), but this is only the frosting.

Deep in the batter of Sendak's book lies the real story—a boy about three years old visualizing his own conception and creation. Moreover, I believe the book is an autobiographical odyssey through the womb. The hero's name is Mickey, and one feels Mickey is the mouthpiece for Maurice. The dedication page reads "For Sadie and Philip" with an illustration of Mickey flying his airplane made of dough, exclaiming: "Mama, Papa!" Are these two Sendak's parents? (I suspect so, but I know nothing of the author's personal life.)

The story opens as Mickey is awakened in his bed by sounds from another part of the house: thump, dump, clump, lump, bump. He shouts: "Quiet down there!" The scene evokes a three-year-old being upset by a sound that is both foreign and primordially familiar (his parents' lovemaking). It is these sounds which provide the catalyst to the womb fantasy odyssey. After issuing his command for quiet, Mickey falls "through the dark, out of his clothes, past the Moon and his Mama and Papa sleeping tight. The key word, dually intended, is "tight."

As he falls past them, the naked Mickey ecstatically coos, "Ooh," "Mama," "Papa," and falls "into the light of the Night Kitchen?" into a pan of batter. Sendak provokes thought by placing a question mark after "Night Kitchen," a place where there are "bakers who bake till dawn so we can have cake in the morn."

The Night Kitchen is beautifully illustrated as a brightly lit place where kitchen staples such as milk containers, jam jars, and boxes of cake mix are drawn to resemble houses—a culinary city—with chimneys made of kitchen utensils (eggbeaters, corkscrews, funnels, etc.). There are three bakers dressed in white, all looking like Oliver Hardy. First the night kitchen, then the identical bakers. What is brilliantly bright and adorned with shiny utensils besides a kitchen? An operating room and an all-night bakery would look very much alike in the fantasy world of a child. And could the insistence of a *night* kitchen with "bakers who bake till dawn so we can have cake in the morn" be concurrent with the myth that children are always born in the wee hours of the morning? And since all doctors look the same in surgical masks, why shouldn't the child's mind conceive of three bakers who look the same—selfishly and delightfully like Oliver Hardy!

It is at this point in the book that parents' faint hearts must become stout. Mickey sits in the batter with the three bakers pouring various ingredients over his head until he disappears (except for one forlorn hand sticking up through the batter), while the three bakers stir it with wooden spoons and chant: "Milk in the Batter! Milk in the Batter! Stir it! Scrape it! Make it! Bake it!" (Could these be surgical goings-on?) They then "put that batter up to bake a delicious Mickey-cake." But the odd thing is that the batter, as yet unbaked, has risen and looks like a pregnant stomach as it is about to be popped into a "Mickey Oven." The word "oven" has an earthy, sexual significance pertaining to pregnancy—"She has something in the oven." One wonders if Sendak wouldn't have given his allegory away if he had called the stove a "Sadie Oven" instead.

"But right in the middle of the steaming and the making and the smelling and the baking, Mickey poked through and said: 'I'm not the Milk, and the Milk's not Me. I'm Mickey!' " Is Mickey now announcing he is no longer a merger of egg and sperm (cream?), but almost the finished product as his head pokes out from a womb of dough?

The next series of illustrations are the most poignant in the book. Mickey is out of the "oven," but he still is half-immersed in a pile of dough. He stands with hand on chin pondering if he is ever going to complete the last leg of his journey. Mickey's look of exasperation is sheer beauty which turns to earnestness, then to glee as "he kneeded and punched it (the dough) and pounded it and pulled till it looked okay."

Possibly this is the infant's and mother's final physical exercise to bring forth life. One can almost hear the pediatrician's exhortations of "push" and "bear down" in the above lines.

Finally, Mickey has sculpted the dough into an airplane, a vehicle to complete his odyssey. One of the buildings in these pages is lettered "Patented June 10, 1928" (Sendak's birthday?), and the patented product is "Coconuts." Is the creative milk now in Mickey? Is the coconut a skull with hair? Endless ruminations here. Also, earlier in the book, a container of pure cream with a Brooklyn address appears—possibly Sendak's birthplace?

So Mickey is off in his plane of dough, clad in a suit of batter to fly over the Night Kitchen's Milky Way. The bakers present him with a cup, howling: "Milk, Milk, Milk for the Morning Cake!" As they watch apprehensively, Mickey flies over a giant bottle of milk (the birth canal) and dives in with his cup, as his suit of batter breaks away from his body. He is naked as he shouts: "I'm in the Milk, and the Milk's in Me. God Bless Milk and God Bless Me!" He then swims to the top of the bottle and pours milk into the bakers' batter below. Since the book basically has been an ode to mother and child, is the fertilizing flow of milk a bow to the father's role in creation? Also, "I'm in the Milk, and the Milk's in Me" could be the child's recognition that once he has been created, he also is capable of the same feat.

As the bakers below celebrate their successful cake: "Milk in the Batter, We Bake Cake, and Nothing's the Matter!" Mickey smugly looks down on the proceedings, reclining on the side of the milk bottle with his creation-giving cup jauntily rising from his stomach like a penis.

The next illustration shows Mickey triumphantly standing on the milk bottle at dawn's creation, chauvinistically crowing: "COCK-A-DOODLE DOO!" with his "novel article" (as Miss Millett dubbed it—or snubbed it) sticking out for all to applaud. His fantasy odyssey over, he slides back into his bed "cakefee and dried," the last remains of the mother's creative juices wiped from his body.

So ends my Christmas Valentine to the genius of Mr. Sendak, an artist who, as the reformed Pierre would say, makes one care. Moreover, I would like to bow to Sadie and Philip, who had the genius to know when he was coming and to bake a cake.

December 24, 1970

God Bless Our Boys in Red

On Tuesday night last, the momentous eve when the striking force of the New York City Police Department decided to return to legal cooping, I traveled out to the Bushwick section of Brooklyn to the Stephen Decatur Chapter of the American Legion where Patrolman James "Battlin' Jimmy" Devaroe was to receive the chapter's annual Law and Order Award for service above and beyond the call of duty. Devaroe was to deliver an address titled "My Parity Right or Wrong—It's My Parity."

The twenty-seven-year-old Devaroe has been something of a local legend in those parts, since his National Guard unit was activated four years ago for the Vietnam conflict over the protest of the local parish priest and Devaroe's assemblyman. There also was economic pressure brought on Washington by the local bars and bowling alleys to keep the unit at home to fight inflation. But duty called, and Devaroe's unit, known as Shirker's Raiders, was shipped overseas to Governors Island, where Devaroe compiled an enviable service record, becoming the heavyweight champion of his medic unit, "The Fighting Ferries."

The dinner was slightly delayed while Legionnaires bailed the master of ceremonies, the Reverend Ignatius Kiley, out of jail. The Reverend Mr. Kiley had been arrested before the strike ended by a Protestant vigilante group who had glimpsed the good father running across a playground in his purple cassock and thought that this servant of the Lord was in drag.

Devaroe began his address by denouncing "all those who are trying to divide us." Then, dramatically looking in the direction of Governors Island (a difficult thing to do from Bushwick), he said: "If I can serve over there, why can't they?" At this juncture, the entire membership (who were still physically able) rose and toasted "Battlin' Jimmy" with 10-cent beers.

Seizing the interlude, the post commander quickly circulated among the crowd selling chances on a basket of cheer. The receipts were to go to the widow and children of the past finance chairman, who had killed himself on Armistice Day when it was discovered that he had been cutting 10 percent off the top of the Tuesday night bingo games.

Devaroe then went on to explain his part in the arrest which won him the Law and Order Award: "My partner, Tony Bennetti, and I disembarked from the K-15 bus on the northeast corner of Bushwick Avenue and walked to the southeast corner, where Tony said something about Sid Davidoff's mother and departed. As I began walking easterly, I heard a loud commotion behind me, westerly, and turned to see ten to fourteen youths, approximately thirteen to sixteen years of age, predominantly Caucasian, running from the sound of a loud crash—a window breaking. The explosion was similar to what was described in *Scanlan's Magazine* as

200

a pipe bomb, and I presumed the alleged perpetrators to be part of a faction known as the Weathermen, a group dedicated to fostering anarchy on our democracy.

"It was now that I took up my westerly chase while the alleged perpetrators ran southerly off Bushwick Avenue. It was at this juncture I observed that the alleged perpetrators were all wearing sneakers (a revolutionary tactic for quick escape which we learned about in the academy) and brandishing sticks, purportedly to perpetrate havoc on citizen or citizens unknown above the head and shoulders. At this point in the chase, the alleged perpetrators ran to an intersection where the northeast corner merges with that of the southwest, giving access to the main thoroughfare which runs north and south (except for commercial traffic). I pulled my service revolver and rapidly fired three warning shots into the air, while at the same time instructing the alleged perpetrators of their constitutional rights. When the party or parties in question failed to cease and desist their flight, I dropped to one knee and discharged three rounds from my service revolver, slaying one I alleged and one I assumed to be perpetrators.

"Fellow Americans, you know all too well the sad end of this story. I am now under indictment on charges brought by the ACLU [a chorus of boos from the audience] who claim I murdered alleged stickball players. They are basing their case on the flimsiest of evidence—circumstantial in every charge, hearsay beyond the shadow of a doubt.

"What do they have to offer a jury in exchange for my good name? A pink 'Spaldeen' found behind a broken window, a box score scribbled in chalk on Bushwick Avenue, clubs that they claim are broom handles, and, purportedly, they allege they have nine witnesses who insist it was the top of the seventh, and the ball through the window constituted a base-clearing ground rule double—thus explaining the fleeing action of the alleged perpetrators. Comrades in arms, if this travesty of justice can happen here, all I can say is 'May God help America tonight.' "

The Legionnaires burst to their feet and began to stomp and clap while the band broke into a medley of America's favorite songs. Devaroe beamed till they struck up "Take Me Out to the Ball Game" when, according to various witnesses near the podium, he wept.

Devaroe moved mummylike through the crowd toward the door where I approached him. "What do you want?" he asked. "Nobody gives a shit about us guys anymore." I assured him that I was interested both in his and his fellow patrolmen's plight, and we walked to his car, a powder blue Pinto. "Do you like it?" he asked. "I got thirty percent off from a dealer on my beat."

As we drove around his beat, he mournfully complained that "everyone hates the cops since we struck." He continued: "The *Daily News* turned against us. Even Jim and Mario took the Fifth on us this time. Who would have expected Buckley to cop out on us after we endorsed him? I thought he was a class guy. Jeez, with that crew cut and white raincoat, he looked like a detective first grade.

I asked him about Bill Buckley. "He's all right, I guess. He says the right things—when you can understand him," replied Devaroe. "But those eyebrows and that smile! We lock up a lot of guys that act like that. Look, the simple matter now is everyone wishes we would disappear for good."

And in all fairness, perhaps Devaroe wasn't dealing in patrolman paranoia. A rumor had reached my desk that Environmental Commissioner Jerome Kretchmer had been on the side of the dissidents during the strike because cars were being allowed to park illegally rather than cruise for parking spaces. Thus, the pollution was reduced by half. It was reported that this gambit was to launch Kretchmer's anti-Lindsay campaign in 1973: "A Fresh Breath of Sweet Air After Old Badmouth."

"No one," Devaroe lamented.

Unable to stand the human despair, I said: "Come on, someone out there loves you."

"Find one," he cryptically countered.

Davaroe switched on his car radio to WPAT, which was playing a Kitty Kallen record, and his spirits picked up. He rhythmically tapped the steering wheel with his American flag pinkie ring, and his identification bracelet, laden with numbered charms, clinked like castanets. I was fascinated by the bracelet and asked if the numbered charms were the dates of his kids' birthdays. "Naw," he replied. "That's the numbers of my six biggest busts since I was on the job. My old lady gave it to me for Christmas. You know how sentimental broads are."

Trying to make him feel better, I complimented him on his black shantung suit, and it seemed to work: "You like it, huh? Half price from a great little Jew tailor on the beat." I asked him if his dress wasn't a bit excessive for a patrolman, but he responded: "What are you talking about? Most of the guys dress like this. You want to know the biggest compliment I ever got on my clothes? Three times, three, mind you, I got picked out of a lineup as a Mafioso button man."

But Devaroe's momentary good mood wouldn't hold, and he lapsed into a constant monotone: "Nobody, nobody." He tried to induce me into going home with him: "Come on, I got some great Irish whiskey—got it for only four dollars a quart. We can watch the hockey game on my color TV —it's a Sony. A Jap on the beat gave me a great discount." I refused, and he was disconsolate.

I told him I was going to walk his beat and was sure I would find someone who welcomed the cops back to work. "No one," he muttered. I bade him a cheery good-night, and, as he was driving off, I heard him say: "Are you sure about the hockey game? You can stretch out on the Castro. I got it. . . ."

I entered a local luncheonette and tried a positive approach, exclaiming: "Great to have the boys back on the beat!"

A bald little man dressed all in white, looking like Casper the Ghost, shot back: "Great for who? Not for me! In the last five days, I realized there was no recession in this country—it was my coffee and danish all along."

"Your what?" I incredulously asked.

"My coffee and danish," he shouted. "Every day for fourteen years, I've been handing out forty-seven containers of coffee, twenty-two cheese danish, fourteen cherry, ten pineapple, and one prune to that momzer Kaufman. They want parity? Then I want parity. They should add up their tabs and retire me and Sylvia to Miami. For me, mister, they should freeze their asses off in the Antarctic and suck on coffee popsicles and break their teeth on frozen danish."

I left the luncheonette and despondently walked down the street, thinking Devaroe had been right—the milk of human kindness *is* two days old. It was then I spotted a figure in a doorway who, I presumed—as our British cousins would say—was a lady of the evening. At first, she refused to talk to me. But I showed her my *Voice* press card, and she said she knew of the paper, though she only read Andrew Sarris. "What's your name?" I asked.

"Lola Montes," she replied.

It turned out that Miss Montes wasn't enthusiastic about the cops' return either: "Jesus, what creeps! Some of these Irish are nice-looking kids who I wouldn't mind throwing a free trick for. But they're sick. All they talk about is how pure their wives are and what they won't do. Well, I don't mind telling you, I got a complete repertoire—that's French, by the way."

"What's French?" I asked.

"Not what their old ladies do, Johnny," she replied. "I fell head over heels for one of those babyface bastards. For months, I was dying to shake out between the sheets with him, but no dice. He wouldn't even let me put my hand on his pecker—he kept mumbling something about the Irish girls from Rockaway with white gloves. Then, one night he buys me a beautiful Spanish mantilla and whispers how he's going to take me to a dim candlelit place with a hint of incense in the air. So I'm all hot to trot, and where do you think he takes me? The sonnuvabitch waltzes me into St. Patrick's Cathedral and wants me to go to confession. I've been known to hit my knees, baby, but not in that scene. For my money, cookie, the cops can go screw themselves—with white gloves, I hope," she added as she flounced down the street.

So that poor, tormented devil Devaroe was right. Nobody wanted the cops: the *Daily News*, Jim and Mario, dealers in danish, and tarts alike. I couldn't believe mankind could be so harsh to these beleaguered men.

I began to meander aimlessly through the streets in a funky gloom. Suddenly, I heard the sounds of uproarious talk and laughter. The commotion was coming from a small storefront with an Algerian flag in the window and a Cadillac with DPL plates parked outside. The door was slightly ajar, and I pushed it open. Much to my wonderment, inside were three cops being embraced by a bunch of black men in berets and a foreign-looking gentleman in a pinstripe suit-and-vest ensemble.

Upon questioning, I found out the black men were members of the Bushwick Panthers, and the foreign gent was a diplomat from the Russian Embassy. They were pouring gin and vodka for the three cops and embracing them effusively. Incredulous, I queried: "Are you guys happy the cops are back on the beat?"

The head brother spoke up: "Man, I've never been so happy in my whole life. The last five days have been hell for the brothers. Those mothers from the Jewish Defense League have been laying heavy shit on us." Looking lovingly at the three white cops, he added: "May Muhammad luck out my beautiful ofay brothers' asses."

The Russian diplomat very drunkenly raised a jelly jar filled with vodka and shouted: *"Pros't, pros't!* The police return to protect our embassy from these meshugginers. As you would say in this superstitious country. 'God bless our boys in red!' "

In his new water bed, which he purportedly got at 17 percent off, Devaroe rolled in his troubled sleep and suddenly emitted a minor sigh, not out of contentment at being well loved, but loved.

Allegedly.

January 28, 1971

Asexuals Have Problems, Too

By Harold Nederland

This piece was written under the outrageous pseudonym Harold Nederland in hopes it would stem, indeed cut off at the pass, the glut of sexual whining that was finding its way into print. After its publication, the opposite proved true. "Harold" received endless letters praising his leap from the asexual closet and, in one instance, a Voice *reader asked if he could write a weekly column on "ASEXUAL CONSCIOUSNESS RAIS-*

ING." *With apologies to George S. Kaufman, it is not "Saturday Night" but the* Village Voice *that rings down the curtain on satire.*

I'm sick and tired of the constant whining going back and forth in your pages between heteros and homos. After all, these people have their sex to keep them warm.

But what about us asexuals? Is there a Merle Miller or an Andrew Sarris around to champion our cause? You bet not.

They must think it's a big thing to confess how many broads they've laid or boys they've buggered. Where is the man or woman with the courage to say the whole sex business leaves them feeling like a limp noodle? What we need is an Antonioni of the Organs, and since I am the founder of the Asexual Inactivists, I would like the opportunity to speak my mind.

Does anyone realize the early torment of an asexual? To have his father buy him a bike for Christmas, and when the salesman asks, "A boy's or girl's model?" his father replies, "It doesn't matter." Or to have his father reach the ultimate peak of frustration and scream at him: "Grow up and become *something.*" Oh, you lucky heteros and homos.

Do you know what it is to grow up in a society polluted with sex? At every turn, the asexual is assaulted with fucking and sucking in movies, music, books, and newspapers. I'm an educated man, but the last film I was able to enjoy was *101 Dalmatians.* Music is always mooning over love and advocating "letting it all hang out." (God, what a disgusting thought!) And forget books! In his latest effort, Norman Mailer has even managed to rocket sex to the virgin moon. NASA and nausea to the critical asexual.

And among newspapers, the *Voice* is the biggest offender to asexual rights. One is interested in reading about dance, but your terpsichorean Lolita, Jill Johnston, instead recites a litany of the motels across the country she's balled in. How about a little news from outside—London and the like? All we get in your paper is the mating habits of limey shopgirls. Who does Zwerin think he is anyway—George Sanders? Vivian Gornick and her vaginal vigilantes are more interested in clitoris raising than in consciousness raising. And what about the safe areas of politics and sports? Safe, maybe, in some other publication. But not in the *Voice* where that boorish Joe Flaherty writes metaphors with his prick rather than his brain. Damn you, you oppressive smut sheet.

And what about the whines of these fathers asking homo or hetero friends not to make advances at their children? Well, would you like it any better if every parent on the block desported their children with you to mind (including their seventeen-year-old daughters) and said nothing but "Thanks, good old Harold." Good old Harold at thirty-one years old! My house is now known as Harold's Romper Room.

Miller bitched that a faggot is a homosexual gentleman who has just left the room. Well, tough shit is all I've got to say—when I leave the room, people don't even notice.

Then these dirges are never complete without the heteros and homos rendering us their mauve, maudlin first encounters with sex. Would you like to hear about mine? When I was a teen-ager, a whore on Forty-second Street grabbed me by the cock, and I thanked her for adjusting my zipper! And there was the time I went to boys' camp and was gang-banged in my bed. I didn't even realize what had happened until the next morning when my camp counselor told me about it—I slept through the whole damn thing! Oh, you unfeeling cocks and cunts out there.

And the social life of an asexual? I am continually invited to orgies to pour the vin rosé and roll the joints. (My friends call me a sexual lazy Susan.) When a friend's wife gets drunk early at a party, the husband not only asks me to take her home, but queries whether I would mind being sure she gets into her pajamas! And God, the agony of the family Thanksgiving dinner when someone says, "Pass the mashed potatoes to It."

Oh, the hell with you. You'll never understand anyway. My hatred and contempt for both heteros and homos are so deep I ought to fuck every one of you, but my tragedy is that such desire is not under my realm.

February 25, 1971

The Potboiling of the Purloined Papers

Last Friday I received a document that may or may not have national significance from a longtime confidante, Lola, the hairdresser at the Hotel Pierre. The document had been left behind by a customer, a middle-aged woman reeking of some unidentifiable odor who had come in for a bouffant tease and who fell asleep under the hair dryer while making a series of raucous phone calls.

The papers themselves were in good order, except for multiple stains which, by licking them, I ascertained to be bourbon. The woman in question had been wearing sling-back pumps with a rhinestone letter M embroidered on each toe.

The document contained the minutes of a meeting that had taken place in a location called the Oval Room with five gentlemen in attendance, identified only by their first names and last initials. Also included were descriptions of the gentlemen in action at the meeting. The papers are classified in my files as the case of "The Lady with the Bun On." What follows is for perversity or posterity, depending on the reader:

RICHARD N.: Well, gentlemen, I guess you know why we're here. 1972 is pretty near at hand.

JOHN M.: Chief, perhaps we should list our strong points first.

RICHARD N.: Do we need memo pads, gentlemen?

JOHN M.: Don't bother. I've got a matchbook handy.

RONALD Z.: The way I see it, Chief, 1972 will be a conflict of image.

RICHARD N.: You mean mine against Hubert's, Edmund's, or Teddy's?

RONALD Z.: No. Your old image against your new one.

RICHARD N.: The same old shit again, eh?

SPIRO A.: The way I see '72, Chief, is a moral muscle maneuver between the lovers of law and the fanatics of ferment.

JOHN M.: Save that shit for when you're on tour, Spiro.

SPIRO A. (obviously hurt): It went over big in Buffalo.

RONALD Z.: How many times do I have to tell you, Spiro baby, 1972 is the big time, the Palace? That Orpheum circuit act is only for the road.

RICHARD N.: Don't quibble, gentlemen. We're in trouble. For chrissake, I've got a cousin in California on welfare. If we win in '72, we keep our jobs for another five years. Nobody in his right mind wants to go out and look for a job in this economy.

JOHN M.: How about playing up our space program?

RONALD Z.: I'm afraid that's out, baby. That son of a bitch Nader is releasing a study about how the space capsule's windows cloud over and louse up the view, that the food is crummy, and that there are no movies on board.

RICHARD N.: (petulantly): What do you mean, no movies?

RONALD Z.: Now, now, Chief.

RICHARD N.: Well, if we've got nothing positive going for us, who has an opinion on where we're the most vulnerable? (A collective silence, except for a voice unheard till now.)

HENRY K.: It's ze var.

RONALD Z. (muttering): Christ, I thought Lady Bird's accent was bad.

RICHARD N.: The var? I mean, the war, Henry?

HENRY K. (smiling knowingly): It's contagious, isn't it, mein Herr?

RICHARD N.: That's impossible, Henry. Everyone around here knows it was the other guys' fault, not mine.

HENRY K.: Precisely, mein leader. Everyone around *here,* but what of ze people?

RICHARD N.: But it's me who has ground this thing down. Don't the voters realize it?

HENRY K.: All zat ze people realize is zat you're contemptible.

RICHARD N. (starting to weep uncontrollably): I want to be loved.

HENRY K. (rises from the table, walks through the french doors, and begins to shout): A typical, sentimental American idea. Great leaders are meant to be despised and loathed. History has shown zis. Is zis ship of state to be paddled with an Erich Segal mentality? No! In the Fatherland. . . .

JOHN M.: Henry! Come in off that balcony and sit down.

RONALD Z.: Cool it, Johnny baby, the *Wunderkind* might be on to something.

RICHARD N.: All right, Henry, the floor is yours.

HENRY K.: Today ze floor, tomorrow. . . . Vell, ze vay I see it is zat ve have ze goods on ze Democrats. Mein leader, in our possession, ve have files on zeir bungling of zis affair since 1961.

RONALD Z.: Do you mean, Henry, we should release the files and indict the opposition as warmongers?

HENRY K.: Exactly. Though, mein God, forgive me, zey don't deserve zat esteemed title.

SPIRO A.: A baffling but brilliant battle plan of colossal chicanery.

JOHN M. (looking at Spiro A. with disgust): Jumping Jesus!

SPIRO A.: It's contagious, isn't it?

HENRY K.: Vith vun swoop, ve smear ze lot of zem. Ve release ze Camelot coup, and zese brothers look like ze Borgias, which vill eliminate zat young snotnose. Ve have enough on zat crazy cowboy to keep him out to pasture forever, along with zat babbling saddle tramp who vas his sidekick. To boot, ve got McNamara, Rusk, Bundy, Taylor, Hilsman—which contaminates zeir whole house.

RICHARD N.: What about the man from Maine?

HENRY K.: Zat neo-Lincoln schlepped in ze same bed vith zese curs. Zere's an old saying zat even ze janitor in a whorehouse can't be flushed clean. I believe *Il Duce* said it.

JOHN M.: But it's illegal to release secret documents. After all, we're the party of law and order.

HENRY K.: Exactly. After ze files are released and do zeir damage, ve go to court and try to suppress zem. To coin a phrase—a Yankee Reichstag.

SPIRO A.: Notwithstanding it's nebulous nihilism, Chief, I would note that's a Nazi nifty.

HENRY K.: *Danke,* mein dolt.

RONALD Z.: Jesus, Chief baby, think of the sweet revenge.

RICHARD N. (warming to the idea): Yeah. I would love to get back at that long-legged bastard for embarrassing me and my state at that library dedication in Texas. (hurt beyond repair) Do you know that that thing was two stories higher than Sleeping Beauty's castle in Disneyland?

RONALD Z.: Now, now, Chief.

JOHN M.: Besides, by releasing the coup, Chief, you could get back at that snobby Henry Cabot for the way he looked down on you in 1960.

RICHARD N. (wistfully): That's a thought. But you have to give a guy who can wear those striped pants the way he does credit.

HENRY K.: In ze old country, he vould have been a vaiter.

JOHN M.: Martha said he's a Brahmin.

SPIRO A.: That's right, Chief. We're checking out that organization right now.

RONALD Z.: But we'd need someone beyond reproach to leak these files.

RICHARD N.: How about the Reverend Billy?

RONALD Z.: No good, Chief. I've been meaning to talk to you about that guy.

RICHARD N.: What do you mean?

RONALD Z.: He has to be dumped, Chief. The guy just has a low Jesus profile. He doesn't suffer enough. Why, he hasn't even served time for his beliefs! Now, take a guy like Dan Berrigan—there's real Christ clout. Look at those great photos he takes, with his Thomas More haircut and his black turtleneck, and that look—I don't know how to describe it.

HENRY K.: Sex-starved.

RICHARD N.: Now, Henry, we've decided to declimax that issue.

RONALD Z.: Well, you know what I mean, Chief. Billy just stares at people with those weird eyes and frightens them. I mean, those eyes are spooky.

HENRY K.: Very Bavarian. Did you notice zat he shuns mirrors?

RONALD Z.: Too bad Checkers isn't alive. We could teach him how to bark in Morse code and do the whole gig over national TV.

HENRY K.: Ze papers must reach ze New York *Times*.

SPIRO A.: What! That rag for the rich, the reformed, and the refined? Revolting!

HENRY K.: Precisely. Ve must feign ze fink is foreign to us. (looking at Spiro) Mein God, vill someone alleviate zis alliterative ass from ze room before ve all suffer from syntactical symptoms?

JOHN M.: Hm-m, the *Times*. How about that bastard who baked the cake, Chief?

RICHARD N.: I don't think that would sit too well with Pat.

RONALD Z.: Besides, suppose they test the files in the oven? Our whole recipe for victory will go up in smoke.

JOHN M. (chortling): I just said it to get a rise out of you, Chief.

SPIRO A.: How about leaving a copy around for a radiclib to lift?

HENRY K. (his right arm bolting in the air): *Jawohl!*

RICHARD N.: Goddammit, Henry, I warned you about those antics around here.

HENRY K.: I simply vish to leave ze room, mein leader.

JOHN M.: Perfect, Spiro. The State Department is full of them. In fact, one of them is always mooning about, declaring himself a war criminal.

SPIRO A.: You mean the guy who walks around with that glass vegetable bin over his head?

JOHN M.: That's our man.

RICHARD N.: How do we expose him after the damage is done?

HENRY K.: Ve don't. Zion does.

RICHARD N.: Henry, this is no time to bring up the Jewish question. I promised you that in the near future.

JOHN M.: No, Chief. Zion, the reporter.

RONALD Z.: Perfect. This is better than the Trotsky caper.

SPIRO A.: What will we call the documents? You know how those liberals love those cloak-and-dagger names: the Catonsville 9, the Chicago 8, the Panther 21.

JOHN M.: Sounds like Martha with her fucking bingo.

HENRY K.: Enough. It is concluded. Zey all have blood on zeir hands but you, mein leader. A name vill come to us.

209

SPIRO A. (rising to leave): Chief, I've got to call Bob with this one. Maybe he can work it into a routine for his next TV special.

(Spiro leaves. The rest sit in deep thought, trying to divine a name for the documents. There is a knock on the door, and Spiro sheepishly sticks his head into the room.)

SPIRO A.: Chief, how about the Pentagon Papers?

(The group smiles as Spiro retreats. Moments later, there is another knock. Spiro again.)

SPIRO A.: Sorry, Chief, but it just struck me. When the papers disappear, we can call them the Purloined Pentagon Papers.

RICHARD N. (rises and hugs him): You alliterative angel. (Spiro exits.)

RICHARD N.: One contingency we didn't cover. What happens if the guy in New York jumps the fence?

HENRY K.: Ve shall replay his nominating speech for zat imbecile who just left on prime time for a week.

(They all sit back contented.)

RICHARD N.: I feel glorious. I have never had a filthier day in my whole career.

HENRY K.: It's a shame, mein leader, ve couldn't have held zis meeting in a beer hall.

(They all rise, except for Richard N., and exit, whistling "Hail to the Chief." Richard N. goes to a private screening room where he watches the film *Patton* for inspiration. He then returns to the Oval Room, passes through the french doors, and enters the garden, where he kneels in the grass, his bare head bathed in sunlight and humbly asks the Lord to let the snow job begin.)

July 8, 1971

The Pieties of Pinocchio

It becomes more and more difficult on this planet to avoid confrontations with the Lord.

On Sixth Avenue at Nathan's one gets his hot dog heavily relished with Hare Krishna chants from the singers who gather outside. On television Jimmy Durante appears in an Oral Roberts' special, raising speculation that "Ink-a-Dink-a-Do" might have been a Gregorian chant all along. Out of doorways freaks appear with a "ps-s-st," peddling Jesus as if he were a hot Timex in flight from Korvette's.

Priests and nuns are accused of trying to cop Henry Kissinger (the *Wunderkind?*) to save the soul of the nation; Billy Graham will be with us until a new administration pulls a Martin Luther and nails another savior to the White House door; and Gene McCarthy, conceived without sin in 1968 and cloaked in swaddling philosophies, finds Lindsay's primary conversion lesser than St. Paul's on the road to Damascus. It's enough to drive an atheist to exclaim "What in heaven is happening here?"

And it doesn't stop there. The once-pleasant pastime of watching a Sunday football game *avec* beer and drawers is a bygone thing. The half-time shows are so solemn one is compelled to don his Sunday best for these Yankee Doodle Diety spectacles. Even the mob isn't ecclesiastically exempt. Every time some Mafioso feels he has been maligned he is on television that very evening invoking justice in God's name and reducing Himself to one of their own, a sort of Kid Bethlehem.

But all this noted, I was not prepared for what I found at the movies the other day. With my son Liam in hand I discovered the Pieties of Pinocchio.

So, in the classic mode of children's storytelling: If you sit still, my little readers, Father Flaherty will tell you what that fanciful fable is all about. In short, it is, with some strings attached, the odyssey of Jesus Christ.

I am now talking about the Disney film, not the original book (which I haven't read), written by an Italian named Carlo Collodi. (For those interested in an interpretation of the original work I would enthusiastically recommend Donald Phelps' brilliant collection of essays on various subjects, Collodi's book included, titled *Covering Ground,* published by Croton Press.) But it is safe to assume that Disney and his screenwriters found the genesis of their tale in that work, since everyone knows any Italian writer from Dante through Fellini worth his pepper could cache religious symbolism in the writing of his laundry list. What I'm most interested in is the merging of these two moralists, Italian and American, or what happens when the Crown of Thorns gets entangled with Hollywood and Vine.

The film opens in a Bethlehem setting, an unnamed town with a brilliant star standing out in the heavens. It then switches to the interior of the woodcarver Gepetto's shop (or that of the carpenter Joseph of Nazareth). Gepetto has carved a wooden puppet he wishes was "real," a wish made to the Wishing Star. As Gepetto sleeps, the Star materializes into the Blue Fairy (an angelic apparition), a scene that leans heavily on the Annunciation. The Fairy gives Pinocchio mortal (*i.e.,* wooden) life as a wooden boy but holds out the promise of real (immortal) life, if he is "good, courageous, and truthful," the Bible as interpreted by the *Boy Scout Manual*.

Thus, we have the Virgin birth, a boy "conceived without sin," a son born outside woman's womb, which sets the insidious, chauvinistic theme of the universe. A theme suggesting that liberated women are perhaps a little wooden-headed themselves, if they take their children to see *Pinocchio*. One also should note the boy is made of wood which strikes me as old rugged symbolism.

Disney is not too kind to Gepetto either, portraying him as a silly old nebbish. But one wonders if there isn't some Biblical accuracy in this. Of all the saints in my catechism I always felt St. Joseph was devoid of drama and clout (for this reason I've never cared for my Christian name). Anyone with sidewalk smarts is moved to snickers at the way Joseph was chosen to be Christ's earthly father. The bit of the lily (the "pure" flower of death) popping out of his staff seems to me the supreme supernatural (never mind Freudian) put-down of the penis.

In fact, Joseph seems to have been the prototype for many Jewish writers who have portrayed him in contemporary literature as the sad, unquestioning shlep, the good-time Charlie uncle who marries his brother's widow, mother of seven kids, and foots the grocery bills but sleeps alone in a separate bedroom.

As for Jiminy Cricket, what else is a conscience but a nagging little bastard that is continually chirping at you?

But back to the Salvation via the silver screen. Gepetto discovers his animated little shaver and is delighted. After some celebration he orders "his son" to go to bed since he has to get up early for school the next morning. Of course, those familiar with the story know Pinocchio never reaches school because en route he runs into that sly old fox Honest John, who convinces him school is a drag and he really should strut his stuff or carve his niche upon the stage. Thank the devil for Honest John, because if Pinocchio ever reached school, the story would fall on its face, like a puppet unstrung.

Indeed, the tale would truly become grotesque and terrifying to children. Imagine this wooden horror, hinges *et al.*, sitting in a classroom with "real" children. Would the children not be tempted to carve their initials in Pinocchio rather than in their desks? Or would they not stick his nose in the pencil sharpener or make scatological jokes about excreting sawdust? Bible or no Bible, boys will be boys.

The way in which Disney grants Pinocchio a modicum of normality is to juxtapose him constantly with grosser grotesques than himself: Honest John, the menacing puppeteer Stromboli (a cruel surrogate father figure), and the evil Coachman of Pleasure Island (a puritanical metaphor for earth where one carouses and dissipates, where humans not only act like jackasses but become them, more stridently christened Boobyland in Collodi's original).

And what is Honest John's sin? A dual one, one supposes: He is realistic (earthbound), for surely a wooden boy would be more at home on a stage than in a classroom with flesh and blood, but, more grievously, he leads Pinocchio away from his heavenly and fatherly dictates. (At this point my son asked, "Daddy, why is he bad?" And one of the foremost truants in the Western world who was tutored by his own Honest John, one Tommy O'Donnell who taught him how to crash into movie houses as a boy, who easily could have adopted Pinocchio's song of the road, "Hi-Diddle-Dee-Dee, An Actor's Life for Me," solemnly answered with a lump in his throat, "Because he is keeping Pinocchio out of school." So much for aging Brooklyn juvenile delinquents.)

So Pinocchio's sin is simply that he spurns the wishes of his father and goes about his own business; ignoring you know whose. But be forewarned, my little readers, he pays, he pays. After he is a critical and financial success with the Stromboli troupe and wants to go home at night to sleep at his father's, Stromboli (who looks like a hairier David Merrick) locks him in a birdcage, presumably inaugurating the first run-of-the-play contract known to man.

Then, once again, the Blue Fairy intervenes in one of her many spiritual roles. We have seen her as the angel at the Annunciation, as the Madonna giving birth (by the way Disney's vision of her is predictably mid-American—he draws her as an aging carhop), and now as a messenger from God the Father. Pinocchio, like any erstwhile actor (substitute human), tries to cop a plea about his adventures by lying. The Fairy, in her benevolent wrath, makes him even more grotesque by extending his nose to the length of a pool cue and then weakens (like heaven she does) and gives the mortal woodenhead *one* more chance. *One,* mind you!

But Pinocchio, like the rest of us, is a creature of multiple failings, and he is conned by Honest John into joining an orgy on Pleasure Island which looks, in Phelps' memorable phrase, like "Warner Brothers reform school stuff." On the island he engages in some rather innocuous deviltry (beer drinking, cigar puffing, and pool shooting—the seventh circle as seen by the residents of River City) with a Mickey Rooney-type sidekick named Lampwyck. He is rescued by Jiminy Cricket, his conscience, before he is turned completely into a jackass (he spouts only the ears and tail, devilish that), thus being only partially damned and leaving room for redemption. The heart is not yet hairied over. Conscience and boy escape by jumping off a high cliff into the sea, a spectacular, baptismal plunge from the giddy heights of mortal high jinks into the eternal sea itself. From that moment on Pinocchio is clear in his purpose: He must reunite with his father.

But when he returns home, Gepetto is gone, swallowed by a whale while searching for his wayward son, a warning to one and all that when one is looking for absolution, he just can't simply go home again. The pearly gates are not to be opened by knocking or picking but are only to be crashed by "courage, truthfulness, etc.," so now Pinocchio must prove his mettle by rescuing his father.

So into the resurrecting sea he plunges once again to do battle with the monstrosity of his ways (the whale is called Monstro) that has enveloped his father. He springs his father (and mankind) from this purgatorial cavern (a netherworld between life and death, salvation and damnation) of the fish (an old Roman symbol) by using Satan's weapon of fire, the smoke forcing the whale to sneeze Gepetto and Pinocchio out upon the sea. The son had the courage to enter into this semideath state to free his father, but courage in the universal theme is not a flirtation with finality—fathers are more demanding than that.

As the whale pursues them across the sea, Gepetto falters and urges the boy to save himself. (Didn't that other son also have a free choice to step down from his cross?) But Pinocchio, true to divinity, chooses to save his father. The wooden, mortal son dies in the doing. Disney depicts him drowned, face down in the water, his arms outspread—a floating crucifix.

Gepetto carries the wooden boy home and places him on a bed, then kneels and weeps. The Blue Fairy now appears satisfied with the boy's sacrifice and grants him real (immortal) life. For his efforts Jiminy Cricket receives an "official" conscience badge, made of 18-carat gold, which may be Hollywood's idea of a 10 percent moral agent's fee. The badge scene was my son's favorite, perhaps an early recognition that the conscience has a hell of a job in this life. The Blue Fairy, no longer needed, since she has united father and son, is dismissed to the ethereal role in which Christianity has doomed women.

So if you take your child to see this movie, and he falls on the floor, don't assume it's from laughter. The little shaver has just witnessed a celluloid chip off the old Pop play out the oldest refrain known to man. The tyke, through the magic of Edison, might have done seen the light.

September 9, 1971

The Men of Local 1268, God Bless Them All, the Last of a Bad Breed

Come St. Patrick's Day, even the most cynical Irishman gets a tear in his eye, dons the green, gargles too much, and warbles a little.

Gone for the day are the memories of working-class poverty, priests in the confessional boxes giving with the third degree for capers committed between the sheets (if you grew up in the fifties, these usually were felonies with no accomplices), and the specter of the "good" nuns beating the eight-times multiplication tables into your head for the greater glory of

God and academic oneupmanship over those heathen who attended P.S. 130. The dark Irish romanticize the day in somewhat the same way ex-GI's wax poetic about the great doses of clap they caught in France.

Luckily for me, when I think of the Irish, my mind wanders down to the water's edge and shapes up with memories of the men with whom I worked in ILA Local 1268 of the Grain Handlers' Association. But be at ease. What follows is not a tale of populist Celts brimming with *machismo*, like the foam on a pint of Guinness, but a rosary of labor miseries that would make the beads of the Sorrowful Mysteries look, by comparison, like the bricks on the yellow road to Oz.

I came to be a grain trimmer by heritage, not accident. My father, John, was once the president of the local, and his brother Christy succeeded my father after his death. My brother Billy (now a cop) was a trimmer, and my first cousin Bobby was a hatch boss. So when I was discharged from the Army at the age of twenty, my Flaherty blood beckoned me to seek my fortune in the dusty holds of grain ships.

In my memory the local had a membership of 100 men at most—all Irish, with the exception of a couple Swedes, which was considered the height of integration in those days. But in fairness to the democracy of 1268 we were avant-garde in some areas.

We recognized Gay Lib before it officially came into existence. One of our members sauntered up the pier daily in black chinos and turtleneck, treading softly on white tennies, and carrying his work gear in an airline shoulder bag. The old-timers used to peer down from the ship, muttering Hail Marys to the effect that the Celtic sperm must have been diluted by the salt water in the crossing. But he was judged by his work (which was splendid), not by his sexual preference, and there were no closets in 1268. Indeed, the opposite was true. One day our homosexual dockwalloper showed up wearing a headband with a pigeon feather stuck into it to celebrate the acquisition of a new lover, an Indian ironworker. He also rewrote ILA history when he succeeded in getting Tough Tony Anastasia's medical clinic on Court Street to pay for his nose bob. Hernias and hemorrhoids you can understand, but the ILA financially floating a nose bob?

Our union hall was located on Coenties Slip over a saloon (mark the symbolism), and our meetings were held on Saturday mornings around ten o'clock. The strategy was that the members could drink for only two hours before the meeting, but it failed since everyone had usually been out until 4 A.M. the night before, and two hours of boozing was enough to turn their breaths to gasoline and their personalities to napalm.

While other locals argued about the impending threat of automation or better working conditions, 1268 concerned itself with much meatier matters. Some stalwart with his brain adrift in a 90-proof Galway Bay would seize the floor and recount how thirteen years before some boss hadn't hired him (even though he had seniority) just because he had been a "few minutes" late for the shape, and, indeed, the reason for his tardiness had been that he was at the bedside of his Aunt Peg, who had taken a stroke in far off Rockaway during the night. Shillelagh sentimentalism was the rule. Of course, the truth of the matter was that the bastard had been three hours late for the shape and so crippled that he had come up the dock looking like Toulouse-Lautrec.

This would lead to a countercharge that the "cheap cur" hadn't chipped in for the collection for Paddy So-and-So's family when he died and so didn't deserve a day's work, which would segue into an oration from an "old-timer" devoted to the proposition that the "Johnny-come-latelys" were running the job, which ricocheted into a j-c-l stating that if it weren't for the young holding up the end of the dilapidated old fogies, not an ounce of grain would be shoveled out of a ship. The crowning culmination was a punch-out, and our union would go into "trusteeship" to be ruled by the overlords of the ILA.

Of course, that never worked either. The bad blood of numerous families flowed through our ranks, spiced with ould sod geographical hatreds. The Galway men were considered "clannish." The Tipperary contingent, not being bold men of the west, were effete, and the Irish-Americans, like me, genetic disappointments to be endured. ("Sure, you wouldn't put a pimple on your father's ass.")

But the ILA officers tried to forge a brotherhood among us. On one occasion the union president, Captain Bradley himself, graced our humble union hall and pleaded for unity, explaining that ours was the most troublesome local on the waterfront, and we had only 100 members. He went on to say that locals with thousands of members lived in harmony. Finally, in the spirit of ecumenism, he began to utter the Lord's Prayer. But in the midst of his negotiations with the Snapper in the Sky, one of our members bounced through the door like a massé cueball and loudly urged the captain to commit an act with himself that would have been difficult for a man many years his junior to execute. Brotherhood in 1268. Better to try forging a connubial contract between Ian Paisley and Berna-dette Devlin.

Loading and unloading grain from ships and barges was an arduous and dangerous profession. One had to walk through mounds of rye or corn up to his knees, an exercise which makes running along a sandy beach seem like a cakewalk. The dangerous aspect was provided by the grain dust that used to fill the hold, making a smoke screen so thick you couldn't recognize a fellow worker at twenty feet. Then there were the occasional pier rats who were so big from eating the grain and chasing it with the polluted Hudson they could have pulled Cinderella's carriage without that trans-formation hocus-pocus.

216

So one would assume that it would take young Spartans to work at this profession. But preconceived notions were always shanghaied in Local 1268. The majority of the grain handlers were men who nowadays would be relegated to pushing a shuffleboard stick in Kern City.

Their training habits were simple. For decades they had drunk anything that was bottled. (Once on an Italian ship Scat Whalen drank cruets of white vinegar which he'd found on the galley table and pronounced it "a great Dago table wine.") To a man they worked in the dusty hold with pipes clenched between their teeth, and their regular diet could have killed a mule, never mind a man. At noon the old-timers would open their brown paper bags and start with a raw onion for an appetizer. (The onion, like garlic with vampires, was supposed to ward off the evil of the dust.) The main course most often was four meat sandwiches on Wonder Bread, with the sliced meat cut to the thickness of a beaver's tail and embalmed inside a quarter pound of butter.

Le Pavillon for the grain trimmers was Ma Kane's bar in Jersey City ("Ah, Jaysus, a great feed"), where you were served a slice of corned beef so thin you could read the *Morning Telegraph* through it and a boiled potato the size of an incubator baby.

As a novice trimmer another phenomenon was revealed to me: Nobody was called by his Christian name. The Irish, being frustrated curates, baptized everyone with a nickname. My father, I learned, had been known as Young Bush which roughly meant top man. My uncle was the Bull for his penchant to bellow orders. Another old-timer was called Shag, because of his amorous adventures in the old country; another Tokens, because he paid the snapper's subway fare. The first day I shaped I was sporting a beard and was so christened. "By Christ," crooned an old harp, "he looks like Haile Selassie."

Then there were the father-and-son teams. One man was the Horse, so named in Orwellian fashion for his capacity for hard work. Naturally, his son was called the Pony. There was Big Joe Taylor, who looked like the eighth dwarf, and his son Little Joe, who looked like the World Trade Center.

We also had a resident spiritualist, the hatch boss, Paddy the Priest, who could forgive anything but moral slackness. A young dude named Ace Gillen was quick to notice this, and when the going in the hold got tough, he would retreat to a clear corner and pull out a newly acquired string of rosary beads. When the Priest reprimanded him for dogging his work, Gillen would piously apologize, saying he had only taken a blow "to say the Angelus." Paddy, touched to find such devotion in the young, would exhort the rest of the gang to work harder to take up the slack for the "saint" in the corner of the hatch.

The Pied Piper of the young men on the pier was the General, an old rogue of grand dimensions. He was a small man with a button nose, white hair, and the most beguiling blue eyes I've ever seen. The truth was an intrusion he couldn't bear, and over a drink he would reminisce: "To be young again and move across the desert with Lawrence of Arabia. Now there was a man! We left a river of blood behind us as long as the Nile." He could recite the seductive splendors of harem girls and desert goats in the same breath, and his sexual fantasies would make anything Girodias has published look pale. He swore that the eleventh-century Irish chieftain Brian Boru had been such a broth of a boyo that when he got an erection it reached all the way across the land, and it took the men of six counties to jerk him off.

The pious old-timers constantly advised us youngsters of his corrosive nature. He was aware of this and always managed to find a moment for revenge. He was a notorious drinker, and when any of them inquired about his wife, they always put "poor" in front of her name. To one patronizing inquiry he replied: "The woman is in desperate straits. I came home drunk last night, and she stole the last penny out of my pockets. When I woke up this morning, I was shocked to find I had a hard-on. The first one in three years. I walked out to the kitchen, showed it to her, then tucked it in my pants and left for work. The poor woman won't see the likes of it for another three years."

But the gem of our polluted ocean was our labor committee, or "comitty" as the old-timers called it, or "comedy" as the perceptive saw it. It was headed by John J. Moriarty aka Calhoun (after Amos and Andy's mouthpiece) and John "Woodenhead" Regan.

Calhoun was granted intellectual status, because he read publications other than the racing form and smoked Parliament cigarettes. He also separated himself from the vulgar herd by daintily sipping Irish Mist while we indulged with a ball and a beer. When he condescended to our level and talked about horse racing, he referred to the classic in Kentucky as the "Darby" and wanted to know if a particular charger's bloodlines went "back to Blenheim, that magnificent English sire." He not only read the minutes of our meetings but wrote them to boot, which put him in the enviable position of Joyce with *Finnegans Wake*. How could we remove him from his post? We wouldn't have known what had gone on in the union for the last ten years.

Woodenhead was our great orator. In his best moments, when he was calling for a strike, he shaped up to William Jennings Bryan in his Cross of Gold speech. And, my God, did we strike! We struck when there was a gossamer layer of snowflakes on the hatch covers (removing snow, like Lindsay in Queens, wasn't in our contract); we struck when friends weren't hired or were fired; we struck for clean drinking water, though in memory I can't recall anyone putting that foreign substance to his lips. Yearly on opening day at Aqueduct the gang could be found draped over winches, claiming that scurvy had hit the ship (pity the paltry imagination of city employees with their "Asian flu" slowdowns).

Woodenhead scaled high C one freezing night when we were unloading a barge for the United States Lines. The barge sprung a leak that was considerably smaller than the dribble of a near empty seltzer bottle, but Woodenhead, running around the deck wildly, turned the incident into a maritime tragedy. "Get those men out of that barge," he screamed. "My God, get those men up before they drown like rats! This will be worse than the *Titanic!* Get the Fire Department. Never mind the Fire Department, get a priest!" Two hours later, after a U.S. Lines official plugged the hole (with Fleers Double Bubble Gum, I presume) we went back to work, a lot warmer, a lot drunker. Like Gepetto, I have loved woodenheads ever since.

As I noted, it was a dangerous thing to fire a worker, because of the threat of a strike. I once played the lead in such a drama. A ship was late docking in Jersey one morning, and we idled our waiting hours ("up the streets") in a bar. When we returned to the ship, all carrying much ballast, an old-timer fell overboard. My drunken brain reacted as if I were in a bad two-reeler, and I dived (wearing work boots) to the rescue. Calhoun, spotting the victim and the hero's condition, ran to the foc's'le, pulled out his rosary, and started to pray for the repose of our soused souls. I started to scream for a heaving line, but some good Samaritan flung me a breast line so heavy it could have been used as a leash for a dinosaur. The line hit us both on the head, and we sunk, and I began to wonder about the merits of sober discretion over drunken valor.

When they finally fished us out, I conked out for three hours and, when I woke up, was told I was being fired for drunkenness. The boys rallied around my flag and delivered an oration to my gallantry, spiced with the threat that the whole damn gang might retire to the high stool if I was fired. Needless to say, I remained on the payroll, and Calhoun, his rosary temporarily squandered, profusely kissed me, like a French general, on both cheeks.

But no story about Local 1268 would be complete without a mention of my first cousin Tommy "Lulu" Fleming. ("That one was well named," the Bull used to mutter.) We were unloading a "dead" (mothballed) grain ship in Brooklyn, and Lulu was fired for that sin the Irish flesh is heir to. But true to his nature, Lulu didn't take it lying down. In fact, he rewrote employer-employee relations forever.

After he left the ship, we heard this strange whacking sound. When we looked over the side, it was even stranger than we'd thought. Lulu was chopping the lines that held the ship to the pier with a fire ax! The thought of a gang of grain trimmers afloat at sea in a ship without engines, endlessly damned to the wavy limbo of the Flying Dutchman, was enough to have the employer "reassess" his position. Next to Lulu, Mike Quill was a pussycat.

But one day he went too far. Lulu was working a hatch with Salty Murphy, who had gained Brooklyn immortality by swimming bare-assed with the seals in Prospect Park Zoo. Lulu and Salty had been under suspicion all day, because every time they descended the ladder the contents of their pockets chimed like the Bells of St. Mary, and it was finally discovered they were working on a wine load. Salty was spraying grain from the open part of the hatch under the decks where Lulu was directing the stream. All that could be heard from the hatch was the sound of "dead soldiers" breaking and loud cursing. When Lulu didn't appear from between decks for about a half hour, the boss inquired where he was, and Salty matter-of-factly replied: "I buried the bastard."

The ship immediately took on the appearance of a January white sale at Korvette's. The flow of grain was stopped, and everyone charged down into the hold with hand shovels to dig Lulu out of his grainy crypt. After an endless time of futile digging, dark imaginings of breaking the "news" to the family, and scores of mental mass cards being written out, lo and behold, the dust cleared. As if the giant stone had been rolled back, there in a far corner of the hatch sat the resurrected Lulu, sipping muscatel and laughing maniacally. Like the Father and His Son, Salty and Lulu ascended the ladder to take body and spirit to the heavenly reaches of a Jersey saloon, a chorus of curses giving them wings. But such exploits must be put in perspective. As Tough Tony Anastasia once said: "That goddamn whiskey mixes with the dust in their Irish heads and drives them all mad."

It is all gone now. Grain hasn't been loaded in this harbor for years. In a way it's a shame. I've never worked at a job I liked so much or with men I loved more. Every day was a trip to the circus, and never will such grand clowns be assembled under one tent again. As Frank Skeffington said in *The Last Hurrah*, "How do you thank a man for a million laughs?"

But it is possible the end was fitting. In the prissy labor field of today, composed of slick four-flushers and punky bureaucrats, these men would be lost. Like Sam Peckinpah's cowboys, their time has passed. These were the urban cowboys.

So may God bless them this St. Paddy's Day wherever they're scattered. And forgive and understand them, too. Their sins were unavoidable—like Willie Loman's, they came with the territory. As old Mike Regan used to say ruefully: "Ah, they're the last of a bad breed."

March 13, 1972

Grimm and Bear It: Sexism in "Snow White"?

The world of letters in these "frabjous" times seems to be in tougher shape than—for want of a better phrase—the real world. Subject matter seems to be diminishing, if not disappearing.

Only a lout would cast a piece of work with an ill-mannered Pole, an Italian with a penchant for crime, an Irishman with a proclivity for poteen, or a Jew with a flair for making money. Gone too are blacks, Puerto Ricans, and Indians whose intentions might be less than celestial. A portrait of a woman a notch below Joan of Arc is inconceivable, and there isn't an unhappy homosexual left on the planet.

And if you have a notion to conjure a man who likes hunting, you'd better believe a chorus of critics will inform you his gun is a substitute for his waning wand and his desire is not venison but Vietnamese. The censorship of sensitivity is upon us.

The lot of an adult is to endure through such times by sporting a benign grin. But enough is enough already. A story a few weeks back in the Sunday *Times* by Fred M. Hechinger was headlined thus: "Grimm's Chauvinist Pigs!" It seems one Marcia R. Lieberman, who is an assistant professor of English at the University of Connecticut, charged that there are damaging links between feminity and passivity in fairy tales. The Grimm reaper cited Snow White, Cinderella, and Sleeping Beauty as cases in point. The only solace to be found in this is that Professor Lieberman is adhering to her profession's historical role—that is, murdering literature.

As a lover of fairy tales, I was taken aback by the professor's charges and decided to reread "Snow White" and "Cinderella." And, by God, the woman was right! The two tales *were* sexist, but not the gender she suspected. What follows is another view of the new criticism, which will prove only that boobery is in the eye of the beholder.

The "Snow White" I read was the translation from the Brothers Grimm by Randall Jarrell with glorious illustrations by Nancy Ekholm Burkert. As any indoctrinated sibling knows, Snow White's natural mother died at birth, and her father, the King, took a second wife. The potent King's (he is mentioned but once in the course of the story) only claim to fame is that he sired a daughter and remarried. As far as I can tell, he was the Calvin Coolidge of his day.

The beauteous Queen has a guru of a mirror which informs her that her stepdaughter is *numero uno* in the land (a bit like Friedan being upstaged by Steinem), and this docile doxie orders a huntsman to kill Snow White: "You kill her, and bring me her lung and liver as a token."

The huntsman, a romantic sexist to the tip of his dirk, just can't cut this scene. Instead, he kills a wild boar and cuts out its lung and liver. (If the professor was the victim, a tame bore could have been substituted.) And our little lamb takes it on the lam through the forest till she comes upon the cottage of the Seven Dwarfs.

The cottage is empty, and the passive Snow White, without as much as an invite, nibbles food from each of their seven plates and swigs wine from each of their little mugs (she was Irish on her father's side). It must also be noted that throughout the story (forget the Disney version) the dwarfs remain nameless—abbreviated sex objects, so to speak. And when Snow White encounters them, she doesn't give her invasion of their home a second thought. I ask you, wouldn't the most aggressive of males perchance think he was intruding on a sanatorium for the handicapped or disturbing a thriving gay commune? But not this little exile.

True, a sexist deal is struck between them. Snow White is to keep house for the seven in exchange for a hideout. But in all fairness it must be admitted that these duties do not seem awesome, given the chaps' size. The dwarfs' sheets were probably the equivalent of Orson Welles' dinner napkin, and a can of Spam would glut the whole crew. It also should be noted that the dwarfs were gold miners. Just a thought, mind you.

But back to our story. The Queen, on further consultation with the Yaqui Indian in her mirror, learns that Snow White is still alive. With all the passivity Bella Abzug displayed at moratoriums to end the war, the Queen plots Snow White's demise. (Cease Now! Cease Now!) Displaying the acting talents of Duse and the laboratory genius of Jonas Salk, she begins her campaign.

Employing a variety of disguises that would have been a boon on Baker Street, the Queen makes two unsuccessful attempts on Snow White's life. First, she tries suffocating her by tightening her bodice laces, which the dwarfs loosen, restoring her to life (no fondling is recorded). The second time around she peddles her a poisoned comb (the message here is to keep an eye on your passive Avon lady). But once again the dwarfs come to the rescue. What a scene to come home to every night after a hard day's work: "Dammit! Dead again!"

Finally, reverting back to the original founder of the sisterhood, the Queen slips Snow White a malevolent McIntosh. This time the dwarfs are stymied. Totally overcome by grief, they construct a beautiful coffin of glass and place Snow White in it on a mountainside. Now, from Snow White's track record, you know that if one of the dwarfs kicked the bucket (or perhaps a shot glass, again considering size), it is dubious that this broad would give him such a sendoff. Cold logic tells us she probably would wrap the corpse in Saran Wrap, like a shriveled gherkin, and toss it in the bushes.

Enter the Prince. He wants the coffin and corpse for his own. "I'll honor and prize her as my own beloved."

It is time for a pause. We must check the males we have encountered so

222

far. A ball-less king, a sentimental slob of a huntsman, seven nameless runts, and, forsooth, a necrophiliac! Hardly the repertory company for *The Ages of Man*.

Indignities enough, you say? Enter the Prince's servants, who, while carrying Snow White's coffin, stumble over a bush. The shock knocks the piece of poisoned apple from Snow White's throat, bringing her back to life. I ask you, was there ever such an ungracious epitaph: "Here lies a man who went through life stumbling from bier."

Our tale ends with our make-believe Monica Vitti indulging in such languid, torpid ennui as marrying the Prince, taking over his castle, and giving her stepmother a deadly hotfoot. One can only give thanks our little Snow White had an underactive thyroid gland, or she might have been shouting at story's end: "Today the forest, Tomorrow . . . !"

But these sagas shall continue. There is still Cinderella and Sleeping Beauty. Can This Conniving Connecticut Cutie Keep Conning the Kids? Stay tuned for the next episode of Glum Girl vs. Grimm Brothers.

March 15, 1973

A Goy in Wonderland: My First Bar Mitzvah

The lamentable thing about life is that it is devoid of fanfare. Man's odyssey more times than not is heralded by a kazoo rather than a trumpet.

The spiritual milestones of my own life have been accompanied by none of the drama one finds in the Old Testament. No seas parted, no stones rolled back, and the closest I've ever come to an ark is when another longshoreman and I walked up a gangplank two by two.

But maybe, I have reasoned, such is the lot of being born a Catholic in Brooklyn. Surely, they do it better in Rome, where one can pass off shaving nicks as stigmata. But in my barren borough you were slapped on the ass at birth, slapped in the face at confirmation (when you became a man), and dirt was thrown over you when you departed. It was early in life that I suspected someone was trying to tell me something.

Of course, there was the trauma of holy communion. I spent endless months in front of a mirror flicking out my tongue, like a frog shagging flies, in preparation to receive the blessed wafer. The nuns warned me that an error on that day would be recorded in black in my fielding stats by the Scorer in the Sky. I even had foreboding fantasies that Dick Young would write a lead column in the *Daily News,* titled "Rookie Muffs the Lord in Key Contest, Soul Sent to Minors Indefinitely."

So when, at an age the ripe side of mellow, I received an invitation to attend my first bar mitzvah, my spiritual curiosity was aroused. The invite came from Marty and Sheila Shaer to celebrate their son Andrew's plunge from puberty. And what an invitation! Not one of those chintzy goyisch numbers written in hand, but a document of such girth it would not fit into my svelte mailbox. The tissue paper separating the various parts of the announcement alone could have been used as a dropcloth for the painting of the Sistine Ceiling.

For the uninitiated, Marty Shaer is my friend and landlord who daily blends business and socializing at the Lion's Head Pub. He is a visionary who sees beauty in condemned buildings, failing pizzerias, and defunct go-go joints. Politically, he hasn't decided whether the Emancipation Proclamation or the bill to remove rent control is the most important document in the American experience. You could trust him with your wife, but never with a vacant room and a half.

With gross insensitivity to the cosmic events of life, Shaer scheduled the boy's bar mitzvah on Kentucky Derby Day. Now, if the child wanted to become a man, he could have waited for the following Saturday. After all, Riva Ridge had been training for his coming-out party for three years. But Shaer assured me he was not about to bow to something which ate oats, even if they were Nova Scotia oats. Whether I liked it or not, Andy was going postward on May 6.

At ten-thirty Saturday morning my lady and I arrived at the Midchester Jewish Center in Yonkers. I selected a skullcap and tried to emulate Peter Finch's dignity in *Sunday, Bloody Sunday,* cautioning the WASP I was with to stop calling the synagogue "the church." Andrew said his prayer with éclat, and I found myself, like a surrogate father, rooting for him. Marty sat through it with a smug look that said it was all in the bloodlines.

The rabbi's turn was next, and to be truthful, I was not looking forward to the sermon. I spent too much of my childhood listening to abstractions about "the Shepherd and His flock" and "If you are miserable, you are fortunate, because God is testing you." (Better he should tinker with the bastard in the pew behind me, I thought then, seeing no grace in being a spark plug.) These spiritual forays usually were interrupted by bingo game announcements, games in which the old biddies, bowing to Freud, used to shout at the priest presiding over the pills, "Shake up your balls, Father."

But I soon discovered that the rabbi was a man to be dealt with. Taking his cue from the Torah on "the spirit of man," he applied it to the South Vietnamese. "They have more men," he thundered, "more equipment, more weapons and B-52's. But without spirit, it's all for kaputz!" Good God, the man knew more than three Presidents.

Then, launching into what Norman Mailer calls an "existential caper," he gave the congregation a going-over. "Many people," he intoned, "tell me I should run this center more like a business. Some members of the Board of Directors even refer to me as 'my rabbi.' They think they own me. Me, a holy man! We don't need business in the temple. Business is what you find in your daily newspaper. The other day I read where the A&P, Finast, and Daitch-Shopwell were caught giving short weight. Is this what you want in your temple?"

The Holy Man had just reduced Ann Page, the Blessed Virgin of the comparative shopper, to a hooker. I was a goy in wonderland. One circumcised, though, I remembered, and a late-inning redemption was not beyond speculation. If Sammy Davis, Jr., could pull it off, why not me? I whispered, "Shalom, me bucko," just to hear how it sounded.

The rabbi then said that employers should treat employees like brothers (a Marxist with a mezuzah?), not slaves. At this point Marty seemed to slide lower in his seat. The rabbi concluded: "If one of your brothers has financial difficulties, don't tell him to leave Westchester and go back to the Bronx, come to his aid." He then blessed us all and told us that sponge cake and wine were waiting in an anteroom.

It was here I learned two tenets of Jewish lore. First, don't badmouth the Bronx when an assemblyman from that borough is sitting in your congregation. The assemblyman let the rabbi know that he did not represent a shlock Sodom-and-Gomorrah and that Westchester, in his mind, was hardly the land of milk and honey. Second, when it comes to the sponge cake and wine, many are called, but few are chosen.

The reception was held in a layout called the Fountainhead in New Rochelle. The only way to describe the place is to say that you could get the gout from the drinking water. Even the cigarette smoke smelled as if it had calories. As we went in, Marty approached and asked if I had understood the sermon. "The crux of it," he informed me, "was that goyim can't fight."

A buffet was laid out on a circular table approximately the circumference of the Astrodome roof. I could have used the help of Supp-Hose just to walk around it. My love, a Lutheran from Montana whose idea of spiritual grandeur is the use of soft wood in kneelers, thought this feast of lox, whitefish (sculpted into a swimming position), corned beef, sweetbreads, sweet and sour chicken, chopped liver, stuffed cabbage, deviled eggs, fruit salad, gefilte fish, fried rice, and circular towers of bread resembling the Guggenheim was the main meal. "No, my dear," Marty patiently explained as I was downing a whiskey. "With the Irish it's the liver, with the Jews the gallbladder."

Meanwhile, for the kids in attendance, there was a charcoal grill in another room, serving up hot dogs and hamburgers. As my lady and I lamented our paltry past, Marty explained that this was a "modest" affair as such things go. He recalled Super Bowl bar mitzvahs, lasting a weekend, in hotels where the hosts rented suites for their guests and those where the Sunday New York *Times* was given to each guest as he was leaving at the end of the evening—an inky bromide to get you through the wee hours of digestive disaster.

He also said the caterer had offered him a "theme bar mitzvah." It so happens that Marty's son Andy is a blossoming basketball player (he reduced this old man's lungs to a wheeze one day), so the caterer was prepared to create a basketball theme. A hoop and a net would be hung above the boy's table, guest tables would not be numbered but christened the "Kareem Abdul Jabbar Table," the "Walt Frazier Table," etc., and the *pièce de résistance* would be a waiter decked out in uniform dribbling a ball in with the cake!

Roy, an old friend of Marty's and one of those philosophical, witty Jews who used to dissect the Dodgers' box score on Ocean Parkway when I was a boy, remarked: "If you don't want the chicken soup, a waiter comes in and stuffs it—WHOOSH!" Marty, realizing that the Lord can get nasty about such tampering with His ground rules, decided not to go one on one with tradition and passed on the theme.

The prelims past, we waddled to the tables for the main event. A chicken crepe, salad, rare roast beef with rice and bamboo sprouts, a green pear ("It tastes like a giant Cloret," someone said) with chocolate sauce and ice cream, mocha cake, dessert cookies, mints, coffee, brandy, and cigars. Roy turned to me and remarked: "The Vietcong are through. The Communists will surrender tomorrow. How can you beat a country which goes to this much trouble for a thirteen-year-old?"

I nobly upheld the Hibernian honor by eating, drinking, and smoking everything in sight. Andy's presence was felt everywhere—toasts in his honor, monogrammed "Andy" menus and matchbooks. I was terrified that some mad stenciler was going to emblazon an "Andy" on my forehead.

To ward off a cholesterol clot I shook a leg to a few horas, disgraced myself with a polka, and antiquated myself with a lindy. For safety's sake I hid out between sets in the bathroom, where the real business of the day was being conducted. "I'm not offering you a deal," one gent loudly declared. "I'm offering you a caveat!"

The most beautiful time of the day was when the old men gathered to do the hora with energy and grace that amazed me. Later, in the shank of the evening (without the Sunday *Times*) I stood in my bathroom, like Jekyll opting to become Hyde, pouring bubbling Bromo from one glass to another. I thought of the rich, glorious Jewish experience I had missed. But it was too late. My mind kept saying: "Try it, you'll like it." But my stomach growled back: "You are not yet a man, my son."

Shalom, Andy.

May 25, 1972

226

Love Thine Enemies List

The White House "enemy list" is now, to coin a phrase, water under the bridge. But in its wake lie dozens of drowned delicate egos. As a social snub, the horror of being left off the list can only be compared to being 86ed from Truman Capote's historic Masked Ball. (Was this the genesis of the Watergate Caper?)

There is a rumor that at the *Village Voice* alone there were three suicide attempts, while up at Elaine's souls are shrouded in black crepe instead of their usual tinsel.

I really don't mean to make light of this calamity, since I once wept openly when the clerk at my local market told me he couldn't decipher my written grocery list. So, to soothe the bruised egos of the "in people," I contacted a gifted medium (medium rare) to ferret out the feelings of the famous, both living and dead, past and present, about the Executive Exorcism. What follows is that doxie's dossier.

I always knew Zelda's penchant for jumping nude into the Reflecting Pool would eventually hurt me with the Social Register.
—F. Scott Fitzgerald

It's just another example of *Patriotic Gore.*
—Edmund Wilson

I wouldn't lose my head over it.
—Anne Boleyn

With Oriental stoicism I can endure, but it's killing my number two son.
—Charlie Chan

You want to know how they could leave off a long-haired peace freak? Well, I was on the list till I promised Peter Brennan I'd deliver the Carpenters' Union. I learned a long time ago that you look out for *numero uno* on this planet.
—Jesus of Nazareth

It's quite simple—I'm on the *Camp* David list.
—Susan Sontag

I hope he takes a walk in the dank Roman night.
—Henry James

Hell, I couldn't be on the list. I was technical adviser on Watergate.
—Gaylord Perry

It was more than I could swallow.
—Linda Lovelace

Who cares about the White House? I hear you need a key to use the bathrooms.

—ALEXANDER PORTNOY

No, 'tis not so deep as a well, nor so wide as a church door, but 'tis enough, 'twill serve.

—WILLIAM SHAKESPEARE

It was a grudge. I wouldn't give him Marvin the Torch's phone number.

—JIMMY BRESLIN

You can lead a horse to. . . .

—SECRETARIAT

Why should I care? I didn't put him on the list for my fiftieth birthday party. It's a simple case of tit for tat. (I just bet Kate Millett will take that as a salacious, chauvinistic metaphor.)

—NORMAN MAILER

It was excruciating. Like a kick in the, uh. In the—uh . . .

—CHRISTINE JORGENSON

Crap. He can keep his list, sport. He's not the kind of guy you call at three in the morning.

—HOLDEN CAULFIELD

That dumb kid don't know what the hell he's talking about.

—MARTHA MITCHELL

It was just a case of misunderstanding a lepidopterist's remark. I simply suggested that someone should throw a net around him.

—VLADIMIR NABOKOV

It was because I admonished him that his administration was going around in circles.

—DANTE

Alice wouldn't give Pat her recipe for brownies.

—GERTRUDE

I can't comprehend it, but dollars to doughnuts he'll never carry old Main Street U.S.A. again.

—RED

He just never forgave Maryland—for some reason.

—MENCK

Son, any wickiup that houses poltroons so possessed by the demon water may passé on my purified persona.

—W. C. FIELDS

228

Unequivocally, unquestionably, and unconstitutionally I have suffered perdition from potentates (never mind Dick Young of the *Daily News*). Moronic minor league mendacity and malevolence have always been the albatross of the anointed. I'm a Star!

—HOWARD COSELL

All I did was request a chauffeur for his Inaugural.

—PROUST

Was it my fault that neither Didi nor Estragon would get off their asses to register?

—SAM BECKETT

Forget the list, it's John Dean I'm interested in. Never have I felt such empathy with a man. I know how he feels. I futilely tried to tell them the other eleven were implicated.

—NAME WITHHELD

Th—tha—that's All, Folks!

—PORKY PIG

July 5, 1973